Bryen Lorenz

FUNDAMENTALS OF MICRO-PROCESSORS

Henry O. Daley

HOLT, RINEHART AND WINSTON

New York   Chicago   San Francisco
Philadelphia   Montreal   Toronto   London
Sydney   Tokyo   Mexico City   Rio de Janeiro   Madrid

Address correspondence to:
383 Madison Avenue, New York, N.Y. 10017

Library of Congress Cataloging in Publication Data

Daley, Henry 0.
   Fundamentals of Microprocessors.

   Includes bibliographical references and index.
   1. Microprocessors.   I. Title.
TK7895.M5D34   1982   621.3819′58   82-15612

ISBN 0-03-059934-2

Printed in the United States of America
Published simultaneously in Canada
345   038   987654321

CBS COLLEGE PUBLISHING
Holt, Rinehart and Winston
The Dryden Press
Saunders College Publishing

PREFACE

In 1970 the first microprocessor was built. Since that time, microprocessors have become a pervading influence on our lives. The first were basically intended as controllers, but as technology developed the uses of these microprocessors increased to the point where they are now the brains of small computers known as microcomputers.

A microprocessor-based microcomputer can be constructed on specifically designed pieces of silicon dioxide (sand) one square inch in area that is capable of more and faster calculations than older computers that occupied the space of a table.

We are truly the computer generation. Computers are all around us, influencing our daily lives from calculating our purchases in large chain stores to directing our children's toys. In this text we are interested in the smallest computer, the microprocessor-based microcomputer.

Microprocessors are also the heart of digital watches, calculators, and TV video games. They control the radar ovens and the street lights at many intersections. They are found in some typewriters used for automatic typing, in word processors, and in automobiles to control gas flow and cylinders for better gas mileage (e.g., the clean-burn engine).

The field of microprocessors and microcomputers is developing so rapidly that it is difficult to keep up with the changes. A large push now is in the field of home computers, which are all run by microprocessors.

In the science fields more and more instruments are being built that are microprocessor controlled. For many scientists it has become necessary to understand the fundamentals of microprocessors and microcomputers in order to use these instruments. Though a basic scientist (biologist, chemist, physicist, etc.) need not know how to construct a microprocessor from its parts (this is a job for an engineer), scientists must be aware of the terminology used so that they can communicate with the engineers.

A person interested in the hobby or home computer field should also have some knowledge of these fundamentals in order to make comparisons between the different computers available and to use the computer to its maximum ability.

The objective of this text is to teach the basic fundamentals of microprocessors and microcomputers. It was developed around the Motorola MC6800 microprocessor, though discussion and comparisons with other microprocessors are made throughout. Comparisons are also made with the MC6809, a newer Motorola microprocessor that can be considered an enhanced version of the 6800. A laboratory experience is a vital part of any course, although the material given here can be studied without experiments.

The 6800 was chosen since it is a relatively simple microprocessor to understand, it is readily available in inexpensive kit forms (Heath Company), and it is one of the three most popular microprocessors. It is also found in certain home computers, for example, the "Imagination Machine" of APF Electronics. The 6809 is also part of various home and business computers. It is the microprocessor in Radio Shack's new "color" computer.

In addition comparisons are made with the LSI-11 microcomputer of Digital Equipment Corporation to show the differences between a "chip" microcomputer and a "board" microcomputer. These comparisons also illustrate some of the differences between an 8 bit and a 16 bit microcomputer.

The material presented in this text has been developed over a period of years from lecture notes used in teaching this course at Bridgewater State College. I would like to extend my appreciation to my many students for their various suggestions as the material was developed. In addition, I would like to thank the people who originally introduced me to this field: Dr. Raymond Dessy of Virginia Polytechnic Institute and State University, Dr. Fred Scalny and Douglas Fulrath of the Commonwealth Center for High Technology/Education, and Mike Odom of Digital Equipment Corporation. I would also like to thank my wife for helping me proofread the material and for drawing the original diagrams, as well as Carol Beckwith for typing the final manuscript.

CONTENTS

CHAPTER 1

NUMBER SYSTEMS AND COMPUTER ARITHMETIC

LEARNING ACTIVITIES

Study lecture material on number systems.
Read resource materials listed at end of unit.
Complete exercises.
Self-check answers to exercises.
Consult instructor for assistance as necessary.

OBJECTIVES

By completing these requirements, you should be able to achieve the following objectives for this unit when formally evaluated.

Objective 1

Given binary numbers, define binary, word, nibble, and byte, and locate the least and most significant bit, for any microcomputer.

Objective 2

Given numbers from different bases, convert the numbers from

Decimal to binary
Binary to decimal
Binary to octal
Octal to binary

Binary to hexadecimal
Hexadecimal to binary

based on standard conversion procedures.

Objective 3

Given binary numbers, add and subtract any combination of numbers, and convert to their one's and two's complements.

Objective 4

Given decimal numbers, convert them to binary coded decimal (BCD), or given BCD numbers, convert them to decimal.

EVALUATION

Your ability to demonstrate achievement on these objectives will be assessed after all instruction on this unit by multiple-choice items.

ANALOG VS. DIGITAL

The world around us is composed, basically, of analog signals (e.g., temperature and pressure). This is a signal that can be continuously varied. Analog computers handle these signals directly. A microprocesssor and digital computers deal with digital signals. Digital signals are discrete signals. That is, they can have only certain specific values (see Figure 1.1). Before a digital computer can handle an analog signal, it must be converted into an equivalent digital signal. There are numerous ways in which these signals are stored in a digital computer. All depend upon a device existing in one of two possible states, which can be thought of as "on" or "off." These two states are represented by the numbers 1 or 0—the numbers that make up the binary number system. To learn how a computer stores information, we must learn to work in the binary number system.

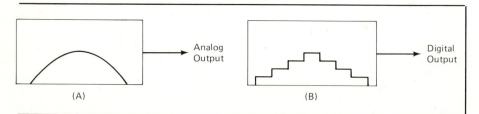

FIGURE 1.1. *Example of (A) an analog signal and (B) a digital signal.*

DECIMAL VS. BINARY NUMBERS

Normally we work with decimal numbers, that is, numbers in base 10. Here ten different digits are used to represent numbers. They are 0, 1, 2, 3, 4, 5, 6, 7, 8, and 9.

$$\text{Decimal number} \quad 42_{10 \leftarrow \text{Base}}$$

The base, 10 in this case, is also known as the "radix."

In a microprocessor or computer, binary numbers are used. These are the numbers in base 2 (0 or 1).

$$\text{Binary number} \quad 101010_2$$
$$42_{10} = 101010_2$$

Both represent the same number but in different bases. Each binary number is a *binary digit* or a *bit*. As in the decimal system, the number is read from left to right with the leftmost bit representing the highest number.

The leftmost bit is called the most significant bit, **MSB** (or most significant digit, MSD).

The rightmost bit is called the least significant bit, **LSB** (or least significant digit, LSD).

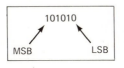

Remember, a bit is one binary digit: 0 or 1.

An interesting or useful property of binary numbers is that, if the LSB of the binary number is 0, the number is even, whereas if the LSB is a 1, the number is odd.

EXERCISE 1-1

1. Select the binary number(s) in the following list.
    a. 101_{10}
    b. 111_8
    c. 1101_2
    d. 1101_{16}

	A		B	C			D

2. Which letter represents the *MSB* in the number 1 1 0 1 0 1 1 0?
   a. A
   b. B
   c. C
   d. D

	A		B	C		D

3. Which letter represents the *LSB* in the 1 1 0 1 0 1 1 0?
   a. A
   b. B
   c. C
   d. D

4. State, in your own words, the difference between decimal and binary numbers.

WORDS, BYTES, AND NIBBLES

Microprocessors and computers are built to handle or store different size binary numbers referred to as words.

Computer Memory Size		Example	Name
a.	4 bits	1010	4-bit word
b.	8 bits	11010111	8-bit word
c.	12 bits	101010101010	12-bit word
d.	16 bits	1101011101110001	16-bit word

Figure 1.2 is a rough, though arbitrary, breakdown of microprocessors by word size. Many operations with computers involve the moving of 8 bits of information. Because of this, a group of 8 bits is often referred to as a *byte*. A computer whose word size is 8 bits is sometimes referred to as a byte computer. A 16-bit computer handles 2 bytes, as shown in Figure 1.3.

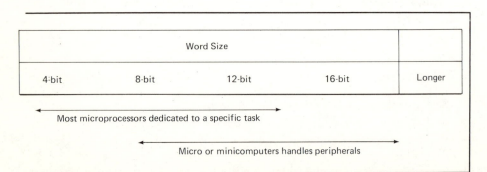

FIGURE 1.2. *Arbitrary classification of microprocessors and microcomputers.*

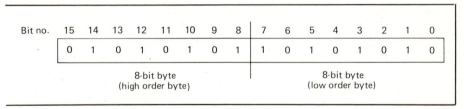

Bit no.	15	14	13	12	11	10	9	8	7	6	5	4	3	2	1	0
	0	1	0	1	0	1	0	1	1	0	1	0	1	0	1	0

8-bit byte
(high order byte)

8-bit byte
(low order byte)

FIGURE 1.3. *A 16-bit word.*

The lowest 8 bits are called the low order byte, while the highest 8 bits are referred to as the high order byte. Each bit in the word is assigned a bit number. The LSB is called bit 0, the eighth bit is bit 7, and the highest bit in a 16-bit word is bit 15. There are times when only 4 bits are used. A group of 4 bits is called a *nibble* (sometimes spelled nybble); thus 2 nibbles make a byte.

EXERCISE 1-2

1. Define the term "word" as used for any microprocessor.
2. Define the term "byte" as used for most microprocessors.
3. Given the 16-bit word 1100100111100011, select the high-order byte.
   a. 11100011
   b. 11001001
   c. 11010011
   d. 10011110
4. Define the term "nibble" as used for a microcomputer.

CONVERTING FROM ONE BASE TO ANOTHER

Decimal to Binary

To convert a decimal number to binary, either of two procedures may be used. One is based on repetitive subtractions, the other method is based on a division process. Let us use 42_{10} and convert it to its binary equivalent which was previously stated to be 101010_2.

Subtraction method.
1. Prepare a weighing table to convert the powers of 2 to their decimal equivalents. A weighing table consists of three rows. The first row is a decimal number and the second row is the binary number expressed as a power of 2 that is equal to the decimal number. [The binary number is aligned directly under its corresponding decimal number.] The third row is a series of binary bits (0 or 1) obtained by the procedure below. The third row gives the binary number that corresponds to the decimal number being converted. The largest digit (MSB) is on the left and the smallest (LSB) is on the right. Table 1.1 is an example of the weighing table needed for this conversion.

TABLE 1.1. *Weighing Table to Convert From Decimal to Binary.*

Decimal value	32	16	8	4	2	1
Binary power	2^5	2^4	2^3	2^2	2^1	2^0
Result	MSB					LSB

The largest value in the table should be the highest power of 2 that is nearest, but does not exceed, the decimal number that is to be converted. In this example,

$$2^6 = 64, \quad \text{which exceeds } 42$$

so the table stops at $2^5 = 32$.

2. Subtract the number in the weighing table closest to 42—that is, 32—and place a 1 in this column in the table.

$$42 - 32 = 10$$

3. Take the remainder from step 2 and again find the closest number to it in the weighing table. This is 8 in this case. Subtract this number from the remainder from step 2. and put a 1 in the column in the table under the 8.

$$10 - 8 = 2$$

4. Repeat this process until no decimal digit is left.

$$2 - 2 = 0$$

So a 1 goes into the 2^1 column.

5. Put a 0 in any column not occupied by a 1. The result is shown in Table 1.2. The binary equivalent is the number in the bottom row. This is

$$101010_2 = 42_{10}$$

The number is read from left to right.

To find the binary number corresponding to 71, we would prepare the weighing table given in Table 1.3. Thus, $71 - 64 = 7$ so a 1 is entered in the 2^6 column: $7 - 4 = 3$; another 1 is put in the 2^2 column: $3 - 2 = 1$; a

TABLE 1.2. *Final Result of Weighing Table for Conversion of 42_{10}.*

Decimal value	32	16	8	4	2	1
Binary power	2^5	2^4	2^3	2^2	2^1	2^0
Result	1 MSB	0	1	0	1	0 LSB

1 is put in the 2^1 column: $1 - 1 = 0$; so a 1 is put in the 2^0 column. The rest are filled with 0's.

$$71_{10} = 1000111_2$$

This method can be used to convert a decimal number into any base. A similar weighing table must be prepared for the other base.

TABLE 1.3. *Weighing Table for Conversion of 71_{10} to Binary.*

Decimal value	64	32	16	8	4	2	1
Binary power	2^6	2^5	2^4	2^3	2^2	2^1	2^0
Result	1	0	0	0	1	1	1

Division method. In this method the number to be converted to another base is repeatedly divided by the new base, and the remainder is put in a special column. The remainder from each division gives the number in the new base. To convert 42_{10} to base 2 we go through the following steps (Table 1.4.).

Divide 2 into 42 and put the remainder in the R column. Repeat this process on the decimal number until no decimal digit is left. When you divide 42 by 2, you get a result of 21, which is placed in the third column, and a remainder of 0, which is placed in the fourth column. Now, divide 21 by 2, which is 10 (third column) with a remainder of 1 (fourth column). Continue dividing until 1 is divided by 2, which gives 0 (third column) and 1 remainder (fourth column).

The binary number is the number in the remainder column with the

TABLE 1.4. *Conversion of 42_{10} to Binary by the Division Method.*

Base	Number	Result	Remainder (R)
2	42	21	0 LSB
2	21	10	1
2	10	5	0
2	5	2	1
2	2	1	0
2	1	0	1 MSB

smallest bit (LSB) at the top and the largest bit (MSB) at the bottom; that is, the number is read from bottom to top.

$$101010_2 = 42_{10}$$

The division method can also be used to convert a decimal number into any base. To convert to base 8, repeat this same procedure but divide by 8 instead of 2; to convert to hexadecimal, divide by 16 instead of 2. Just remember that there are no 8's or 9's in base 8.

EXERCISE 1-3

Convert each of the following decimal numbers to its binary equivalent.
a. 25_{10} b. 97_{10} c. 174_{10} d. 110_{10} e. 44_{10}

Binary to Decimal

There is one basic method used to convert binary to decimal. This method is based on the weight of a number using positional notation. The number 6321_{10} can be written in terms of positional notation as

$$6321_{10} = 6 \times 10^3 + 3 \times 10^2 + 2 \times 10^1 + 1 \times 10^0$$

To determine the value of a number in positional notation, multiply each digit by the weight of the position and add each number together.

$$
\begin{aligned}
6 \times 10^3 &= 6000 \\
3 \times 10^2 &= 300 \\
2 \times 10^1 &= 20 \\
1 \times 10^0 &= 1 \\
\hline
\text{Add} \quad & 6321
\end{aligned}
$$

For a number in base 2:

$$101010_2 = 1 \times 2^5 + 0 \times 2^4 + 1 \times 2^3 + 0 \times 2^2 + 1 \times 2^1 + 0 \times 2^0$$

Note that:

$$2^0 = 1$$
$$2^1 = 2$$
$$2^2 = 4$$
$$2^3 = 8$$
$$2^4 = 16$$
$$2^5 = 32$$

Carrying out this process involves two steps: (1) multiplication of each bit by its weighted position, and (2) addition of the results from step 1.

It is most convenient if you start from the right and work to the left.

MSB   LSB

$$1 \quad 0 \quad 1 \quad 0 \quad 1 \quad 0_2 = x_{10} \ ?$$

$$= 0 \times 2^0 = 0$$
$$= 1 \times 2^1 = 2$$
$$= 0 \times 2^2 = 0$$
$$= 1 \times 2^3 = 8$$
$$= 0 \times 2^4 = 0$$
$$= 1 \times 2^5 = \underline{32}$$
$$42_{10} = x_{10}$$

EXERCISE 1-4

Convert each of the following binary numbers to its decimal equivalent.

a. 1100_2 b. 11101_2 c. 1101100_2 d. 110110_2 e. 010111_2

Binary to Octal

Although computers store information in the form of binary numbers, it is awkward to communicate with the computer in binary. There are too many numbers to remember. It is easier to work in some other base. Computers such as the Heath H-8 and the Digital Equipment Corporation LSI series allow you to communicate with the computer in octal.

Octal is a number representation in base 8. Here there are eight digits: 0, 1, 2, 3, 4, 5, 6, and 7. The relationship between an octal number and its binary equivalent is given in Table 1.5.

TABLE 1.5. *Octal Numbers and Their Binary Equivalents.*

Octal Number	Binary Equivalent
0	000
1	001
2	010
3	011
4	100
5	101
6	110
7	111

Each octal number can be represented by three binary numbers. To convert from binary to octal, group the binary numbers in threes, starting from right and going to left, and replace each group with its octal equivalent. Remember, zeros can be added to the left of the MSB without changing the number. ($200_{10} = 0200_{10}$ and $110_2 = 0110_2$.)

Combine the octal digits from right to left.

Example 1.1:

$$1001010_2 = x_8$$

$$1001010_2$$

001   001   010   Break the binary number into groups of three.

 1   1   2 $= 112_8$

Convert the following number to base 8.

Example 1.2:

$$10101101_2 = x_8$$

10   101   101

010   101   101

$x_8 =$ 2   5   5 $= 255_8$

EXERCISE 1-5

Convert each of the following binary numbers to octal.

a. 110_2 b. 1101_2 c. 111001_2 d. 11001_2 e. 111011_2

Octal to Binary

To convert an octal number to binary, change each octal digit into its 3-bit binary number and combine the bits.

Example 1.3: 75_8

$$5_8 = 101_2$$

$$7_8 = 111_2$$

$$\text{Combine } 111 \quad 101_2 = 75_8$$

$$\text{MSB} \qquad \text{LSB}$$

In the above case, since 5_8 is the LSD, its bits go to the right when combined with the 7_8 bits.

EXERCISE 1-6

Convert each of the following octal numbers to its binary equivalent.
a. 65_8 b. 72_8 c. 174_8 d. 35_8 e. 246_8

Binary to Hexadecimal

Many other computers such as the Apple II, PET, ATARI, and TRS-80 allow you to work in hexadecimal instead of octal. Hexadecimal is a number representation in base 16. The following are the 16 hexadecimal digits.

$$0, 1, 2, 3, 4, 5, 6, 7, 8, 9, A, B, C, D, E, F$$

Note that the letters A, B, C, D, E, and F represent numbers.

In counting in hexadecimal be careful to insert these numbers in their proper place. For instance, after 19 comes 1A and after 29 comes 2A then 2B. An example of counting backward would be 101, 100, FF, FE, and so on.

Table 1.6 shows the relationship between the hexadecimal numbers and their binary equivalents. Note that any hexadecimal number can be represented by 4 binary bits. This makes converting from binary to hexadecimal easy. To convert from binary to hexadecimal, group the binary numbers in blocks of four, starting with the LSB, and replace each group with its hexadecimal equivalent. Combine the hexadecimal digits in the same manner that was used to form octal numbers.

Example 1.4:

$$1001010_2 = x_{16}$$

$$1001010 \rightarrow 0100 \quad 1010$$

$$x_{16} = \quad 4 \qquad A \ = 4A_{16}$$

TABLE 1.6. *Hexadecimal Numbers and Their Binary Equivalents.*

Hexadecimal Number	Binary Number
0	0000
1	0001
2	0010
3	0011
4	0100
5	0101
6	0110
7	0111
8	1000
9	1001
A	1010
B	1011
C	1100
D	1101
E	1110
F	1111

EXERCISE 1-7

Convert the following binary numbers to hexadecimal.
a. 11011101_2 b. 10111001_2 c. 1101001_2 d. 10011111_2
e. 10011001101_2

Hexadecimal to Binary

To convert from hexadecimal to binary, write each hexadecimal digit in its binary equivalent and group the bits together.

Example 1.5: $1A_{16}$

$$1_{16} = 0001_2$$

$$A_{16} = 1010_2$$

$$\text{Combining} = 00011010_2$$

$$1A_{16} = \quad 11010_2$$

Since A_{16} is the LSD, its bits are placed to the right of the bits from 1_{16}.

EXERCISE 1-8

Convert the following hexadecimal numbers to binary.
a. E5   b. C2   c. AA   d. F3   e. BC

With modern calculators available to convert from one base system to another, it might seem superfluous to learn the preceding material. When working with modern microcomputers, an understanding of the octal and hexadecimal system will enable you to write programs for the computer that operate much faster than programs written in a high-level language such as Basic.

BINARY ARITHMETIC

Addition

Addition with binary numbers follows the same general rules that you have been using all your life. The rules here are simplified as there are only three possible combinations of 1's and 0's; thus three rules need to be remembered.

Rule 1: $1 + 1 = 0$ with one carry

$$\begin{array}{r} 1 \\ 1 \\ \hline 10 \end{array}$$
↑
carry

Rule 2: $1 + 0 = 1 = 0 + 1$
Rule 3: $0 + 0 = 0$

Example 1.6:

101	01001101	10111110
001	00101011	10101010
110	01111000	[1]01101000

↑
ignored in an 8-bit computer

Any carry beyond the word size is ignored by the computer. (There is a device in the computer that detects this and warns you it happened.)

EXERCISE 1-9
Add the following binary numbers.

a. 1010010   b. 1111101   c. 1110110   d. 11001110   e. 11000011
   +0101101   +1100111   +1101001   +00101011   +01010100

Subtraction

Some computers and microprocessors cannot do subtraction directly. In order to subtract on these instruments, you take the two's complement and add. The easiest way to form the two's complement is to form the one's complement and add 1.

To form a one's complement, the following two rules are necessary.

$$\text{Change } 1 \rightarrow 0$$

$$\text{Change } 0 \rightarrow 1$$

Change all bits in the number. All 1's become 0's and all 0's become 1's. Examples of one's complement are:

Binary Number	One's Complement
01100100	10011011
11111111	00000000

To form the two's complement, add 1 to each one's complement.

10011011	00000000
1	1
10011100 two's complement	00000001

Binary Number	One's Complement	Two's Complement
10010010	01101101 Every bit is complemented	01101110 1 is added to one's complement

A quick way of finding the two's complement of any binary number is to start at the LSB and copy the original numbers as you go up through the bits until you reach the first 1. Every bit after this 1 is complemented.

Example 1.7

0100 0100

100   first 1 is reached

10111100   every bit after is complemented

Example 1.8

Find the two's complement of 10011101.

1001110|1

0110001|1

all complemented to the left of this line so the two's complement of 10011101 is 01100011.

EXERCISE 1-10

Find the two's complement of each of the following binary numbers.

a. 10011101   b. 11001101   c. 11110100   d. 10101101   e. 11001011

    To subtract two numbers take the two's complement of the subtrahend and add it to the minuend.

Example 1.9

Decimal	Binary	
15	1111	1111
		$\rightarrow$
-9	-1001	0111
6		[1]0110
		↑
		ignored

The number $0110_2 = 6_{10}$.

    The "1" is ignored in the carry. The presence of a "1" here means the result is a positive number. If a "0" had been formed, the result would have been a negative number. An examination of the two's complement of the subtrahend will show why this is so and thus why the carry can be ignored.

    In forming the two's complement of a number it should be kept in mind that leading zeros up to the word size of the computer are present; for example, $100 \rightarrow 00000100$ for an 8-bit computer. When the two's complement is formed, these 0's become 1's. When the "1" carry occurs, all the leading 1's now become 0's again. If we repeat Example 9 using 8 bits, we get:

Example 1.10

Decimal	Binary	
15	0000 1111	0000 1111
		$\rightarrow$
-9	$-0000\ 1001$	1111 0111
6		[1]0000 0110
		↑
		ignored

Thus the "1" carry is carried off indefinitely.

EXERCISE 1-11

Carry out subtraction on the following numbers using two's complement addition.

a.	11011011	b.	11110111	c.	11110001	d.	11011010	e.	10110010
	-10011101		-11100011		-10001111		-10010101		-10011101

MULTIPLICATION AND DIVISION

Multiplication can be done by repetitive addition.
　　Multiplication: To multiply 3×2:

Example 1.11

$$
\begin{array}{ccc}
3 & & 0011 \\
& \rightarrow & \\
\times 2 & & \times 0010
\end{array}
$$

As 3×2 is the same as $3 + 3$, to carry out this multiplication simply add:

Decimal		Binary
3	$\rightarrow$	0011
+3	$\rightarrow$	0011
		0110

and 0110 is 6.

To multiply 3×3; this is $3 + 3 + 3$, so simply add:

Example 1.12

Binary	Decimal
0011	3
0011	+3
0011	+3
1001	9

　　Multiplication can also be carried out using rules similar to decimal multiplication. In binary there are fewer rules.

$$0 \times 1 = 0 \qquad 0 \times 0 = 0 \qquad 1 \times 0 = 0 \qquad 1 \times 1 = 1$$

Any number times 0 is 0 and 1 times 1 is 1.

Example 1.13

Binary	Decimal
0011	3
0011	$\times 3$
0011	
0011	
01001	$= 9$

Division can be done by repetitive subtraction. In this method the divisor is subtracted from the dividend until there is no remainder. The number of times the subtraction is done gives the answer.

Example 1.14

$$4 \div 2 = 2 \qquad 4 - 2 = 2 \qquad 2 - 2 = 0$$

Here 2 must be subtracted twice before there is no remainder, and so the answer is 2.

Division can also be done in the same way you would in decimal. The four general rules are

$$\frac{0}{0} \quad \text{have no} \qquad \frac{0}{1} = 0$$

$$\frac{1}{0} \quad \text{meaning} \qquad \frac{1}{1} = 1$$

Example 1.15

Using this method $\dfrac{4}{2} = \dfrac{100}{010}$

$$\begin{array}{r} 10. \\ 10{\overline{\smash{\big)}\,100.}} \\ \underline{10} \\ 00 \end{array}$$

or

$$\frac{100}{10} = 10 = 2_{10}$$

in binary

NEGATIVE NUMBERS

Computers do not store the plus $(+)$ or minus $(-)$ signs to identify positive or negative numbers. In most computers the leftmost bit is used to designate the sign of the number

Sign	MSB				.			LSB
Bit	2^7	2^6	2^5	2^4	2^3	2^2	2^1	2^0

8-bit word

If the sign bit is a 1, the number is negative; if it is 0, the number is positive. Using this convention, there are two ways in which positive and negative numbers can be stored. One method is known as sign-magnitude and the other is two's complement format.

Sign-Magnitude

Using sign-magnitude representation, the MSB tells the sign of the number whereas the other bits represent the actual number. The largest numbers that can be stored in an 8-bit computer with this format are $+127$ and -127 as shown in Figure 1.4. This leads to two zeros: $+0$ and -0.

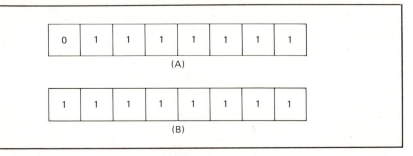

FIGURE 1.4. *Sign-magnitude representation of (A) $+127$ and (B) -127.*

Some computers use this type of representation, but most use two's complement format.

Two's Complement Format

In two's complement format a positive number is represented the same way as it would be in sign-magnitude representation. Thus the largest positive number that can be stored in 8 bits is still $+127$. Negative numbers, however, though are stored in two's complement form. The largest negative number that can be stored this way in 8 bits is -128. This representation is shown in Figure 1.5.

The 1 in the MSB identifies this as a negative number in two's complement form. The two's complement of 10000000 is still 10000000 and

$$10000000_2 = 128_{10}$$

Thus 10000000_2 is -128_{10}, with the minus sign coming from the MSB. Table

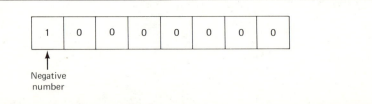

FIGURE 1.5. *Two's complement form of -128.*

TABLE 1.7. *Decimal Numbers Stored in Two's Complement Format.*

Decimal Number	8-Bit Binary Number
+127	01111111
.	.
.	.
.	.
+3	00000011
+2	00000010
+1	00000001
0	00000000
−1	11111111
−2	11111110
−3	11111101
.	.
.	.
−128	10000000

1.7 gives the binary representation of some positive and negative numbers in two's complement format.

The computer thus stores positive numbers in their normal format, while negative numbers are stored in two's complement format.

EXERCISE 1-12

Identify each of the following numbers stored in a computer using two's complement format. Express these numbers in base 10.

a. 11100110   b. 11000100   c. 00101101   d. 10001110   e. 11100010

BINARY CODED DECIMAL

Many times it is convenient to work in a computer with binary numbers that represent decimal numbers. Such representations are known as binary coded decimal (BCD) representations. There are different coding schemes available to do this. The most common is the 8421 binary coded decimal (BCD) format. The number 8421 comes from the decimal equivalent of the bits in a 4-bit binary number. Table 1.8 gives the BCD representation of the decimal numbers.

All BCD numbers are 4 bits long. In an 8-bit storage device, two BCD numbers can be packed. Normal addition of two BCD numbers is *not* the same as binary addition. Let us look at the addition of 7 to 8 decimal.

TABLE 1.8. *8421 BCD Representation of the Decimal Digits.*

Decimal Number	BCD Representation
0	0000
1	0001
2	0010
3	0011
4	0100
5	0101
6	0110
7	0111
8	1000
9	1001

Decimal	BCD	
7	0111	
+8	1000	
15	1111	15 in binary, but F in hexadecimal

Although the number 1111 is a valid binary number, it is not a valid BCD number. This type of problem occurs any time two decimal numbers are added and their sum exceeds 9. To correct for the six letters between 9 and 10, a 6 is added to the result.

$$
\begin{array}{r}
1111 \\
0110 \\
\hline
10101
\end{array}
$$

This now becomes two BCD numbers 0001 and 0101, which is 15_{10}. Other arithmetic operations are also more complicated in BCD but routines can be written to handle them.

Various other types of BCD format are also used. Two of the more common are known as Gray code and excess-3 code. Table 1.9 lists the values of the decimal digits in these two formats.

The excess-3 code is formed by adding 3 to the 8421 BCD format. Its complement is found by simply inverting each bit. An examination of Table 1.9 shows that in excess-3 code a number plus its complement always equals "9."

The Gray code was devised so that, as you go from one number to the next, only one bit changes in the number. This makes it useful for analog-to-digital conversions.

TABLE 1.9. *Additional BCD Codes.*

Decimal	Excess-3	Gray
0	0011	0000
1	0100	0001
2	0101	0011
3	0110	0010
4	0111	0110
5	1000	1110
6	1001	1010
7	1010	1011
8	1011	1001
9	1100	1000

EXERCISE 1-13

1. Convert the following decimal numbers to 8421 BCD numbers.
    a. 25   b. 86   c. 91   d. 2
2. Convert each of the following 8421 BCD numbers to its decimal equivalent.
    a. 0110   b. 1001   c. 1000 0110   d. 1100 0001   e. 0110 0101

REVIEW QUESTIONS

1. Convert the following values to binary.
    a. 174_{10}
    b. $C9_{16}$
    c. 71_8
2. Complete the following and convert your answer into hexadecimal code.

    a. $\quad$ 11011011   b. $\quad$ 11001110   c. $\quad$ 11011001
    $\quad$ -10011101 $\qquad$ $+00101011$ $\qquad$ -00111011

3. Find the signed decimal equivalents for the following two's complement formatted numbers.
    a. 00000111
    b. 10000111
    c. 10000000
    d. 01110000
4. Find the two's complement format for the following signed decimal numbers.
    a. $+32$
    b. -26
    c. -7
    d. $+73$

5. Find the sum of the following octal numbers.
   a. 234   b. 670   c. 777
      111   143   111

6. Find the sum of the following hexadecimal numbers.
   a. 48   b. FF   c. 99
      48   AB   24

7. What is the largest positive number that can be stored in a computer that has a 12-bit word length and uses two's complement arithmetic?

8. What is the largest positive number and the greatest negative number that can be stored in a computer that has a 16-bit word length and uses two's complement arithmetic?

9. The result obtained when 225_8 is subtracted from 332_8 is
   a. 11001001   b. 01000111   c. 01000101   d. 10101100

10. The result obtained by the subtraction of $E3_{16}$ from $F7_{16}$ is
    a. C6   b. B5   c. 32   d. 14

11. Find the one's complement of each of the following.
    a. 01100011   b. 10001000   c. 10101010

12. Find the two's complement of each of the numbers in question 11.

13. The following numbers were transmitted using 8421 BCD format. What are their decimal equivalents?
    a. 10010010   b. 01011000   c. 01110001

14. What would the numbers in question 13 look like if they were transmitted using Gray code?

REFERENCES

1. *Digital Computer Principles*, Burroughs Corporation. McGraw-Hill Book Co., New York, 1969, Chapter 3.
2. Introduction to Minicomputers, Digital Equipment Corporation
   a. Numbering Systems
   b. Computer Arithmetic
3. Sam Perone and David Jones, *Digital Computers in Scientific Instrumentation*. McGraw-Hill Book Co., New York, 1973, Chapter 2.
4. Heath Corporation. Individual Learning Program in Microprocessors, 1977, Chapters 1 and 3.
5. Ron Bishop, *Basic Microprocessors and the 6800*. Hayden Book Company, New York, 1979.

GLOSSARY

Analog computer	Data represented by electrical voltages are acted upon by combining and measuring voltages through connections on a patch-panel. Quantity of data stored is small and precision is limited.
Base	See Radix.

BCD (binary coded decimal)	A system of representing decimal numbers in binary.
Binary digit (bit)	A digit used to express a number in base 2; that is, 0 or 1.
Binary number system	System of counting and representing quantities in base 2. All digital computers use this system.
Byte	A group of 8 bits.
Complementary addition	Process by which many computers perform subtraction in which two's complement of a negative number is added to a positive number.
Decimal number system	Traditional system of counting and representing quantities in base 10.
Digital computer	Data represented by 0's and 1's are counted and computed according to stored programs.
Direct subtraction	A negative number is subtracted from a positive number directly, without complementing.
Excess-3	A BCD code formed by adding 3 to the binary equivalent of the decimal number.
8421 code	A BCD code in which the binary equivalent of the digital number is used.
Gray code	A BCD code that needs only 1 bit changed as you go from one digital number to the next.
Hexadecimal number system	System of representing data to computer of radix 16. The 16 characters are 0, 1, 2, 3, 4, 5, 6, 7, 8, 9, A, B, C, D, E, F.
Least significant digit (or bit)	(LSD or LSB) Rightmost bit
Most significant digit (or bit)	(MSD or MSB) Leftmost bit
Nibble (nybble)	A group of 4 bits.
Octal number system	System of counting and representing quantities in base 8. Used by programmers as shorthand for binary. Eight characters are 0, 1, 2, 3, 4, 5, 6, 7.
One's complement	Formed by reversing all the digits in a binary number. Change 0 to 1 and 1 to 0.
Place value (positional value)	Base of number system raised to some power. Indicates weight of each digit.
Positional notation	The value of a digit in a number depends on its location. Each digit acts as a coefficient for integral powers of the same base.
Radix (base)	Fixes the number of digits or characters in a particular number system.
Sign bit	Most significant bit in a number. When 0, means the number is $(+)$; when 1, means the number is $(-)$.

Sign-magnitude	A system of representing positive and negative numbers in binary. The MSB is the sign bit, the rest is the number.
Two's complement	Formed by subtracting number from smallest power of base greater than number. Also equal to one's complement $+1$.
Weighing table	Easily constructed table useful in converting numbers of base 10 to binary using positional notation.

ANSWERS TO EXERCISE 1-1

1. c
2. a
3. d
4. Answers should include:
   a. Decimal is base 10, binary is base 2.
   b. Decimal uses 10 digits (0–9) to represent numbers.
   c. Binary uses 2 digits (0 and 1) to represent numbers.
   d. Binary numbers are used by computers. Decimals are used by people.

ANSWERS TO EXERCISE 1-2

1. The term "word" refers to the size of a binary number. Different microprocessors use different size numbers or words. For example:
   4-bit number (1101) = 4-bit word
   8-bit number (11101001) = 8-bit word
2. Some processors split words into smaller units, which are called bytes. One half of a 16-bit word is called a byte. For example:
   $$1101100111001001 = \underbrace{11011001}_{\text{BYTE}} \quad \underbrace{11001001}_{\text{BYTE}}$$
3. b
4. 4 bits

ANSWERS TO EXERCISE 1-3

a. 11001_2 b. 1100001_2 c. 10101110_2
d. 1101110_2 e. 101100_2

ANSWERS TO EXERCISE 1-4

a. 12_{10} b. 29_{10} c. 108_{10}
d. 54_{10} e. 23_{10}

ANSWERS TO EXERCISE 1-5

a. 6_8 b. 15_8 c. 71_8 d. 31_8 e. 73_8

ANSWERS TO EXERCISE 1-6

a. 110101   b. 111010   c. 1111100
d. 11101   e. 10100110

ANSWERS TO EXERCISE 1-7

a. DD_{16} b. $B9_{16}$ c. 69_{16} d. $9F_{16}$ e. $4CD_{16}$

ANSWERS TO EXERCISE 1-8

a. 11100101_2 b. 11000010_2 c. 10101010_2
d. 11110011_2 e. 10111100_2

ANSWERS TO EXERCISE 1-9

a. 1111111   b. 11100100   c. 11011111
d. 11111001   e. *100010111
* Computer will not "see" this bit.

ANSWERS TO EXERCISE 1-10

a. 01100011   b. 00110011   c. 00001100
d. 01010011   e. 00110101

ANSWERS TO EXERCISE 1-11

a. 00111110   b. 00010100   c. 01100010
d. 01000101   e. 00010101

ANSWERS TO EXERCISE 1-12

a. -26 b. -60 c. 45   d. -114 e. -30

ANSWERS TO EXERCISE 1-13

1. a. 0010   0101
    b. 1000   0110
    c. 1001   0001
    d. 0000   0010
2. a. 6
    b. 9
    c. 86
    d. Not a valid 8421 BCD number
    e. 65

ANSWERS TO REVIEW QUESTIONS

1. a. 10101110
    b. 11001001
    c. 111001
2. a. 00111110   3E
    b. 11111001   F9
    c. 10011110   9E
3. a. $+7$ b. -121 c. -128 d. 112
4. a. 00100000   b. 11100110   c. 11111001   d. 01001001
5. a. 345_8 b. 1033_8 c. 1110_8
6. a. 90_{16} b. $1AA_{16}$ c. BD_{16}
7. 2047_{10}
8. $+32767$; -32768
9. c
10. a
11. a. 10011100   b. 01110111   c. 01010101
12. a. 10011101   b. 01111000   c. 01010110
13. a. 92   b. 58   c. 71
14. a. 10000011   b. 11101001   c. 10110001

If you had any difficulty with these problems, you should review your lecture notes, the workbook, and/or discuss your concerns with a classmate or your instructor. Use this procedure after every exercise in this book.

CHAPTER 2

DIGITAL LOGIC

LEARNING ACTIVITIES

Study lecture material on digital logic.
Read resources listed at end of chapter.
Complete exercises.
Self-check answers to exercises.
Consult instructor if necessary.

OBJECTIVES

By completing these requirements, you should be able to achieve the following objectives for this unit when formally evaluated.

Objective 1

Given voltage information, identify positive and negative states according to conventional rules.

Objective 2

Given partial truth tables and diagrams, complete the tables and name basic gates according to their operating rules.

Objective 3

Given tables and diagrams, name and identify the logic states for three common flip-flops and tell how they are combined to form registers according to their rules of operation.

Objective 4

Given abbreviations for standard integrated circuit designs, state the proper names and uses according to standard descriptions.

EVALUATION

Your ability to demonstrate achievement on these objectives will be assessed after all instruction on this unit by:

- Multiple-choice items
- Completion items

INTRODUCTION

Microprocessors and computers operate using three basic logic devices:

1. Inverters
2. Gates
3. Flip-flops

Binary numbers are sent through or stored in these logic devices using voltages (Figure 2.1). Commonly, a voltage of +5 is used to represent a binary 1 and 0 volts to represent a binary 0. This is referred to as positive logic. In negative logic the reverse relationship is used: +5 volts is a binary 0 and 0 volts is a binary 1. In practice a voltage between +2.8 and +5 can be used to generate a 1, while less than +0.8 volt is used to represent a 0. Some manufacturers use negative logic states in their computers, but most use positive.

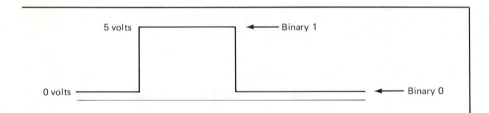

FIGURE 2.1. *Binary numbers as voltages.*

EXERCISE 2-1

1. Negative logic is applied to a data line. A voltage reading taken at the end of the line indicates +5 volts. The binary code on the line is _____ .
2. Complete the following table.

Voltage Measured	Positive Logic Binary Code	Negative Logic Binary Code
4.5 volts	a. _____	e. _____
0.2 volt	b. _____	f. _____
0 volts	c. _____	g. _____
3.9 volts	d. _____	h. _____

3. Positive logic is applied to a circuit. Zero volts is read on the output. The binary code is _____ .

INVERTERS

Inverters are simple logic circuits with one input and one output. The inverter is a *not* circuit. The output is always the reverse (or complement) of the input. In Figure 2.2 $\bar{A}$ means the complement of A. Table 2.1 shows a typical way of summarizing the results known as a truth table. Figure 2.3 shows a typical waveform for an inverter.

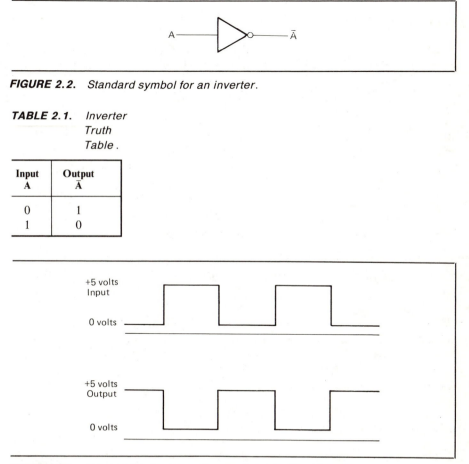

FIGURE 2.2. *Standard symbol for an inverter.*

TABLE 2.1. *Inverter Truth Table.*

Input A	Output $\bar{A}$
0	1
1	0

FIGURE 2.3. *Input and output waveforms of an idealized inverter.*

EXERCISE 2-2

1. Positive logic is fed to an inverter (not gate). Complete the table.

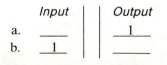

	Input		Output
a.	____		1
b.	1		____

2. For any type of logic fed to an inverter, the output is always the _____ of the input.
3. Sketch the standard symbol for an inverter. Label the inputs and outputs.

GATES

Gates are decision-making logic devices containing two or more inputs and one output. There are two basic types of gates. All discussions of gates that follow assume *positive* logic.

AND Gate

Figure 2.4(A) is a standard symbol for an AND gate with two inputs. Figure 2.4(B) shows the equivalent circuit in simple electrical terms. (This is *not* the

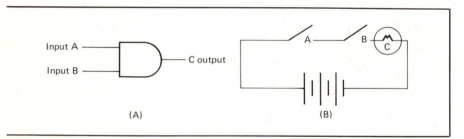

(A)   (B)

FIGURE 2.4. *AND Gate (A) and equivalent circuitry (B).*

actual circuitry in an AND gate.) In order for a current to flow through the light bulb, both switch *A* and switch *B* must be closed before the light (*C*) can be lit.

In an AND gate, both A and B must be 1 for C to be 1. Under these conditions the gate is said to be "enabled" (or opened). In general, when a gate is enabled, data present at the input are transferred to the output. If either A or B or both are 0, C is 0. Table 2.2 gives the truth table for an AND gate.

There are four rows in the truth table since there are two inputs to the gate. In general, the number of rows in a truth table is given by

$$2^n$$

where *n* is the number of inputs.

TABLE 2.2. *Truth Tables for an AND Gate.*

Input		Output	Input		Output
A	**B**	**C**	**A**	**B**	**C**
0	0	0	1	1	1
0	1	0	1	0	1
1	0	0	0	1	1
1	1	1	0	0	0

(A) Positive Logic   (B) Negative Logic

FIGURE 2.5.   *AND gate with three inputs.*

For the AND gate with three inputs (Figure 2.5), there are eight corresponding rows in a truth table (Table 2.3). In this type of gate only when all three inputs are 1 is the output a 1.

TABLE 2.3.   *Truth Table for three-Input AND Gate (Positive Logic).*

| Input | | | Output |
A	B	C	D
0	0	0	0
1	0	0	0
0	1	0	0
0	0	1	0
1	1	0	0
0	1	1	0
1	0	1	0
1	1	1	1

OR Gate

Figure 2.6(A) gives the standard symbol for an OR gate. Figure 2.6(B) shows the equivalent circuit in simple electrical terms.

With this gate, a high on either input A or B enables the gate. Thus a 1 on A or B, or on both A and B at the same time, produces a 1 for output. This is

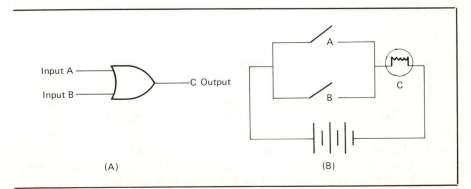

(A)   (B)

FIGURE 2.6.   *OR gate and equivalent circuitry.*

TABLE 2.4. *Truth Tables for an OR Gate.*

Input		Output	Input		Output
A	B	C	A	B	C
0	0	0	1	1	1
0	1	1	1	0	0
1	0	1	0	1	0
1	1	1	0	0	0

(A) Positive Logic   (B) Negative Logic

known as an inclusive OR gate. The truth table for this gate is given in Table 2.4.

Note that the positive logic for an AND gate gives the same result as negative logic for an OR gate. Also, negative logic for an AND gate gives the same result as positive logic for an OR gate. Thus either gate can act as the other, depending upon how logic levels are assigned.

Exclusive OR (XOR)

Another form of the OR gate that is used is the exclusive OR. Figure 2.7(A) gives the standard symbol for this logical device, and Figure 2.7(B) shows the equivalent electrical circuit.

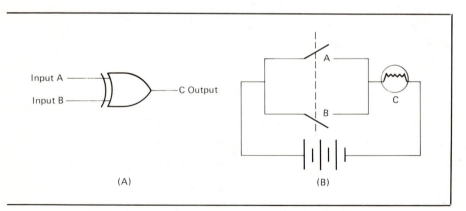

(A)   (B)

FIGURE 2.7. *Exclusive OR gate (A) and equivalent circuitry (B).*

Here switches *A* and *B* are tied together so one switch or the other may be closed, but not both. If either is closed, current will flow in lamp *C*. If neither switch is closed, no current will flow. Since both switches cannot be closed at the same time, this is again a state of no current flow. The truth table for this logic device is given in Table 2.5. An examination of the truth table shows the gate is enabled if either A or B, but not both, is a 1.

TABLE 2.5. *Truth Tables for an Exclusive OR Gate.*

Input		Output	Input		Output
A	**B**	**C**	**A**	**B**	**C**
0	0	0	1	1	1
0	1	1	1	0	0
1	0	1	0	1	0
1	1	0	0	0	1

(A) Positive Logic   (B) Negative Logic

NAND Gate

If an inverter is put at the output of an AND gate, a new gate is formed called a NOT AND, or NAND, gate. Figure 2.8 shows the standard symbol for this gate along with an equivalent electrical circuit.

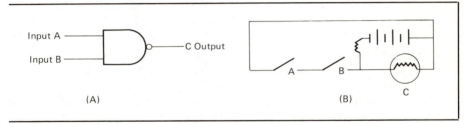

(A)   (B)

FIGURE 2.8. *NAND gate symbol (A) and equivalent circuitry (B).*

In the standard symbol, the small circle (o) at the output shows an inverter. This complements all the 1's and 0's at the output in the truth table (Table 2.6) from that of the AND gate. An inverter at an input would complement the input to the gate.

Note that in the circuit diagram, if both switches are closed, the path of least resistance for the current is through the switches, and thus the lamp (C) will not be lit. If either or both switches are open, the current will flow through

TABLE 2.6. *Truth Table for a NAND Gate.*

Input		Output	Input		Output
A	**B**	**C**	**A**	**B**	**C**
0	0	1	1	1	0
0	1	1	1	0	0
1	0	1	0	1	0
1	1	0	0	0	1

(A) Positive Logic   (B) Negative Logic

the lamp lighting it. If an inverter is put on an input, it changes the logic from positive to negative.

NOR Gate

If an inverter is put at the output of an OR gate, a NOR gate (*NOT OR*) is formed. Figure 2.9 gives the standard symbol for this gate and its equivalent in terms of a simple electric circuit.

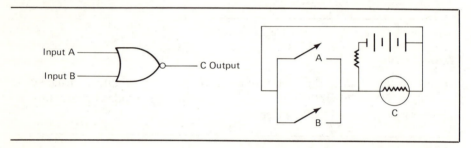

FIGURE 2.9. *NOR gate symbol (A) and simple equivalent electrical circuit (B).*

As with the NAND gate, the inverter complements all the 1's and 0's at the output of the NOR gate and thus all the 1's and 0's are complemented in the output column of the truth table (Table 2.7).

Because certain electrical properties of NAND and NOR gates make them superior to AND and OR gates, the NAND and NOR gates are the

TABLE 2.7. *Truth Table for a NOR Gate.*

Input		Output	Input		Output
A	**B**	**C**	**A**	**B**	**C**
0	0	1	1	1	0
0	1	0	1	0	1
1	0	0	0	1	1
1	1	0	0	0	1
(A) Positive Logic			(B) Negative Logic		

basic units used in many circuits. In fact, it is possible to build AND, OR or NOR gates from NAND gates. Similarily AND, OR and NAND gates can be built from NOR gates.

Example 2.1:

Build an inverter using NAND gates.

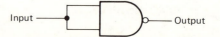

By feeding a single input to both the inputs of the NAND gate, the output is the inverse of the input. The NAND gate is now acting like an inverter.

Example 2.2:

Using NAND gates, build an AND circuit.

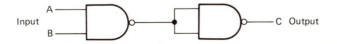

In the above circuit, if either A or B or both A and B have a low (0) input, there is a high (1) as an output from the first gate. The second gate acts as an inverter, thus making the output at C low (0). If both A and B are high, a low is output from the first gate, which is then inverted to a high by the second gate. This circuit is now acting as an AND gate.

Gates are used in various parts of a computer to make logic decisions. They are also used external to a computer to make decisions on an input to the computer.

Example 2.3:

Suppose you wish to build a device that will ring a buzzer if either of two doors is opened. Show a simple circuit diagram that will do this.

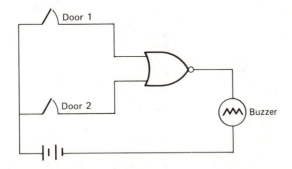

In the above diagram, if both doors are closed, the output from the NOR gate is a low. If either door is opened, the output goes high and the buzzer will ring. This type of circuit could be used with a computer replacing the buzzer. The output from the gate would be fed as an input to the computer. Since the number of input lines to a computer is limited, circuits like this one are very useful.

EXERCISE 2-3

1. Sketch the standard symbol for a two-input AND gate. Label all inputs and outputs.

2.   In terms of positive logic, which AND gate(s) are "enabled"?

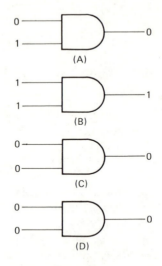

3.   For an AND gate with six inputs the truth table would contain _____ combinations of inputs (rows).
4.   Sketch the standard symbol for a two-input inclusive OR gate. Label all inputs and outputs.
5.   Fill in the correct logic levels on the following symbols. Assume positive logic.

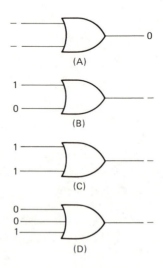

6.   Sketch the standard symbol for a two-input exclusive OR gate. Label all inputs and outputs.
7.   Using positive logic, complete the following table for a two-input NAND gate.

INPUTS		OUTPUT
A	B	C
A) 1	0	
B) 1		0
C) 0	0	
D) 1	1	

8. The NAND gate is made by connecting a _____ gate to the output of an _____ gate.
9. Sketch the standard symbol for a two-input NOR gate. Label all inputs and outputs.
10. Fill in logic levels on the following standard symbols. Assume positive logic.

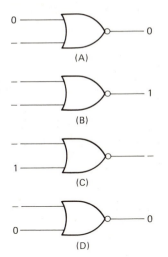

FLIP-FLOPS

A flip-flop is a digital logic device that can exist in either one of two stable states. These states represent a binary 1 or binary 0.

Once a flip-flop is put into a state, it stays in that state until changed by a signal, or until power is lost. The state of the flip-flop is determined by examining its outputs.

There are three basic types of flip-flops: the RS (or latch), the D, and the JK.

RS Flip-flop

The RS, latch, or set–reset flip-flop is illustrated in Figure 2.10. It is referred to by all three names.

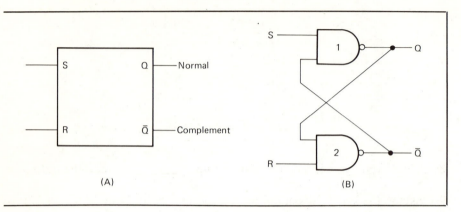

FIGURE 2.10. *The RS flip-flop: block diagram (A) and schematic diagram of one type of RS flip-flop using NAND gates (B).*

Figure 2.10(B) is a diagram of a common version of the RS flip-flop using NAND gates. This flip-flop is also built using negative NOR logic.

The S stands for set and R for reset in the inputs. Q is the normal output while $\bar{Q}$ is the complement of Q.

If this flip-flop is storing a binary 0, the Q output is 0 while the $\bar{Q}$ output is 1. Examine Figure 2.10(B) for the following discussion.

Suppose a 0 is put in the flip-flop and the following voltages are applied to R and S.

	Q	$\bar{Q}$	R	S
Binary number	0	1	1	1
Voltage	0	+5	+5	+5

At gate 2 there is a 0 at one input from Q and a 1 at the other input R. This means the output is a 1. At gate 1 the 1 from $\bar{Q}$ is fed into one input and $S = 1$, therefore a 0 comes through the gate to Q. Under these conditions there is no change in the flip-flop.

Now, assume the voltage at S is dropped to 0.

	Q	$\bar{Q}$	R	S
Binary number	1	0	1	0
Voltage	+5	0	+5	0

We have a 0 and a 1 as inputs to the first gate and thus a 1 as an output to Q. This gate has been enabled then by a low input. There are now two 1's being applied to gate 2, therefore a 0 is seen at $\bar{Q}$. The RS flip-flop has changed states and is now in the set or 1 state. By examining the voltages at Q or $\bar{Q}$, the flip-flop can be read without altering its state.

TABLE 2.8. *Truth Table for RS Flip-Flop. (Note that when both inputs are low (0) the flip-flop is in an undefined state; it could be either 1 or 0.)*

Original State of Flip-Flop		Signals to Inputs		Output Result	
Q	Q̄	S	R	Q	Q̄
0	1	0	0	Undefined	
0	1	0	1	1	0
0	1	1	0	0	1
0	1	1	1	No change	
1	0	0	0	Undefined	
1	0	0	1	1	0
1	0	1	0	0	1
1	0	1	1	No change	

Table 2.8 gives the truth table for the RS flip-flop when either a 0 or 1 was originally latched in the flip-flop.

Some books refer to this as an $\overline{R}$ $\overline{S}$ flip-flop since the outputs are the complement of the inputs. The RS flip-flop made from negative NOR logic gives a normal RS truth table. Here Q follows the input on the S line. When S is a 1, Q is a 1, and when S is 0, Q is 0. There are more complicated forms of the RS flip-flop having more inputs. These will not be discussed in this text.

D Flip-flop

Like the RS flip-flop, the D flip-flop has two input lines labeled D and C and two output lines Q and Q̄. See Figure 2.11. In diagram B the gates to the right of the dotted line are essentially the RS flip-flop.

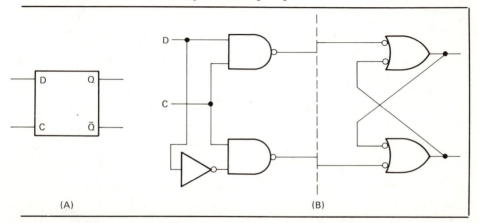

(A)

(B)

FIGURE 2.11. *The D flip-flop: (A) block diagram and (B) schematic diagram of a typical D flip-flop.*

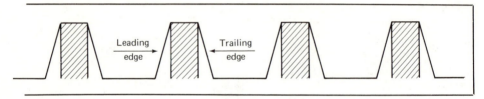

FIGURE 2.12. *Clock pulses; shaded area represents ideal clock pulse.*

The D line is the data line while the C line is a clock line. Data (0 or 1) are placed on the D line but are not stored in the flip-flop until a pulse is sent on the clock line. When the clock pulse goes high, the flip-flop stores the value present on the D line. Figure 2.12 shows the typical pulse on a clock. The clock pulse goes high when the voltage reading goes from 0 to +5 volts and goes low when the voltage goes from +5 volts to 0 volts. Changes in flip-flops occur as the pulse is going high (along the leading edge) or low (along the trailing edge).

The D flip-flop is normally made to change state along a leading edge. Figure 2.13 shows the relationship between the outputs from a D flip-flop and its inputs. In this type of diagram, for convenience sake, all pulses are treated as ideal pulses. At the first clock pulse a 1 is put on the D line, so this is stored in the flip-flop. This value is stored in the flip-flop until the leading edge of the next clock pulse. Even though the D line goes high before the third clock pulse, there is no change until the leading edge of this clock pulse occurs. Again a 1 is stored until the leading edge of the fourth clock pulse. The truth table for a D flip-flop is given in Table 2.9.

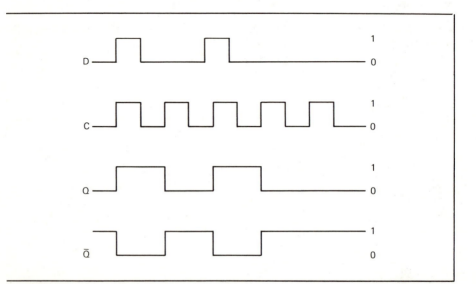

FIGURE 2.13. *Clocked pulses into a D flip-flop.*

TABLE 2.9. *D Flip-flop Truth Table*.

Original State of Flip-Flop		Signals to Inputs		Output Result	
Q	Q̄	D	C	Q	Q̄
1	0	0	0	1	0
1	0	1	0	1	0
1	0	1	1	1	0
1	0	0	1	0	1
0	1	0	0	0	1
0	1	0	1	0	1
0	1	1	1	1	0
0	1	1	0	0	1

JK Flip-Flop

This is the most useful and complex of the three flip-flops discussed. The JK referred to here is called a JK master – slave flip-flop. It is actually two flip-flops combined. One is referred to as the master, and the other the slave. See Figure 2.14.

Gates 3 and 4 make one latch (master) while gates 7 and 8 make the other (slave). Whatever is stored in the slave is read at the outputs Q and Q̄. Data are entered through the J and K inputs. When the clock pulse goes high it is transferred to the master flip-flop and held there. When the clock pulse goes low, the data are sent from the master to the slave flip-flop. Since Q and Q̄ are read from the slave flip-flop, the state of the flip-flop changes only when the clock pulse goes from high to low (1 to 0).

Table 2.10 gives the truth table for the JK flip-flop after the clock goes

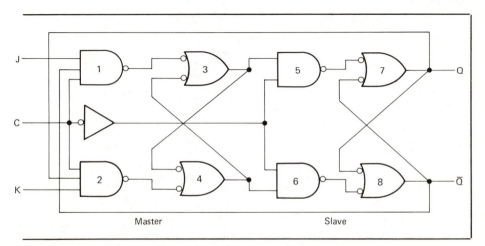

FIGURE 2.14. *Master-slave JK flip-flop.*

TABLE 2.10. *Truth Table for Master-Slave.*

Original State of Flip-Flop		Signals to Inputs		Output Result		
Q	Q̄	J	K	Q	Q̄	
0	1	0	0	No change		
0	1	0	1	0	1	
0	1	1	0	1	0	
0	1	1	1	1	0	(Complement)
1	0	0	0	No change		
1	0	0	1	0	1	
1	0	1	0	1	0	
1	0	1	1	0	1	(Complement)

from high to low. It is not necessary, at this time, to be able to verify the truth table for the JK flip-flop.

Another common form of the JK flip-flop has two more inputs to the slave flip-flop that are the S (set) and (R) reset lines. These gates are then three input NOR gates. By using the S or R line, the flip-flop can be preset to a 1 or precleared to 0.

Both the RS and the D flip-flop come in many other types; some that have master–slave components, and others with a set or reset input. The JK also comes in forms in which the initial change of the flip-flop is triggered by a trailing edge rather than a leading edge. For further information consult a text on digital logic or digital circuits.

EXERCISE 2-4

1. The RS or set–reset flip-flop is also known as a _____.
2. Consider the following diagram for an RS flip-flop.

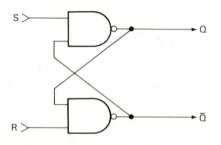

Complete the following truth table.

ORIGINAL STATE		DATA APPLIED		OUTPUT STATE	
Q	Q̄	R	S	Q	Q̄
1	0	0	1		

3. Whether data can or cannot be stored in a D flip-flop is determined by the _____ pulse.
4. Consider the following diagrams and conditions.
   What are Q and $\overline{Q}$?

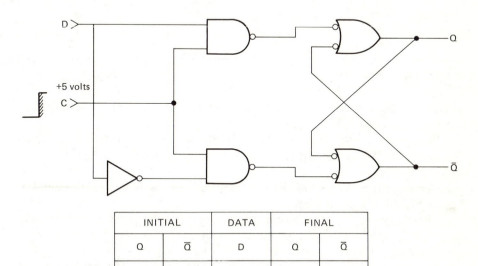

INITIAL		DATA	FINAL	
Q	$\overline{Q}$	D	Q	$\overline{Q}$
1	0	1		

5. The JK flip-flop is made of two latches. The one that receives the data first is called the _____ , and the second to which data are transferred is called the _____ .
6. True or false?
   a. There are data present at the inputs of a JK flip-flop and the device receives a low clock pulse. The data may now enter the master latch.

   _____

   b. Data are stored in the master of a JK and the device receives a low clock pulse. The data may now be transferred to the slave.

   _____

   c. On any low clock pulse the data stored in the master and slave latches of a JK are the same.

   _____

   d. On a high clock pulse new data *can* enter the master of a JK and the data in the slave will not be changed.

   _____

TRISTATE DEVICES

A variation of the logic devices, inverters, and gates introduced by National Semiconductor is called a tristate logic (TSL) device. These devices have the normal logic "0" and logic "1" and a third state called a high-impedance or high-Z state. This third state is equivalent to disconnecting the output of the

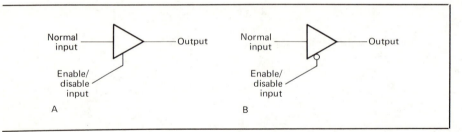

FIGURE 2.15. *Tristate buffer: (A) enabled high and (B) enabled low.*

device from the rest of the circuit. One of the most important of these devices is the bus buffer gate, Figure 2.15.

In Figure 2.15(A) when the enable/disable line is high (1) the buffer operates normally. When it is low (0), this disables the device so it acts as if it were disconnected from the circuit. In Figure 2.15(B) the opposite occurs. Some manufacturers thus refer to the line in Figure 2.15(A) as an enable input and in Figure 2.15(B) as a disable input.

These devices are extremely important on microcomputers as they quite conveniently allow isolation of circuits, exhibit less noise, and operate at higher speeds than other circuits used to do the same job.

Their usefulness will become quite clear when we discuss the ways devices are attached to busses in the computer. Many other tristate devices are available, including flip-flops, memories, and just about any device you would want to use in a microcomputer.

REGISTERS

Since each flip-flop stores a binary number we can put the flip-flops together to store a larger binary number. One flip-flop is needed for each bit that is to be stored. Such a group of flip-flops is called a register or latch. Which type of flip-flop is used depends upon the specific function of the register. Figure 2.16 is an example of D flip-flops being used to store a number. Each data bit is put on one of the D lines. When the clock is pulsed, the value of the binary number on the data line is stored in that particular flip-flop. It can be read later from the Q output lines.

By using gates, logic decisions can be made and thus addition, subtraction, and any other arithmetic operations can be performed. By combining gates to make flip-flops, memory or storage devices can be made. By combining gates, very sophisticated and complex decision-making circuits can be built. These are called combinational circuits. They are used for decoding, encoding, and arithmetic operations, for example.

If combinational circuits are interconnected with more flip-flops and gates, another more sophisticated form of register or memory device is formed; it is called a sequential circuit. Typical uses of sequential circuits are as

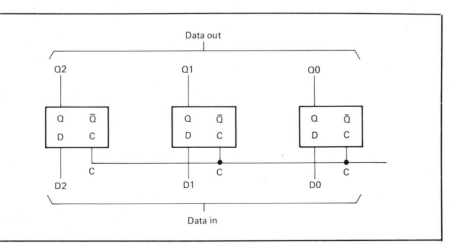

FIGURE 2.16. *A 3-bit register made from D flip-flops.*

counters, shift registers, and other circuits in which binary data are stored and used as a function of time. The last two circuits, combinational and sequential, are studied in more detail in a later unit.

EXERCISE 2-5

1. Draw a diagram of a tristate buffer with a disable input.
2. Define high-Z state.
3. Multiple flip-flops interconnected to form devices capable of storing large quantities of binary data are called _____ .
4. A device that can perform arithmetic operations is an example of a _____ circuit.
5. Memories use binary data as a function of time. They are _____ circuits.
6. Two types of very sophisticated special purpose registers are _____ and _____ .

DIGITAL LOGIC FAMILIES

There are two basic ways in which gates and flip-flops are made. These logic circuits can be made from different types of transistors (NPN or PNP), diodes, or similiar devices. They are known as bipolar devices. The other approach is to use metal oxide semiconductor field-effect transistors (MOSFETs). These are known as unipolar devices. MOS circuits are smaller than a regular transistor, therefore, a larger number can be placed in a given space. Figure 2.17 is a schematic diagram of a bipolar transistor (A) and a MOS transistor (B).

Transistors are made from semiconducting material, usually silicon, doped with another chemical to make the silicon either an N-type (negative) or

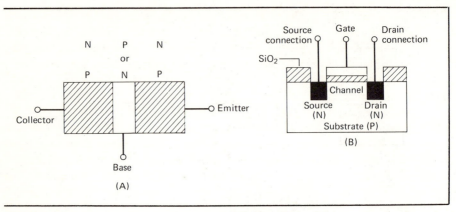

FIGURE 2.17. *Bipolar transistor (A) and NMOS transistor (B).*

P-type (positive) conductor. In a bipolar transistor the charge is carried by both N- and P-type carriers. In the MOSFET the charge is carried by only one type of carrier. In an NMOS transistor a silicon chip is doped to form a P-type substrate. Two islands are formed within this substrate that are N-type and are called the source and drain. Between these islands is a channel through which conduction takes place from source to drain. Above the channel is the gate. This is isolated from the channel by a small area of SiO_2. By applying a voltage to the gate, electrons flow through the channel. This type of MOSFET is known as an enhancement-mode transistor.

There are two different types of MOS circuitry depending upon whether P-type transistors in an N substrate or N-type transistors in a P substrate are used. Early microprocessors used the P type, or PMOS, while second- and third-generation microprocessors use the N type, or NMOS. A third type of MOS circuitry that is becoming more popular and is used by some microsystems is CMOS (complementory MOS). These MOSFETs contain both N- and P-type transistors together.

Because conduction by negative charges (electrons) is two to three times faster than by positive charges (holes), NMOS circuitry works two to three times faster than PMOS and therefore predominates in the field.

These devices are combined in different ways to form an integrated circuit (IC). The most popular form of integrated circuit or "chip" is the dual in-line package (DIP). See Figure 2.18.

FIGURE 2.18. *Illustration of a DIP IC.*

They are available with different numbers of pins, usually between 6 and 64. Depending upon the number of gates or flip-flops in a particular chip, the IC may be referred to as small-scale integration (SSI), medium-scale integration (MSI), or large-scale integration (LSI). Today work is being done on very-large-scale integration (VLSI). A single flip-flop is an example of an SSI circuit. MSI circuits contain numerous gates (perhaps 12 to 100) while large-scale integration may contain from 100 to 1000 or more gates, which means 1000 to 60,000 transistors. VLSI circuits contain as many as 250,000 transistors on a single chip. SSI packages usually have 8, 14, or 16 pins; MSIs have 14, 16, or 24 pins; LSIs have 24, 28, and 40 pins. Large-scale integration has been developed as a result of the discovery of MOSFETs. MOS circuitry predominates in medium- and large-scale applications. Figure 2.19 is a list of some bipolar IC logic families.

Logic Family	Abbreviation	Voltage Levels
Resistor–Transistor	RTL	0V; +3.6V
Diode–Transistor	DTL	0V; +5.V
Transistor–Transistor	TTL	0V; +5V
Emitter–coupled	ECL	−1.55V; −0.75V
High threshold	HTL	0V; 8–30V
Integrated injection	I^2L	0.05V; 0.75V

FIGURE 2.19. *Some bipolar logic families.*

Of these devices, TTL has been the most popular by far. It has so dominated the industry that other devices are made compatible with TTL logic states. Although most microcomputers use TTL logic states, ECL and I^2L are popular with some companies for reasons to be discussed later.

When building a computer from components, there are three fundamental characteristics of the components that must be considered: the operating speed of each chip, the power consumption, and the number of elements per chip, or packing density. In terms of operating speed the bipolar devices are fastest, followed by Schottky TTL, while NMOS is the fastest of the MOS devices, followed by CMOS and PMOS. On the other hand, the reverse order is essentially followed when considering power consumption. CMOS uses the least, followed by I^2L, while ECL and Schottky TTL consume the most. In terms of packing density, PMOS and NMOS are the best, followed by I^2L. TTL and ECL are the worst.

A disadvantage of the MOS circuitry, especially CMOS, is that it is very sensitive to static electricity. Care must be taken in handling these chips as a surge of static electricity through it may "burn" a chip out. A big advantage of MOS devices is the ability to make a microsystem from one chip due to the large packing densities of these devices. Bipolar circuitry requires two or more chips.

For an interesting series of articles on microcircuits and the technology involved, see *Scientific American.* (reference n. 7).

EXERCISE 2-6

1. A circuit made mainly of transistors is said to be employing _____ logic.
2. A circuit made of three RS flip-flops "hard-wired," connected externally, is an example of _____ .
3. The abbreviation IC stands for _____ .
4. Identify the following package by circling the proper letter.

   a. TO-35
   b. DIP
   c. TO-OO epoxy
   d. "Orange crate" package

REVIEW QUESTIONS

1. Complete the following table from voltages read as an output of a gate.

Voltage Read	Positive Logic Binary Code	Negative Logic Binary Code
4.5 Volts	a. _____	b. _____
0.2 Volt	c. _____	d. _____
0 Volts	e. _____	f. _____
3.9 Volts	g. _____	h. _____

2. For a two-input AND gate, where A is at logical 1 and output C is at logical 1, the logic level on input B must be _____ . (Assume positive logic.)
3. Negative logic is applied to an inclusive OR gate such that +5 volts is seen at input A and 0 volts is seen at input B. The voltage level at the output will be _____ , and the binary code would be _____ .
4. Fill in the correct logic levels on the following symbols. Assume positive logic.

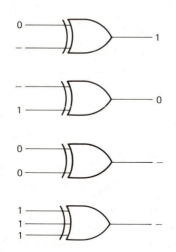

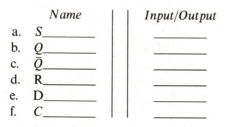

5. In the NAND gate symbol the small circle on the output means that the output is _____ .
6. When negative logic 1 is applied to both inputs of a dual-input NOR gate, the output in binary is _____ .
7. A flip-flop has the ability to _____ data.
8. Name each of the following flip-flop abbreviations and tell if it is an input or an output.

		Name	*Input/Output*
a.	S	_____	_____
b.	Q	_____	_____
c.	$\bar{Q}$	_____	_____
d.	R	_____	_____
e.	D	_____	_____
f.	C	_____	_____

9. A MOSFET is (circle the letter):
   a. A flip-flop
   b. A gate
   c. A transistor
   d. A combinational circuit
10. Using only NAND gates, construct an OR circuit.
11. Using only NOR gates, construct an AND circuit.
12. Assume you want to build a burglar alarm system that checks any of six windows or two doors. Construct a circuit, similar to Example 2.3 that will ring a buzzer if any door or window is opened. Use OR or NOR gates.
13. Draw a diagram of an RS flip-flop made from negative logic.
14. Explain what a tristate device is, and what its purpose is.

15. List an advantage and disadvantage of each of the following.

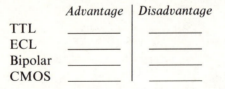

16. Refer to Figure 2.10. If we make the Q output the Q̄, and the Q̄ the Q output, what type of flip-flop is this?

GLOSSARY

AND gate	A two or more input device for which all inputs must be logical 1 to generate a logical 1 output (positive logic).
Binary	Two state. For example, the binary number system has only two digits, 0 and 1.
Chip	Nickname for an integrated circuit.
Clock Pulses	Alternating high and low signals generated by the computer to enable D-type and JK flip-flops, and time its functions. (Also see Chapter 3 glossary.)
CMOS	Complementory MOS transistor containing both N and P types.
Combinational circuits	A series of flip-flops and gates used to make a more complex circuit such as a register.
DIP	Dual in-line package. A popular form of integrated circuit package most often with 14 or 16 connecting pins, seven or eight to a side.
D-type flip-flop	Circuit that will store the binary data present on its D input line upon receipt of a high (or low) clock pulse at its C input line.
Enable	To allow a gate to pass data from its input to its output.
Encoders	Devices that convert from one code to another, usually a complicated or expanded code to a more compact one. Example: A 7-bit ASCII code might be encoded into 4-bit BCD codes.
Flip-flop	An electronic device with two stable states, conducting and not conducting, which can be used to store binary information.
Gate	A simple electronic circuit that can selectively allow the passage of data through it based on its input conditions. Gates in combination are used to form logic circuits.
Inverter	A logic device with one input and one output. When a signal is applied to the input, the signal at the output will be the reverse or complement.
JK flip-flop	Constructed of two D-type flip-flops such that it will store the information on its J and K inputs in its master

section upon receipt of a high clock pulse and will transfer the stored information to its slave upon receipt of a low clock pulse.

Latch	Another term for an RS flip-flop.
LSI	Large-scale integration. The incorporation of hundreds of discrete components onto a small integrated circuit.
MOSFET	Metal oxide semiconductor field-effect transistor. A very small transistor used widely in the computer field because of its low power consumption.
MSI	Medium-scale integration. The incorporation of a number, usually 12 or more, of logic devices into a single package with no external connections between the devices.
NAND gate	An AND with its output coupled through an inverter so that when all inputs are logical 1 the output will be logical 0 (positive logic).
Negative logic	Voltage assignments made in a computer system such that a level of +5 volts represents a binary 0 and 0 volts represent a binary 1.
NMOS	Negative-type MOS transistor.
NOR gate	An OR gate with its output coupled through an inverter so that when at least one input is logical 1, the output will be logical 0 (positive logic).
OR gate	A two or more input device for which at least one input must be logical 1 to generate a logical 1 output (positive logic).
PMOS	Positive-type MOS transistor. Conducting is done by movement of a positive charge or "holes."
Positive logic	Voltage assignments made in a computer system such that a level of +5 volts represents a binary 1 and 0 volts a binary 0.
Register	Combinations of flip-flops used to store binary words.
RS flip-flop	A device with two inputs, a set (S) input and a reset (R) input. If a logical 1 is applied to the set input, the device generates a logical 1 on the Q output. If a logical 1 is applied to the reset input, then Q displays logical 0. The device flip-flops.
Sequential circuits	These store and use data as a function of time. Example: memories that may or may not be made of flip-flops.
SSI	Small-scale integration. The use of discrete components and external wiring to form logic circuits.
Truth table	A row and column arrangement for a logic device showing all of its possible input combinations with their corresponding output states.
TTL	Transistor-transistor logic. A form of logic switching using primarily transistors. It is in the widest use today.

VLSI
: Very-large-scale integration. Latest technique for packing a large number of transistors, 250,000 or more, on a single chip.

XOR gate
: A two or more input device for which one and only one input may be logical 1 to generate a logical 1 output (positive logic).

REFERENCES

1. *Individual Learning Program in Digital Logic.* Heath Corp., Benton Harbor, Mich., 1975, Units 5 and 6.
2. John Young, *Digital Logic Workbook.* Digital Equipment Corp., Maynard, Mass., 1967, Chapter 2.
3. John F. Wakerly, *Logic Design Projects Using Standard Integrated Circuits.* John Wiley & Sons, New York, 1976, Chapters 2 and 4.
4. Peter R. Rony and David G. Larsen, *The Bugbook I.* E&L Instruments, Derby, Conn., 1974.
5. David G. Larsen and Peter R. Rony, *The Bugbook II.* E&L Instruments, Derby, Conn., 1974, Unit 8.
6. Sam Perone and David Jones, *Digital Computers in Scientific Instrumentation.* McGraw-Hill Book Company, New York, 1973, Chapter 2.
7. *Scientific American*, Sept., 237 (3), 1977 (entire issue on microcircuits.)
8. Ronald L. Krutz, *Microprocessors and Logic Design.* John Wiley & Sons, New York, 1980.
9. A. James Diefenderfer, *Principles of Electronic Instrumentation*, 2nd ed. W. B. Saunders Co., Philadelphia, 1979.

ANSWERS TO EXERCISE 2-1

1. 0
2. a. 1   e. 0
    b. 0   f. 1
    c. 0   g. 1
    d. 1   h. 0
3. 0

ANSWERS TO EXERCISE 2-2

1.

	INPUT	OUTPUT
a.	0	1
b.	1	0

2. Complement or reverse.

3.

Remember, $\overline{A}$ means complement of A.

ANSWERS TO EXERCISE 2-3

1. Inputs

2. b
3. $2^6 = 64$ combinations of inputs
4. Inputs

5. a. 0
      0
   b. 1
   c. 1
   d. 1

6.

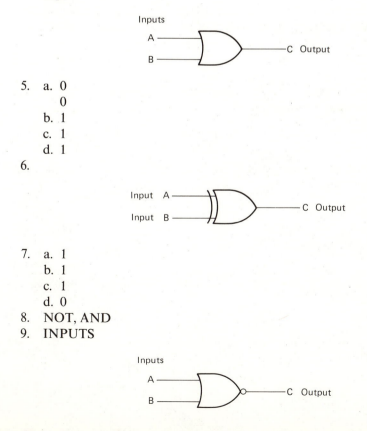

7. a. 1
   b. 1
   c. 1
   d. 0
8. NOT, AND
9. INPUTS

10. a. 1
     b. 0, 0
     c. 0
     d. 1

ANSWERS TO EXERCISE 2-4

1. Latch
2. $\overline{\begin{matrix} Q & \quad \overline{Q} \end{matrix}}$
    $\begin{matrix} 0 & \quad 1 \end{matrix}$
3. Clock
4. $\overline{\begin{matrix} Q & \quad \overline{Q} \end{matrix}}$
    $\begin{matrix} 1 & \quad 0 \end{matrix}$
5. Master, slave
6. a. False
    b. True
    c. True
    d. True

ANSWERS TO EXERCISE 2-5

1.

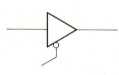

2. Third state a logic device can exist in, which corresponds to an open circuit. (Also high impedence.)
3. Registers
4. Combinational
5. Sequential
6. Sequential and combinational

ANSWERS TO EXERCISE 2-6

1. TTL
2. SSI: small-scale integration
3. Integrated circuit
4. b

ANSWERS TO REVIEW QUESTIONS

1. a. 1   b. 0
    c. 0   d. 1
    e. 0   f. 1
    g. 1   h. 0
2. 1
3. +5 volts: 0
4. a. 1
    b. 1
    c. 0
    d. 0:   On a multiple-input exclusive OR gate, *only one* input can be logic 1 to generate an output of logic 1.
5. Inverted or complemented
6. 0
7. Store
8. a. set   input
    b. normal   output
    c. complement   output
    d. reset   input
    e. data   input
    f. clock   input
9. c
10.

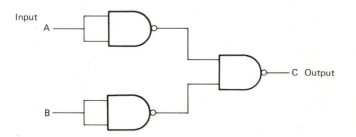

11.

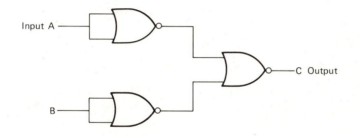

12.

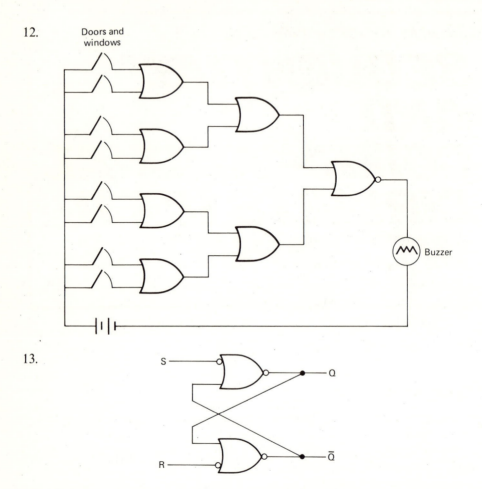

13.

14. A tristate device is a device having three states: high, low, and high Z. In the high-Z state the device acts as if it were disconnected from the line. This allows it to be isolated from other components on line.

15.

	Advantage	Disadvantage
TTL	Most widely used; overall rating one of the best	High power consumption
ECL	Very fast	High power consumption
Bipolar	Very fast	Low packing density
CMOS	Small power consumption; larger packing density	Not as fast as NMOS; more sensitive to static electricity

16. A normal RS flip-flop

CHAPTER 3

SEQUENTIAL AND COMBINATIONAL CIRCUITS USED IN COMPUTERS

LEARNING ACTIVITIES

Study lecture material on sequential and combinational circuits.
Read resources at end of unit.
Complete exercises.
Self-check answers to exercises.
Consult instructor if necessary.

OBJECTIVES

By completing these requirements, you should be able to achieve the following objectives for this unit when formally evaluated.

Objective 1

Given a diagram, identify each of the following parts of a computer.

a. Debouncing circuit
b. Latch
c. Shift register
d. Counter (up and down)
e. Decoder
f. Encoder
g. Multiplexers and demultiplexers
h. Adders

Objective 2

Given voltage signals applied to each of the above devices, identify the state of the device.

Objective 3

Given a memory unit, identify how information is stored in the unit and how units are put together to build larger memory units.

EVALUATION

Your ability to demonstrate achievement on these objectives will be assessed after all instruction on this unit by:

- Multiple-choice items
- Identification items

INTRODUCTION

Gates and inverters can be combined in various ways to form digital logic circuits referred to as combinational circuits. They have many uses in a computer, such as decoders, encoders, and multiplexers.

Digital logic circuits that contain gates, inverters, and flip-flops are referred to as sequential circuits. These are used, for example, to build counters, shift registers, and latches. The use of D flip-flops to build a latch was illustrated in Chapter 2. In this chapter we look at some typical components of a computer.

DEBOUNCING CIRCUITS

When a button is depressed and electrical contact is made, a considerable amount of noise is generated (Figure 3.1), which is called contact "bounce."

Each of the spikes on the leading or trailing edge could be interpreted by the computer to be a separate signal. In Figure 3.1 rather than a single change in state, seven possible changes in state may occur. That is, the computer may interpret this as seven separate depressions of the button. This problem may be eliminated in either of two ways:

1. Using a software program
2. With additional hardware

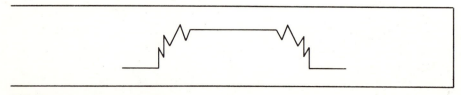

FIGURE 3.1. *Contact bounce.*

With a software program, the computer is instructed to examine a switch closure for a period of time, usually around 20 ms (milliseconds). If the button remains closed during this period of time, the computer assumes it to be a simple legitimate closure. The disadvantage of this is that it uses up memory. Its advantage is that such a system is cheaper to build. Many microcomputers work this way. A suitable hardware circuit for debouncing an input is given in Figure 3.2.

This type of circuit is used in debouncing single-pole double-throw (SPDT) switches. When the switch makes contact for the first time, the data are latched into the flip-flop and repeated pulses now have no further effect on the state of the circuit. An examination of the NAND gate debouncer shows that if the switch is thrown to the lower gate, this causes an input of 0 to occur here and an output of a 1. There are now two 1's going to the upper gate, so its output is 0. The data are now latched into this form of RS flip-flop. If the switch is thrown upward, the opposite happens, that is, a 1 is output through the upper gate and a 0 through the lower gate. This is again latched into this data configuration.

In using this circuit to debounce a switch, the circuit is put into a particular state. That is, the switch is pushed up so a 1 is stored in the latch; when the switch is pushed down, the latch will change state as soon as contact is made on the lower pole. As long as the switch does not touch the upper pole, a 0 is stored in the latch even though contact bounce may occur. The circuit has been debounced. The computer thus treats this as a single switch closure. Other debouncing circuits using inverters can be made for single-pole single-throw (SPST) switches.

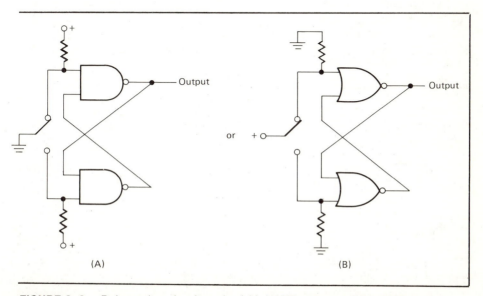

FIGURE 3.2.   *Debouncing circuits using (A) NAND gates and (B) NOR gates.*

Many of the problems encountered in building a computer have this two-fold type of solution — either hardware or software. There is always a trade-off between the two; the hardware solution costs more and the software solution uses up memory. In some cases a combination of hardware and software is used to solve a particular problem.

LATCHES AND SHIFT REGISTERS

Figure 2.16 was an example of a latch (or register) built from D flip-flops. These are often used in a computer to hold the data being transferred from one part of the computer to a peripheral or to another part of the computer. Each flip-flop is capable of holding 1 bit of information. Thus a 4-bit data latch can be built using two 7474 ICs since each 7474 IC contains two D flip-flops. These latches can be made from any type of flip-flop, although the RS and D are most commonly used. Either the original data or the data's complement can be read out from a latch.

By taking the output of a flip-flop and using it as an input to the next flip-flop, a different type of register known as a shift register can be built. Figure 3.3 illustrates a way in which the output of a D flip-flop is used as an input for the next D flip-flop in a serial-to-parallel shift register. In this figure, the rightmost flip-flop contains the least significant bit, while the leftmost flip-flop contains the most significant bit. Let us follow the change in state of each flip-flop through a series of clock signals.

We will alternate the data input 1, 0, 1, 0, etc. The D flip-flop chosen is one that changes state on the leading edge only.

The results are summarized in Figure 3.4. Note that four clock pulses are all that are needed to store the number in the shift register. The number stored is 0101_2. In general, to load a serial-to-parallel shift register, it takes one clock pulse for each bit in the register. By monitoring the output of each flip-flop, it is possible to read the number stored in the shift register. The data have been

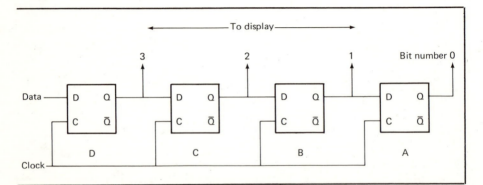

FIGURE 3.3. *Four - bit shift register made from D flip - flops.*

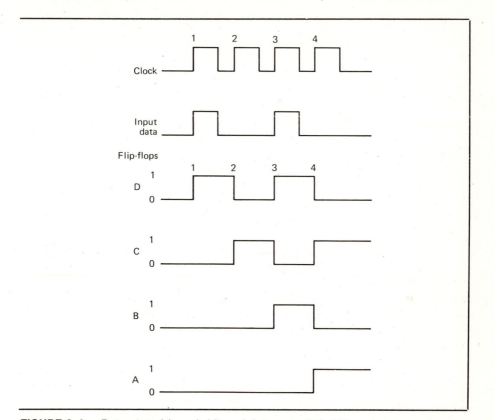

FIGURE 3.4. *Data stored in a 4-bit serial-to-parallel shift register as a function of time.*

entered in serial format and read in a parallel format. This means each bit is read in one at a time (serially), and the result (all 4 bits) is output all at the same time.

Another form of this is the parallel-to-serial shift register. Here all the bits are loaded into the flip-flops at the same time and then read out from the register 1 bit at a time.

Shift registers can be built from D or JK flip-flops but not RS flip-flops since the RS is not a clocked flip-flop.

EXERCISE 3-1

1. Given the following NOR gate debouncing circuit, in which direction (up or down) must the switch be moved to output a 1 through the latch?

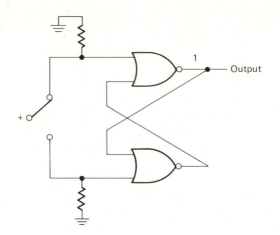

2. The following signals are input to a 4-bit serial to parallel shift register using D flip-flops (see Figure 3.3). What is the value of the binary number stored in this register? Assume the rightmost signal was the first signal.

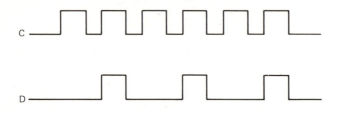

a. 1010   b. 0101   c. 0010   d. 0001

COUNTERS

Many different types of counters are used in computers. The most common is the binary counter. This counter counts in normal binary form. Counters can also be built to count in binary coded decimal or decimal form. Figure 3.5 is an example of a binary counter.

Note that this binary counter is again made by connecting flip-flops together. This time, though, the complement of the normal output ($\overline{Q}$) of each flip-flop is tied to the clock of the next flip-flop. The least significant bit is now the leftmost bit. The complementary output of the flip-flop is also connected to the D input of the same flip-flop. The results of a series of clock pulses to this counter are given in Figure 3.6. Since D flip-flops (FF) change state on the leading edge, if all 0's are stored in the FF's, that is, Q_0 through Q_3, the first clock pulse will cause FF A to become a 1, but the rest will remain 0. The second clock pulse changes FF A to a 0 and B to a 1, and so on.

This same type of circuit is also useful as a frequency divider. Since the flip-flop needs two clock pulses to change state, each flip-flop can be used as a divide-by-2 circuit. This circuit can be used to generate slower clock pulses. If

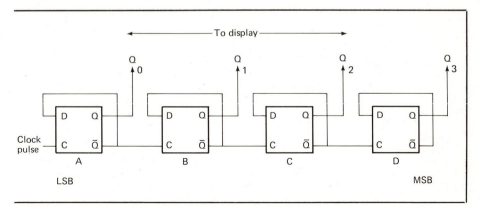

FIGURE 3.5.   *A binary counter using D flip-flops.*

the frequency of input to flip-flop A is 1 MHz (megahertz), then the output at each flip-flop is as follows:

A   0.5   MHz

B   0.25   MHz

C   0.125 MHz

D   0.0625 MHz

The counter in Figure 3.5 is known as an up-counter. Every clock pulse to

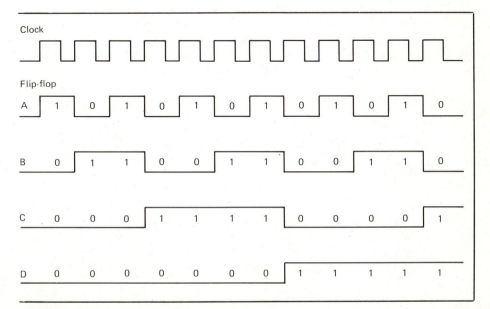

FIGURE 3.6.   *Pulses in a 4-bit binary counter.*

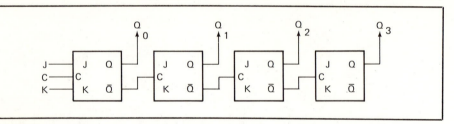

FIGURE 3.7. *Down-counter using JK flip-flops.*

flip-flop A causes the counter to increase by 1. Other types of counters used are down-counters (see Figure 3.7) and up-down counters. An input of a clock pulse to a down-counter causes a decrease in the number stored while an up-down counter can go in either direction, depending upon certain wiring constraints.

The type of counter discussed so far is an asynchronous or ripple counter. It is asynchronous because the same clock pulse does not control all the flip-flops. This type of counter is the easiest to construct and is cheaper since a minimum of hardware is necessary. Another type of counter is the synchronous counter. In this type all the flip-flops are controlled by the same clock pulse. In order to use this as a counter, more gates are necessary for controls. Though a synchronous counter is more expensive than an asynchronous counter, it is much faster at counting than the asynchronous counters since the count does not have to "ripple" from one flip-flop to another. Because there is a small, but definite, time delay involved in the changing of the state of a flip-flop, if a ripple counter gets too large or frequencies that are too fast are used to change states, this type of counter is more likely to give an error than the synchronous counter. By using flip-flops with set or present inputs, it is possible to make sure the counter is cleared or set to maximum count before counting starts.

EXERCISE 3-2

1. Counters can be built using:
   a. RS, JK, or D flip-flops
   b. JK or RS flip-flops
   c. D or RS flip-flops
   d. JK or D flip-flops
2. If a frequency of 4 MHz is applied to an 8-bit binary counter, the output frequency through the last flip-flop is
   a. 0.5 MHz   b. 0.25 MHz
   c. 0.0156 MHz   d. 1 MHz
3. Explain why counters are also referred to as divide-by circuits.

DECODERS

A decoder is a combinational logic circuit that detects the presence of an input signal and generates a unique output that is determined by the input. Figure 3.8 shows a simple single-bit decoder.

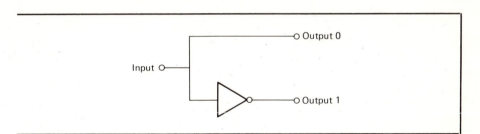

FIGURE 3.8. *A 1-bit decoder.*

Depending upon the input, either output 0 or output 1 is activated. The basic gates used in decoder circuitry are inverters and AND gates. Figure 3.9 is an example of a 2-bit decoder.

This is a two-line to four-line decoder. Decoders such as this are used in BCD to decimal decoding (4 bit to ten lines) as well as binary to hexadecimal

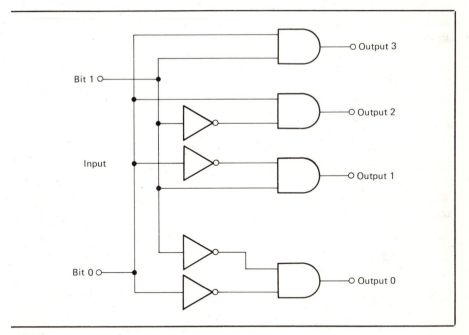

FIGURE 3.9. *A 2-bit decoder.*

decoders. In general, the maximum number of outputs from a decoder is given by 2^N where N is the number of inputs. In some decoders not all the outputs are used.

ENCODERS

The opposite circuitry of a decoder is an encoder. An encoder is a combinational logic circuit that detects the presence of a signal on one input line out of many and generates a specific output determined by the input signal. These are used, for instance, to translate a decimal signal from a pushbutton to

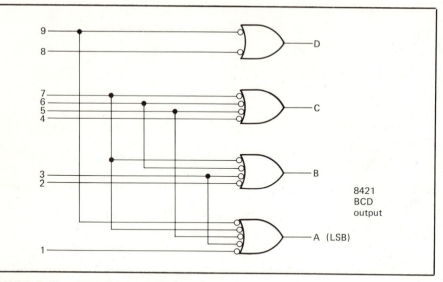

FIGURE 3.10. *Decimal - to - BCD encoder.*

binary or BCD output code. Multiple-input OR gates using negative logic can be employed for this purpose. Figure 3.10 gives an example of a decimal to BCD encoder. With this encoder, the lines (1 through 9) are kept high in their normal state. When a decimal number such as 3 is put on lines 1 through 9, the line 3 will go low, enabling OR gates A and B. The BCD output is thus 0011. A decimal to BCD encoder could be made using this gate arrangement but without the inverters to the gates. This would decode when lines 1 to 9 go high.

In examining Figure 3.10, we can see that if two lines go low at the same time, the output could be meaningless. Some encoders, known as *priority encoders*, handle this problem by outputting the highest number on the inputs. Thus if lines 1 and 2 both went low, only gate B would register an output. Figure 3.10 is not a priority encoder so it could not handle this problem.

Example 3.1:

Examine Figure 3.10. This diagram is typical of encoders. Note that inverters are on the inputs. This means the lines are normally high, and are decoded when the line goes low. Which outputs are high if line 9 goes low?

Answer: Outputs *D* and *A* go high while *B* and *C* remain low. This corresponds to the BCD number 1001. This is a 9 in 8421 BCD format.

Now determine which outputs are high if both 8 and 7 go low.

Answer: All four outputs now become high. This gives the BCD number 1111, which does not correspond to an 8421 BCD code. This is why it is not a priority encoder.

EXERCISE 3-3

1. A device that detects the presence of an input signal and generates a unique output signal is called a(n) _____ .
2. A device that generates a unique output signal that is determined by the nature of an input signal to the device is called a(n) _____ .
3. Refer to Figure 3.10. Which gates are enabled when line 6 goes low?
4. Refer to Figure 3.10. If this were a priority encoder, which gates would be enabled if both lines 7 and 8 went low?

MULTIPLEXING AND DEMULTIPLEXING

It is possible to take a number of different inputs and put them, at different times, on the same line. This process is called multiplexing. A decoder is used with additional gates to selectively place the different data bits on the same line at different times. Such a device is known as a multiplexer or data selector. Multiplexing is used either to keep the number of lines to a minimum or to keep the number of pins needed in a chip to a minimum. Multiplexers are also used to convert parallel data to a serial format or act as a Boolean function generator.

Figure 3.11 is an example of a two-input multiplexer. Inputs A and B are

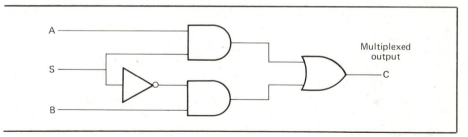

FIGURE 3.11. *A two-input multiplexer.*

the data inputs, while line S is a select input. This line determines which data, from A or B, will be placed on the output line C.

Demultiplexing is the opposite of multiplexing. When a multiplexed signal occurs on a line, there must be logic circuitry at the other end to send the data to the proper place. This device is called a demultiplexer or data distributor. It works in a manner similar to the rotor in the distributior of a car. As the signal comes in, the rotor moves from one place to another, selectively sending the signal to various other lines. A demultiplexer thus takes a signal from one line and distributes it to more than one line. A typical use is as a serial-to-parallel converter.

BINARY ADDERS

Another common combinational logic circuit used in computers is the binary adder. Figure 3.12 shows a simple 1-bit half-adder.

The upper gate is an exclusive OR gate. If A and B are 0, both outputs

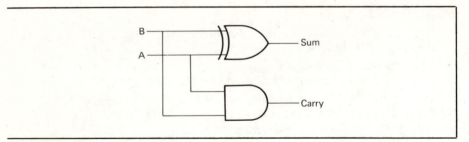

FIGURE 3.12. *A 1-bit binary half-adder.*

are 0; if either A or B is 1, the output of the exclusive OR is 1, while the carry is 0. If A and B are both 1, the sum is 0, and the carry output is 1. This conforms to the rules of adding in binary.

Table 3.1 gives the truth table for a half-adder.

TABLE 3.1. *Truth Table for a Half-Adder.*

Inputs		Outputs	
A	**B**	**S**	**C**
0	0	0	0
0	1	1	0
1	0	1	0
1	1	0	1

Two half-adders can be combined to give a full adder. A full adder differs from a half-adder in that the full adder will also accept a carry from another adder (Figure 3.13).

In Figure 3.13 A and B are the inputs, while C is the carry from another adder. The truth table for such an adder is given in Table 3.2.

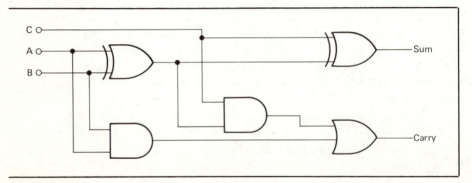

FIGURE 3.13. *A full adder.*

TABLE 3.2. Truth Table for a Full Adder.

Inputs			Outputs	
A	B	C	Sum	Carry
0	0	0	0	0
0	1	0	1	0
1	0	0	1	0
1	1	0	0	1
0	0	1	1	0
0	1	1	0	1
1	0	1	0	1
1	1	1	1	1

EXERCISE 3-4 Multiplexers, demultiplexers, and adders.

1. A device that takes different signals and puts them at different times on a single line is called a _____ .
2. A device that takes various signals on a given line and distributes them to other lines is called a _____ .
3. Examine Figure 3.13, the full adder. Can an AND gate be substituted for the OR gate used to generate the carry from the full adder? How will the truth table differ?

MEMORIES

In order to be functional, computers must be capable of storing large amounts of binary information. In microcomputers this storage is usually accomplished by using semiconductor ICs arranged in groups comparable to the word size of the computer. Figure 3.14 gives a typical arrangement of memory in a chip.

Each memory unit that is capable of storing 1 bit of information is called a "cell." In Figure 3.14 the device is capable of storing 128, 4-bit words. By concatanating two of these chips together, we can build a 128- by 8-bit word-storage device. The proper cell is chosen using a data selector circuit or decoding circuit on lines 1 to 128 as well as a separate set of signals to lines A through D. Memory storage devices come in various sizes and packages. Other common sizes are 256×8 and 256×1. In general, all chips store a number of words that corresponds to a power of 2. The most common are 128, 256, 512, 1024, 2048, and 4096. By combining these chips, various word sizes are built. It is usually cheaper to build an 8-bit memory from eight chips of 256×1, but this uses much more room than a single chip of 256×8.

The cost of an IC is also roughly related to the number of pins on the IC — the more pins, the more complex the circuits in the IC, and the more expensive the IC. In the above IC there are 128 rows of cells holding information. Each has its own specific address. Since $128 = 2^7$, you need a 7-line to 128-line decoder to address each row. A chip holding this memory needs seven

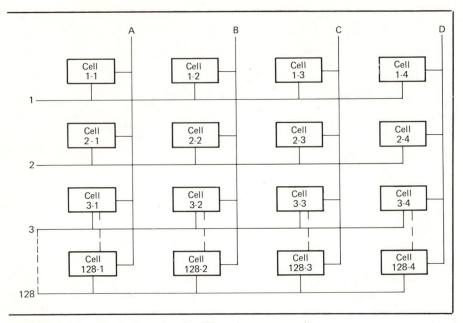

FIGURE 3.14. *Block diagram of a 128 × 4 memory unit.*

pins for addressing. To determine which column the information will enter (A, B, C, or D), another four pins, called data pins are used. In addition, a minimum of two power pins are needed, as well as another pin called a read/write pin. The purpose of this last pin is discussed in more detail in the next chapter. This comes to a total of 14 pins.

If we wish to concatanate two such chips to make an 8-bit word, we usually need another means of selecting the chips since the addresses to the cells must be the same. This means that another pin, called a chip-select pin, must be present. Since every IC has an even number of pins, we need two chip-select (CS) pins. This gives us a chip containing a minimum of 16 pins. A summary follows.

Address pins	7
Data pins	4
Power pins	2
Read/write pins	1
Chip-select pins	2
Total	16

If the memory device is 128 × 1, then only one data pin is needed and a smaller chip containing 12 pins could be used to build this circuit.

Memory units can be made from flip-flops, as well as from many other types of devices. The various types of memory units will be discussed in the next chapter. Further circuitry is discussed in the chapter on interfacing with digital-to-analog and analog-to-digital devices.

Example 3.2:

Suppose you wish to build an IC containing memory cells of 256 × 4. What is the minimum number of pins necessary on the chip?

   Answer: To address 256 cells we need an 8-line to 256-line decoder ($2^8 = 256$). This uses eight pins. Four pins are needed for the four cells on the same line. With two power pins and a read/write pin, this comes to 15 pins. With one chip-select pin we have a total of 16 pins.

Example 3.3:

How many of the above chips would be necessary to build a memory unit of 512 × 8?

   Answer: If we concatanate two chips together we will get a memory unit of 256 × 8. Two of these units will equal 512 × 8, so a total of four chips is necessary.

REVIEW QUESTIONS

   1.   The following signals are input to a 4-bit serial-to-parallel shift register using D FFs. What is the value of the binary number stored?

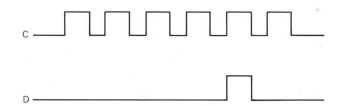

   2.   An 8-bit shift register is built using D FFs. How many clock pulses are needed to load the register?
   3.   What frequency must be applied to an 8-bit binary counter such that the output frequency from the last flip-flop is 1 MHz?
   4.   If you have a decoder with three inputs, what is the maximum number of outputs possible?
   5.   What is a priority encoder?
   6.   Explain how a data distributor works.
   7.   How many chips of 256 × 4 must be put together to make a memory unit of 256 × 16?
   8.   What is meant by the software/hardware trade-off in microsystems?
   9.   The following is a form of the RS flip-flop known as a clocked RSFF.

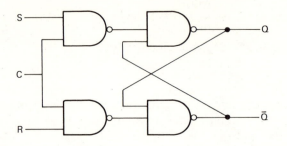

This can be used to make a latch or register since it changes state under the C control and not with every leading edge. Construct a circuit diagram of a 2-bit shift register using this flip-flop.

10. Construct a priority encoder that will take a signal from one of three lines (1, 2, 3) and output the result in BCD format.

11. Complete the following truth table for problem 10.

3	2	1	A	B
1	1	1		
0	1	1		
1	0	1		
1	1	0		
1	0	0		
0	0	0		

12. A new memory chip has recently become very popular. It consists of 65,536 × 1 memory cells. What is the minimum number of pins needed for this chip?

REFERENCES

1. *Individual Learning Program in Digital Logic.* Heath Corp., Benton Harbor, Mich., 1975.
2. *Digital Computer Principles,* new edition, Burrough Corporation. McGraw-Hill Book Company, New York, 1969, Chapter 8.
3. A. James Diefenderfer, *Principles of Electronic Instrumentation.* W. B. Saunders Company, Philadelphia, 1979, Chapters 11 and 12.
4. Sam P. Perone and David O. Jones, *Digital Computers in Scientific Instrumentation.* McGraw-Hill Book Company, New York, 1973, Chapter 7.

GLOSSARY

Adders	Electrical circuit that carries out binary addition.
Asynchronous counter	A counter in which the clock of each flip-flop is controlled by the output of the previous flip-flop.
Cell	Unit in memory capable of storing 1 bit of information.
Counter	Device used to count in binary, which may be up, down, or either way, depending upon the nature of the counter.
Decoder	A device used to detect a unique input and generate a specific output.
Debouncing circuit	A hardware or software circuit that eliminates switch bouncing.
Demultiplexer	A device that will take several signals on a given line and assign them to their proper line.
Encoder	A device used to generate a unique output based on input to one of two or more lines.
Frequency divide circuit	Another use for a counter circuit; divides frequency by 2^N where N is the number of flip-flops.
Full adder	An adder that handles the carry from another adder.
Half-adder	An adder that does not handle carry from another adder.
Latch	Register used to hold binary numbers.
Multiplexer	A device that will take several signals and put them on the same line at different times.
Priority encoder	An encoder that outputs the highest number when two or more numbers reach it at the same time.
Ripple counter	Another name for an asynchronous counter.
Shift register	Register in which a serial word can be converted to a parallel format or a parallel word to a serial format.
Synchronous counter	A counter in which all the clocks of the flip-flops are controlled to change at the same time.

ANSWERS TO EXERCISE 3-1

1. Down
2. 1010 (a)

ANSWERS TO EXERCISE 3-2

1. JK or D flip-flops (d)
2. 0.0156 MHz (c)
3. Because output through a flip-flop is some number of 2's divided into input.

ANSWERS TO EXERCISE 3-3

1. Decoder
2. Encoder
3. B and C 0110 binary output
4. Line 8 enables gate D.
   Line 7 enables gates C, B, and A.
   If only one gate could be enabled, it would be the gate with the highest value, or gate D.

ANSWERS TO EXERCISE 3-4

1. Multiplexer
2. Demultiplexer
3. No. If either A or B is high and C is high, the carry from the OR gate will be lost.

ANSWERS TO REVIEW QUESTIONS

1. 0100
2. Eight
3. 256 MHz
4. Eight (2^N)
5. One that accepts the output only from the highest valued gate.
6. Distributes data to different lines by assuming data is time dependent.
7. Four
8. Electrical problems can be solved using additional hardware, which is more expensive, or software-writing programs, which is less expensive but uses up memory.
9.

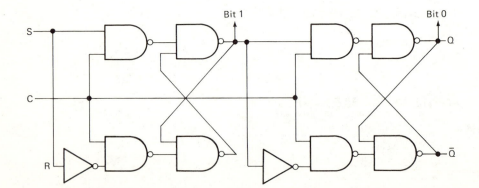

10.

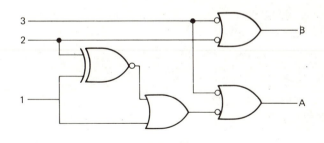

11.

3	2	1	B	A
1	1	1	0	0
0	1	1	1	1
1	0	1	1	0
1	1	0	0	1
1	0	0	1	0
0	0	0	1	1

12. 16 address pins
Two power pins
One read/write pin
One chip-select pin
No pin is needed for the other dimension. In actuality more chip selects are present than just one.

CHAPTER 4

MICRO-PROCESSOR/ MICRO-COMPUTER STRUCTURES

LEARNING ACTIVITIES

Study lecture material on computer structures.
Read resources listed at end of unit.
Complete exercises.
Self-check answers to exercises.
Consult instructor if necessary.

OBJECTIVES

By completing these requirements, you should be able to achieve the following objectives for this unit when formally evaluated.

Objective 1

Given a diagram of a CPU and register, select and define each register and label the parts of the CPU according to standard conventions.

Objective 2

Given an instruction cycle, select the registers involved in an operation according to standard procedures.

Objective 3

Given main memory, define the types of memory and parts according to conventional operations.

Objective 4

Given a list of input and output devices, define the appropriate method of operation according to conventional standards.

Objective 5

Given a list of bus terminology, select the appropriate definition of each function according to standard descriptions.

EVALUATION

Your ability to demonstrate achievement on these objectives will be assessed after all instruction on this unit by:

- Multiple-choice items
- Identification items

MAJOR UNITS

Six major units make up a microcomputer:

1. Central processor or CPU
2. Clock

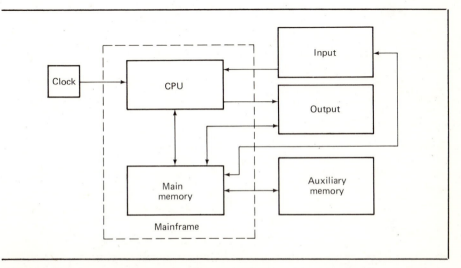

FIGURE 4.1. *Block diagram of a microcomputer.*

3. Main memory
4. Input devices
5. Output devices
6. Auxiliary storage devices

Figure 4.1 is a block diagram of these units.

The main memory and CPU together are referred to as the *Mainframe*.

THE CENTRAL PROCESSING UNIT

The central processing unit (CPU) is the heart of a microcomputer. This is the microprocessor. Some books refer to it as MPU, for microprocessing unit. It does all logical and arithmetic operations, executes the instructions stored in memory, and controls and supervises the other units. Figure 4.2 shows a typical structure of a CPU.

The CPU can be divided into two parts—the control unit (CU) and an arithmetic unit (AU). The control unit executes the instructions stored in

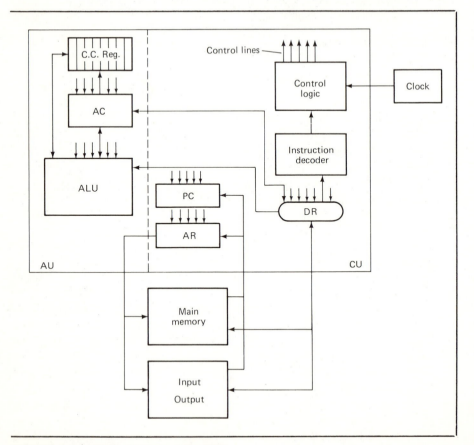

FIGURE 4.2. *Block diagram of the CPU.*

memory and controls and supervises the other units. The AU does the logic and arithmetic operations.

The major components of the AU are as follows:

1. ALC (arithmetic and logic circuits). This unit is composed of gates and registers that can do arithmetic calculations and make tests between numbers. It has three main inputs: the accumulator, the data register, and another register that Motorola calls a condition code register (CC register).
2. AC (accumulator). This is the most useful register in the microprocessor. All arithmetic operations are handled through the accumulator. The AC holds a number after the operation. There may be more than one accumulator in a microprocessor. Typical examples are as follows:

Company	Microprocessor	Word Length	No. of ACs
Intel	8080A	8 bits	1
Intel	8085	8 bits	1
Motorola	MC6800	8 bits	2
Motorola	MC6809	8 bits	2
Zilog	Z80	8 bits	2
MOS Technology	6502	8 bits	1

Some central processors do not have accumulators. Their functions are handled by general-purpose registers (GPRs). The LSI-11 of Digital Equipment Corporation has eight such registers that can function as an accumulator, although only six should be used as such. Some GPRs can act like accumulators, others cannot. The 8080, for instance, has six GPRs that do not act like accumulators but are useful as storage registers, whereas the 6800 has no such registers.

3. Condition code register. In a microprocessor each bit of this register represents the status of a particular operation that has taken place. One bit will check the accumulator to see if it is 0. Another checks for overflow from bit 7. This bit is called the carry bit. In an 8-bit microprocessor, this is an 8-bit register, and so eight different checks can be made. Each bit is referred to as a 1-bit flag. Because each bit represents the status of an event, this register is also called a "processor status word" by manufacturers. Not all the bits need be used. In the MC6800 only 6 of the bits are used as flags. The other 2 bits are permanently locked into a high state.

In general most manufacturers use these flags to check for overflow from bit 7 (carry), overflow into bit 7 (negative), to see if the accumulator is 0, overflow from bit 3 to bit 4 of the accumulator (half-carry), and an interrupt bit. The six flags for the MC6800 are explained in more detail later.

The control unit consists of the following.

1. Address register (AR). This register holds the address of the place in main memory where the CPU is presently obtaining information. This is also known as the memory address register (MAR).
2. Control logic. This device produces a series of electrical signals that enables information to be transferred from one register or unit to another. These electrical signals are usually referred to as data paths. Every instruction produces its own set of unique signals.
3. Data register (DR). This is a temporary storage register for data coming into or going out of the CPU. It also holds an instruction while the instruction is being decoded. In some microcomputers there are two registers that take the place of a data register—a buffer register and an instruction register.
4. Instruction decoder. This circuit examines the instruction in the data register and decodes the instruction into a format the control logic circuitry will understand.
5. Program counter (PC). This is a register that stores the address of the next instruction to be executed. To execute (or run) a program, the starting address of the program is stored in the PC and a command is given to start the program. The instruction at this address is transferred to the data register and the address of the next instruction is put into the PC. Normally the addresses stored in the PC are in increasing order, differing by 1 so the PC need only be incremented by 1 to get the address of the next instruction. The exception to this is when a branch instruction of any type is encountered.

In many microprocessors the logic circuits are hard-wired random logic. The instruction decoder will generate one or more microinstructions that determine which logic circuits are used to generate the data paths. Some newer microprocessors have what is called a programmable logic array (PLA), also referred to as a programmable array logic (PAL). These consist of arrays of AND feeding OR arrays that can be used to change the meaning of the various instructions fed into the computer. In general, the advantage of the PLA over a hard-wired logic is that the PLA can be altered by the manufacturer to increase the efficiency of a micro for a particular task. A more complicated form of PLA is the field programmable logic array (FPLA). This type can be used to some extent by a person using the FPLA in the lab, to alter the meanings of the instructions to the computer. These arrays are also useful in correcting defects in memory. This is referred to as a "patch."

Some computers have all instructions stored in what is called microcode. The microcode then generates the signals to the logic circuits. If a particular logic circuit is defective, corrections can usually be made by changing the microcode rather than changing the hard-wired logic circuits. This speeds up the introduction of the microprocessor and also has the advantage of the possibility of introducing new instructions to the computer at a future time.

EXERCISE 4-1 CPU

1. Draw a block diagram of a basic CPU unit. Label the control and arithmetic logic units along with their appropriate registers.
2. Which register keeps track of the program during operation?
   a. AR
   b. PC
   c. IR
   d. DR
3. Which of the following registers is used as a working area in the CPU?
   a. IR
   b. AR
   c. AC
   d. PC
4. Choose the correct answer in each of the following.

   a. Consists of the CPU and main memory.   A. Accumulator
   b. Where all mathematical and logic   B. Program counter
      functions are performed.   C. Mainframe
   c. This unit supervises each instruction   D. Address register
      in the CPU.   E. Control logic circuits
   d. Where information is held before going   F. Data register
      to the decoder.   G. AU

CLOCK

When a microprocessor executes a series of instructions (called a program), it does so in a particular order and in a certain time. Every microcomputer contains a clock that splits time up into very small and equal intervals, and counts the number of intervals passed since a particular program has started. The output of this circuitry is an electrical pulse, called a clock pulse. This pulse is used, for instance, to set and reset flip-flops and thus change information in registers in a manner determined by the control logic device in the CPU. Figure 4.3 is a diagram of a typical clock pulse. Most microprocessors take the clock pulse and divide it into sections called phases. The 6800, 8080A, and 6502, for instance, have a two-phase clock. Figure 4.3 shows a two-phase clock pulse.

These pulses are split into two separate nonoverlapping phases, $\phi1$ and $\phi2$. Certain parts of the microprocessor are activated by $\phi1$ while other parts are activated by $\phi2$. Both phases combined make one clock cycle. This is an example of nonoverlapping phases since $\phi2$ does not start until $\phi1$ is completed. For most microprocessors $\phi1$ controls events coming from the MPU, while $\phi2$ controls devices external to the MPU. Various changes in the system are triggered by the leading or trailing edges 1, 2, 3, and 4.

In the 6800 and 6502 a machine cycle consists of one clock period as

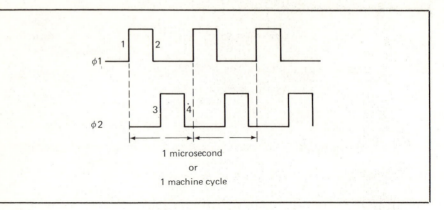

FIGURE 4.3. *Two-phase nonoverlapping clock pulse.*

shown in Figure 4.3. For the 8080A a machine cycle can have anywhere from three to five of these clock pulses, depending upon the instruction being executed. The time for a clock pulse will vary from microprocessor to microprocessor. For the 6800 it is 1 μs (microsecond), but Motorola also makes other models of the 6800 that have different clock speeds. The MC68B00 has twice the speed of the 6800, so its machine cycle or clock pulse would be 0.5 μs.

Other microprocessors such as the 8085 and the Z-80 have a single-phase clock pulse. The MC6809 by Motorola has a two-phase clock pulse that overlaps by 90°.

As a microprocessor executes a program, it goes through two basic cycles over and over again as shown in Figure 4.4.

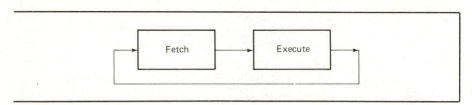

FIGURE 4.4. *Two basic cycles of a microprocessor.*

During the fetch cycle, an instruction is taken from memory and placed in the data register. This operation would take the same number of pulses from the clock no matter what type of instruction were being fetched. In the 6800, this is one clock pulse (or cycle). This process involves many steps.

The following is an example of what would take place during an ADD immediate instruction. The ADD immediate instruction is a 2-byte instruction with the first byte telling the computer that this is an ADD immediate instruction; the second byte is the number to be added to an accumulator.

Operation	Clock Edge
1. The PC contains the address of the instruction to be taken.	(see Figure 4.3)
2. This address is transferred to the address register.	No. 1
3. The PC is incremented by 1 and now contains the address of the next instruction.	No. 2
4. The contents of this address (the ADD immediate instruction, 8B) are now placed on the data bus.	No. 3
5. The contents are latched into the data register and are decoded by the instruction decoder.	No. 4
This completes the fetch cycle.	

Example 4.1:

The ADD immediate instruction for the 6800 is 3B. Let us examine the value of various registers as this instruction is executed. We will assume this instruction is stored in memory at address 0100.

Original state of various registers.

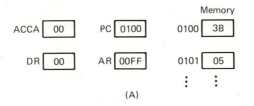

(A)

Along the first clock edge the address in the PC is transfered to the AR.

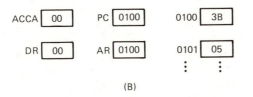

(B)

Along the second clock edge the address in the PC is incremented by 1.

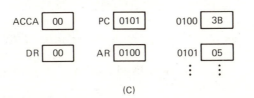

(C)

Along the third clock edge the address in the AR is decoded and the value at this address is placed on the data bus to the DR.

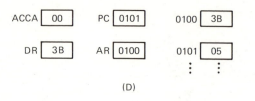

(D)

Along the fourth clock edge the instruction 3B is decoded by the instruction decoder and the control logic circuitry produces the proper signals to carry out the instruction.

This completes the fetch phase. The execute phase goes through a similar cycle.

Unlike the fetch cycle, the execute cycle can take many different number of machine cycles, depending upon the specific instruction being operated on. The basic step in this cycle is the execution of the instruction. If it is a simple instruction such as ADD immediately, then this cycle uses a minimum of time. If the instruction is an indirect instruction that tells the computer to go elsewhere before it can ADD, the execute state takes longer. For the ADD immediate instruction, the fetch cycle would tell the computer that this was an ADD immediate command. The execute cycle would carry out the addition. The following steps would be used.

Operation	Clock Edge
1. The PC now contains the address of the number to be added.	—
2. This address is transferred to the address register.	No. 1
3. The PC is again incremented by 1.	No. 2
4. The contents of the address are placed on the data bus.	No. 3
5. The contents are latched into the data register and executed; that is, the logic control unit has generated signals that cause the AU to take the contents of the data register and ADD these to whatever is in the accumulator and store the result in the accumulator	No. 4

The four edges referred to are used to complete the fetch cycle and another four edges would complete the second half of the ADD immediate cycle. It would thus take an MPU with a 1-μs clock 2 μs to complete this instruction. For an ADD direct instruction, in which the computer has to go to another address to get the data, the execute cycle would take two machine cycles before it was completed.

The total time it takes the microprocessor to go through the two basic cycles, or the instruction cycle as it is called, is referred to as *instruction cycle time*. Obviously this time will differ from one instruction to another, depending upon the complexity of the instructions.

The time it takes for one complete pulse of a clock is called a machine cycle. The fetch cycle takes one machine cycle. Most microcomputers come with a booklet that gives the number of machine cycles for each instruction.

All microprocessors use clocks to synchronize their internal activities. Some microprocessor-based microcomputers use these clocks to synchronize external activities on the bus. These are referred to as *synchronous* computers. In these computers, as with microprocessors, after executing an instruction the CPU waits for the proper clock pulse to trigger the next operation. A small amount of time may be wasted by the CPU waiting for the signal to start the next operation. There is another class of computers that do not depend entirely upon the clock for control of operations on the bus. These are referred to as *asynchronous* computers. Rather than being clock driven, they are event driven. When an operation is completed, a signal is produced that starts the next operation. This type of computer needs much more hardware to generate the signal after each event and to keep track of what the CPU is doing. The advantage of asynchronous computers is they are generally faster than synchronous computers. A 6800-based microcomputer is a synchronous computer, while the LSI-11 is an asynchronous computer.

EXERCISE 4-2: Clock

1. A computer that relies on a clock to set up pulses in order to perform instructions is called
   a. Asynchronous
   b. Synchronous
   c. Sequential
   d. Pulse generation
2. The sequence of operations necessary to fetch and execute information is known as a(n)
   a. Memory cycle
   b. Instruction cycle
   c. TRI cycle
   d. Clock cycle
3. The unit of time that is $1/10^6$ of a second is a
   a. Nanosecond
   b. Millisecond
   c. Microsecond
   d. Macrosecond
4. Which of the following computers generally operates faster?
   a. Synchronous
   b. Asynchronous

MAIN MEMORY

The instructions and data needed by the CPU while going through a program are stored in a part of the computer referred to as main memory. The time it takes a CPU to put into memory or take out of memory an instruction or data word is called the access time. This normally is 1 μs or less. Figure 4.5 is an example of a typical 128×8 memory chip. The pins on the chip have the following functions.

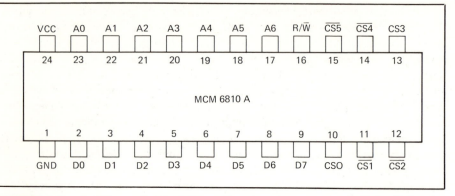

FIGURE 4.5. *A 128- × 8-bit static random-access memory built by Motorola. (Courtesy Motorola Semiconductor Products, Inc.)*

1. Read/write pins. The process of fetching information out of main memory is called *reading*. This process does not alter the contents of memory. Data can be read from a certain memory location as many times as is desired.

   Information can also be stored in a given location in memory. This process is called writing . What was previously in that memory location is now gone. The read/write pin determines whether data are being read into or written from memory. The time it takes to read data is called the read access time. This will depend upon the type of logic family and circuitry used to build the chip.

   The bar over the word write ($\overline{w}$) means that a low to the pin puts the chip in a write state whereas a high would put the chip in a read state.

2. Address-select pins. As discussed in Chapter 3, memory is built up in microcomputers using various size chips. For instance, if we have an 8-bit computer, and wish to have 256 × 8 memory available, we could make this by concatenating two 128 × 8 memory chips or eight 256 × 1 memory chips. To store a word in the eight 256 × 1 memory chips, 1-bit of the word is stored in each memory chip. In order to read/write a word, eight different chips have to be accessed at the same time.

   Each DIP holding the chip has pins known as address pins and chip-select pins. Both these types of pins are used to address a DIP. The address pins select where in memory the computer goes, while the chip select pins, which may be high or low, enable the chip. Since this is a 128 × 8 memory unit, seven address lines are needed to decode all 128 rows of memory ($128 = 2^7$). Pins 23 through 17 are the address pins. Pins 10 through 15 are the chip-select pins (CS). Here we have six CS pins, four of which are enabled low while the other two (pins 10 and 13) are enabled high. By using various combinations of these pins, different chips can be selected at the appropriate time and larger amounts of memory can be combined.

3. Power pins. In this chip two pins are used for power. Pin 24 is +5 volts and pin 1 is ground.

4.   Data pins. Since this is a 128×8 memory unit, there are eight data pins, pins 2 through 9.

MEMORY UNITS

Main memories come in different sizes. Each location in memory can store one word. The total number of locations in memory is the size of memory. It is usually expressed in multiples of K. In the decimal system K means 1000, but in binary it means the power of 2 nearest 1000. This is 2^{10}, which is equal to 1024. A 1K computer has 1024 memory locations. A 4K computer has 4096 memory locations, each of which has its own unique address. In computers memory normally is some multiple of 4K whereas in microprocessors it may be as low as 1/4K, or 256 bytes.

Memories are made of different types of material. Three of the more common media used are magnetic cores, bipolar, and MOS, and bubble memories are just entering the field.

1.   Magnetic core. Core memory is made from very small rings of ferrite, a magnetizable material. The magnetic field may extend in either of two directions. One direction represents the 1 state, the other the 0 state. In order to read core memory, the memory state has to be set to 0 and the change in magnetic field is monitored. The time it takes to do a read or write operation is called a memory cycle time. The process of reading core memory is relatively slow so the memory cycle time here is of the order of a microsecond. The read process is a destructive process in that what was originally in memory has been destroyed. There must be additional circuitry to restore the memory to its original state. The biggest advantages of core memory are that it uses very little power and information is retained in memory when the power is off. Core memory is just about obsolete in microcomputers.

2.   Bipolar. The basic unit in this memory element is the flip-flop. Memory locations are registers made of a series of flip-flops. As mentioned in Chapter 2, voltages are used to set flip-flops. Once set, the value is retained by the memory device as long as the power is on. This type of memory device is called a *static* memory. Its memory cycle time is around 300 ns (nanoseconds).

3.   MOS. These memories contain many MOSFETs combined. There are two ways in which MOS memories can be made. An electric charge can be stored in the memory locations. Such a unit is called a charge-coupled device (CCD) memory unit. This charge dissipates with time and has to be recharged through a process done approximately once every millisecond by a circuit called a refreshing circuit. This type of memory is called dynamic. MOS memories can also be made of flip-flops. This is another example of a static memory. MOS memory cycle time ranges from 300 to 800 ns. Both bipolar and MOS memories lose what is stored in them when the power is shut off.

4. Bubble memories. A recently available device is the bubble memory, in which the absence or presence of bubbles in a magnetic material represents a 0 or a 1. It has only been in the past year or two that the technology has been developed to such a state that these devices are capable of holding sufficient information in a given area. Their advantages are fewer moving parts and the fact that the memory is retained when the power is shut off.

There are two basic ways in which memories function. Some memories are read/write memories (RAM), sometimes called (RWM). Others are read-only memories (ROM). ROM memories have information permanently written into memory. This information cannot be changed, nor is it lost if the power to the circuit is shut off. RAM memories are the read/write memories as previously mentioned. The letters RAM stand for random access memory. This is actually a misnomer as both RAM and ROM are random access memories, but the name for RAM was historically developed before ROM memories were.

Besides the foregoing, there are other special forms of memories.

- PROM. A programmable read-only memory (PROM) is a special type of ROM that can be programmed by anyone. Using a device known as a PROM burner, data or instructions are permanently stored in memory.
- EPROM. An erasable read-only memory (EPROM or EROM) is an example of a read-mostly memory (RMM). These can be programmed using the PROM burner, but also can be erased (cleaned) by exposure to ultraviolet light through a transparent window on top of the chip. This procedure erases all of the memory. It can then be reprogrammed.
- EAROM (trademark of National Cash Register). This is an electrically erasable read-only memory and is another example of RMM. It requires a larger chip to store the same number of bits as an EPROM does, is higher in price, and slower in operation. Its advantage is that it can be selectively erased and rewritten.

EXERCISE 4-3 Main memory

1. Identify the following.
   a. This type of memory can only perform a read operation. _____
   b. The basic unit in a bipolar memory is a _____
   c. This operation is always a destructive one in memory. _____
   d. Memory size is usually referred to in terms of K. K is equal to _____ words.
2. Draw a diagram of a main memory unit and label all parts.
3. Which of the following forms of memory retains its information after power has been shut off?
   a. Core   c. Semiconductor
   b. Bipolar   d. MOS

4. Which of the following is the best example of a dynamic type of memory?
   a. Core   b. Bipolar   c. MOS

INPUT/OUTPUT DEVICES

To communicate with a computer, it is necessary to be able to feed information into the computer from the external world or to have the computer feed information to the external world. Devices that are capable of doing this are called input/output devices (I/O), or peripheral devices.

Input Devices

Each device has its own medium on which the code is stored. On input commands this code must be read off the medium and transformed into a format the computer understands. The major differences between input devices are the manner in which the code is stored and the speed with which it is transmitted to the computer.
Common input devices are

1. Pushbutton switches
2. Teletypewriters (TTYs)
3. Paper tape readers
4. Magnetic tape readers
5. Disks
6. Cassettes
7. Punch cards
8. High-speed readers

Each input device is attached to the computer through an interface. This unit translates the code from the device into the format needed by the computer. There are registers in this unit that hold the data being sent out by the input device. Interfaces are discussed in greater detail in the next chapter.

Output Devices

These devices store or record information being sent out by a computer. They have an interface that translates the information from the computer into the code used by the device. Common output devices are

1. Lights (LED)
2. Teletypewriter
3. Paper tape punch
4. Magnetic tape
5. Video screens
6. High-speed printers

7. Disks
8. Cassettes

EXERCISE 4-4 I/O devices

1. List five types of input devices.
2. List five types of output devices.
3. A magnetic disk device is used as a(n)
   a. Input device
   b. Output device
   c. Auxiliary storage device
   d. All of the above
4. All peripherals are directly connected to the memory and CPU units.
   a. True
   b. False

AUXILIARY STORAGE DEVICES

Some of the peripheral devices listed as input/output devices are used to store large amounts of information (disks, magnetic tapes). These are also referred to as auxiliary storage devices.

There are two ways in which information can be stored in these devices. A *sequential access* means the information is stored in such a way that the computer must start at the beginning of the stored information and move through every bit of information until the desired information is reached. This can be time consuming. In *direct access* devices, any storage location can be accessed directly without going through all the previous locations. Storage devices are discussed in more detail in Chapter 6.

BUSSES

To transmit information from one part of the microprocessor to another, the units must be connected by a group of wires called a *bus*. All data, instructions, controls, etc., are thus transmitted along busses.

Bus systems can be classified as single-bus or multiple-bus.

1. Single-bus. In this configuration (Figure 4.6) one bus is used to transmit all

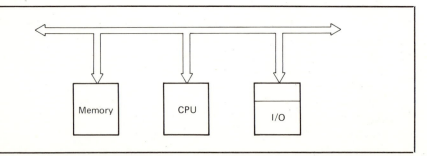

FIGURE 4.6. *A single-bus system.*

signals through the computer. Such a bus must be bidirectional in that at times signals may be moving one way along the bus and at another time they may be moving in the opposite direction.

2. Multiple-bus. In a multibus system, more than one bus is used to transfer data to the various units in the computer. Figure 4.7 shows a typical multibus system.

This is a three-bus system with one bus connecting the CPU to memory (a memory bus), a second between the CPU and I/O devices (I/O bus), and the third between the I/O devices and memory. A three-bus system can be faster than a single-bus system since different signals may be sent along two busses at the same time. In most three-bus systems only one bus can be used at a time. A single-bus system has the advantage of using fewer machine instructions and is thus easier on a person writing a program.

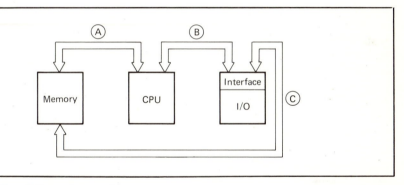

FIGURE 4.7. *A three-bus system.*

In Figure 4.7 bus *C* going from the I/O interface to memory is called a direct memory access (DMA) bus. This allows data to be entered directly into the memory, thus bypassing the CPU. This process takes only one memory cycle to transfer a word from the input device to memory; going through the CPU and then to memory might take three memory cycles.

EXERCISE 4-5 Busses

1. Diagram a single-bus system.
2. The three busses associated with a three-bus system are the memory bus, I/O bus, and the:
   a. Address bus
   b. Data bus
   c. Direct memory access bus
   d. Unibus
3. The single-bus system is generally _____ than the three-bus system.
   a. Slower

    b. Faster

    c. No difference

4. The bus that enables data to flow from the main memory to a peripheral device is the

    a. DMA bus

    b. Input bus

    c. Output bus

    d. Data bus

REVIEW QUESTIONS

1. The location where all mathematical and logic operations are performed is called the

    a. CPU

    b. ALU

    c. CU

    d. AC

2. During an ADD instruction the contents of the AR is 2000_{16}. What are the contents of the PC?

    a. 2000

    b. 2001

    c. 1999

    d. 1FFF

3. A type of memory that must be continuously recharged in order to retain its information is known as

    a. Static

    b. Rechargeable

    c. Core

    d. Dynamic

4. If a memory has 4K capacity, how many addresses does it have?

    a. 4000

    b. 4096

    c. 8000

    d. 2048

5. Which type of memory can be erased in part if an error is detected?

    a. EPROM

    b. PROM

    c. EAROM

    d. EROM

6. How many chips are needed to build a memory unit of 256×8 bits if the only chips available are 128×4 bits?

    a. Cannot be done

    b. Two

    c. Four

    d. Eight

7. The mainframe of the computer is composed of the
   a. CPU and storage devices
   b. CPU and main memory
   c. Main memory and storage devices
   d. CPU and ALC
8. Match the second column with the first.
   1. DMA bus   a. Memory composed of flip-flops.
   2. Sequential access   b. Random-access, read/write memory.
   3. Static memory   c. Access that starts at the beginning
                               and goes through everything
                               without skipping.
   4. RAM   d. Connects main memory and external
                               memory devices.
   5. ROM   e. Random-access read-only memory.
9. What is meant by a "flag"?
10. Identify the term PLA.
11. Complete Example 4.1 by doing a similar analysis of the execute cycle for the ADD immediate instruction.
12. What is the number stored in the program counter when the execute cycle in question 11 is completed?
13. What is the difference between a ROM and a RAM?
14. Explain the difference between a sequential-access device and a direct-access device.
15. What is a bus?

REFERENCES

1. *Individual Learning Program in Microprocessors.* Heath Corp., Benton Harbor, Mich., 1977, Units IV and V.
2. *Introduction to Minicomputers.* Digital Equipment Corp., Maynard, Mass., 1973.
3. Sam Perone and David Jones, *Digital Computers, in Scientific Instrumentation.* McGraw-Hill Book Company, New York, 1973, Chapter 13.
4. Al Halsema, Bubble Memories, *Byte* 4(6), p. 166 (June 1979).
5. Ben E. Cline, An Introduction to Microprogramming, *Byte* 4(4), p. 210 (Apr. 1979).
6. David A. Hodges, Microelectronic Memories, *Scientific American.* 237 (4), p. 310, Sept. 1977.
7. Ronald L. Krutz, *Microprocessors and Logic Design.* John Wiley & Sons, New York, 1980, Chapter 5.

GLOSSARY

Accumulator (AC)   A register in the arithmetic-logic unit of the CPU that is used as a working area for computations.

Address register (AR)	A register in the control unit of the CPU that is used to hold the address of the memory location presently being serviced by the CPU.
Arithmetic-logic circuits (ALC)	The component in the arithmetic-logic unit of the CPU that contains adders and other circuits to perform the actual calculations and logical tests required.
Auxiliary storage	Bulk storage medium used to support the main memory of a computer. Usually used to store programs not currently needed and vast amounts of data.
Bipolar	A type of semiconductor memory that uses a flip-flop to store 1 bit of information.
Bus	A group of wires used to interconnect computer system components. Each group is designed to carry a specific type of information (i.e., address, data, control).
Carry register	A 1-bit register that handles the carry from the MSB.
CCD	Charge-coupled device. MOS memory unit that stores data as a charge.
Central processing unit (CPU)	The major control, logical, and mathematical unit in a computer system.
Chip selects	Pins on a DIP used to enable a chip.
Clock	A device used to generate a repetitive electrical pulse.
Condition code register (CC)	An 8-bit register in which each bit is used as a 1-bit flag to signify events. Also known as processor status word.
Control lines	The bus lines used for control and monitoring functions.
Control logic	The component in the control unit of the CPU that is responsible for switching data paths between CPU components.
Control unit (CU)	The section of the CPU responsible for retrieving and decoding instructions and for controlling data movements throughout the computer system.
Core	A ferrite ring used to store a bit of information. Core is a memory storage area for main memory.
Data bus	The bus lines used for transferring data between two components connected to the bus.
Data register (DR)	A register in the control unit of the CPU that is used to hold an instruction while it is being decoded and executed.
Direct memory access (DMA)	Transfer of data between a peripheral and main memory without intervention of the CPU.
DMA bus	A bus that interconnects main memory with one or more mass storage devices. The bus is *not* connected directly to the device, but rather to the device's interface.
EAROM	Electrically alterable read-only memory. A RMM unit that can be selectively erased and rewritten.

EPROM	Eraseable programmable read-only memory. A type of PROM memory that can be erased, thus enabling it to be used over and over again.
General-purpose register (GPR)	A register in the CPU that is used for different functions such as addressing operands, storing operands, and holding the results of computations.
Input/output bus	A bus that provides a common communication path between the CPU and various peripheral devices. Peripheral devices are *not* connected directly to the bus; rather, they are connected through individual interfaces.
Instruction	A series of bits (usually a word) that tells the computer what operation to perform next.
Instruction cycle	A sequence of operations necessary to fetch, decode, and execute an instruction.
Instruction decoder	A component in the control unit of the CPU that is used to decode the OP code of an instruction. This determines which operation is to be executed.
Instruction register (IR)	See Data register.
Interface	A unit that serves as a translator between a specific peripheral device and the computer system.
Mainframe	The central processor and main memory of a computer system.
Main memory	The high-speed storage of a computer. Usually used for storing current instructions and data.
Memory access time	The time it takes to complete an entire memory cycle.
Memory address register	A part of the location-select circuit in main memory that holds addresses to be referenced by the processor. Also called address register.
Memory bus	A bus connected between the CPU and main memory that permits transfers of information between main memory and the CPU.
Memory cycle	A complete read or write operation.
Microcomputer	A microprocessor containing input and output devices and auxiliary memory.
Microprocessor	From the contraction microprogrammable processor, often understood to mean a one-chip CPU.
Microsecond	A unit of time that is one millionth of a second. Usually abbreviated μs.
Millisecond	A unit of time that is one thousandth of a second. Usually abbreviated ms.
MOS memory	Metal-oxide semiconductor memory. There are two types. One stores data in a flip-flop, a static unit; the other stores data as a charge and needs to be refreshed, dynamic memory.

Nanosecond	A unit of time that is one billionth of a second. Usually abbreviated ns.
Peripheral device	Any part of a computer system other than the CPU and main memory. Input and output devices and auxiliary storage units are included in this category.
Processor status word	See Condition code register.
Program	A complete sequence of instructions for solving a particular problem on a computer.
Program counter (PC)	A register in the control unit of the CPU that indicates which instruction is the next to be executed.
PROM	Programmable read-only memory. A type of ROM memory that can be programmed.
Read and write memory (RWM)	A type of memory in which information may be written or read.
Read-only memory (ROM)	A permanent memory that cannot be changed. This type of memory can only be read.
Register	A common storage element that is usually designed to hold one word of information.
Single-bus system	A system in which a single, common bus is used to interconnect all computer system components. All information is transferred on this single bus.

ANSWERS TO EXERCISE 4-1

1. See Figure 4.6
2. PC
3. AC
4. a = C
   b = G
   c = E
   d = F

ANSWERS TO EXERCISE 4-2

1. b
2. b
3. c
4. b

ANSWERS TO EXERCISE 4-3

1. a. ROM
   b. Flip-flop
   c. Write
   d. 2^{10} or 1024

2. See Figure 4.5
3. a. Core
4. c. MOS

ANSWERS TO EXERCISE 4-4

1. Paper tape readers
   Teletypewriters TTYs
   Magnetic tape readers
   Magnetic disks
   Punch cards
   High-speed readers
   Cassettes
   Switches
2. Video screen
   TTYs
   Cassettes
   Magnetic disks
   Magnetic tapes
   Paper tape punch
   High-speed printers
   Lights
3. d
4. false

ANSWERS TO EXERCISE 4-5

1. See Figure 4.6.
2. c
3. a
4. a

ANSWERS TO REVIEW QUESTIONS

1. a
2. b
3. d
4. b
5. c
6. c
7. b
8. 1—d
   2—c
   3—a
   4—b
   5—e

9. A one bit register that is used to represent the status of a device or operation.
10. Programmable logic array; an array of gates that can be used to patch an error in a ROM or alter the meaning of an instruction.
11.   along the fifth clock edge, the address in the PC is transferred to the AR.

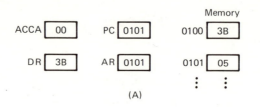

(A)

along the sixth clock edge, the PC is incremented by one.

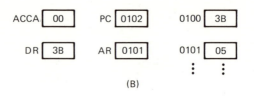

(B)

along the seventh clock edge, the address in the AR is decoded and the value at this address is placed on the data bus to the DR.

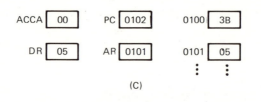

(C)

along the eighth clock edge, the control logic signals add the value in the DR to ACCA.

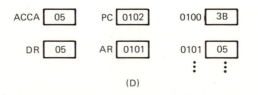

(D)

We are now ready for the next fetch state.

12. 0102
13. Both are random access memory units. A ROM can only be read though. The information in it can not be changed. A RAM can be read or written to. All information stored in it can be changed.
14. Sequential access: one must start at the beginning and move through all information until you come to the desired information. Direct access: or random access allows you to jump anywhere into the information and remove it.
15. A group of wires that connect one part of the computer to another.

CHAPTER 5

INPUT/ OUTPUT I- SIGNALS

LEARNING ACTIVITIES

Study lecture material.
Read resource materials listed at end of unit.
Complete exercises.
Self-check answers to exercises.
Consult instructor for assistance as necessary.

OBJECTIVES

By completing these requirements, you should be able to achieve the following objectives for this unit when formally evaluated.

Objective 1

Given the words bus, bidirectional, undirectional, address lines, control lines, and data lines, define each according to standard usage.

Objective 2

Given the terms memory mapped and I/O mapped, define each and identify how it is used in microcomputers.

Objective 3

Given the words chip select, define them and identify how they are addressed in a standard microcomputer.

Objective 4

Given parallel and serial transmission signals, bit time, and baud rate, define each and identify it as used in a computer.

Objective 5

Given the terms chip computer and board computer, identify each according to standard usage.

Objective 6

Given the terms parallel and serial interface, asynchronous and synchronous communications, and communications protocol, define each and identify each and its use in the LSI-11 and 6800-based microcomputers.

EVALUATION

Your ability to demonstrate achievement on these objectives will be assessed after all instruction on this unit by:

- Multiple-choice items
- Definitions
- True or False items

INTRODUCTION

The various components of a microcomputer (CPU, clock, memory, etc.) are present as IC chips on dual in-line packages (DIPs). In this unit we look at how these components are put together to build a microcomputer, and at the signals sent through the microcomputer to enable the CPU to operate the system.

MICROPROCESSORS

A microprocessor is the central unit in a microcomputer. As we learned in the last chapter, it contains all the circuitry necessary to do the arithmetic calculations and logic decisions. In this chapter we look at the external connections of a typical microprocessor. Figure 5.1 is a diagram of two common microprocessors built by Motorola. Both are based on NMOS technology. The MC6809 is the newest member of the 6800 family of microprocessors. Both of these have 16 address pins and eight data pins and run on a single +5 volts. The MC6800 has its clock signals generated by an external crystal while the MC6809 comes in two versions, one with an internal oscillator and the other with an external oscillator. Signals are sent to and from the microprocessor along busses.

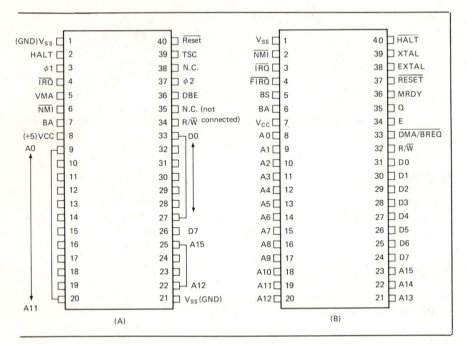

FIGURE 5.1. *Pin assignments for the (A) MC 6800 and (B) MC 6809 of Motorola. (Courtesy Motorola Semiconductor Products, Inc.)*

BUSSES

Microcomputers are highly bus-oriented computers. All devices on the computer are connected together via the bus. The nature of the bus, to some extent, determines the capabilities and limits of the computer. The bus structure used in most microcomputers is the single-bus system described in Chapter 4.

A typical bus is a flat, flexible cable with special connectors at each end to attach to the pins. The pins where the connections are made are called a *port*. The number of wires in a bus and the way signals are carried along the bus vary from one manufacturer to another. Some busses allow signals to move in either direction along the bus. These are called *bidirectional* busses. Other busses (*unidirectional*) allow signals to move in only one direction along the bus. The wires in a bus can be divided into three general groups.

1. Address lines. The CPU sends a signal along these lines that corresponds to the address of the device or memory unit desired.
2. Data lines. These are bidirectional lines along which information or instructions are sent.

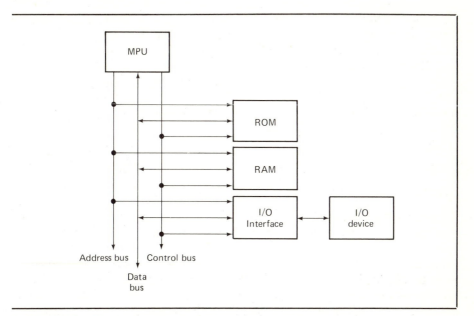

FIGURE 5.2. *Block diagram of a basic microcomputer system.*

3. Control lines. As the name implies, these lines are used to control or monitor the system. These include read/write commands, and start, halt, busy, and similar commands.

Microcomputers refer to these sets of lines as the address bus, the data bus, and the control bus respectively. Manufacturers will thus refer to three busses in the system. It should be noted that this does *not* mean the same thing as the three-bus system described in Chapter 4. Figure 5.2 is a block diagram of a typical microprocessor-based microcomputer with a minimum number of devices connected to the busses.

With this bus system, there are two basic ways in which the CPU can communicate with other devices attached to the bus. These are called memory-mapped input/output (I/O) and input/output-mapped input/output.

Memory-Mapped I/O

In this method every memory unit or peripheral device attached to the bus is assigned a specific address. Both MC6800-based computers and the LSI-11 use this method. Each has 16 address lines, and thus 2^{16} or 65536_{10} (64K) different locations can be addressed with this bus.

Since some of these addresses must be reserved for the peripheral devices, less than this number is available for memory storage. The LS-11 microcomputer of the Digital Equipment Corporation is a 16-bit microcomputer in which each byte of a word can be addressed. Thus there are 32K 16-bit addresses available. The upper 4K, from 28K to 32K, are normally reserved for peripheral addresses, leaving 28K 16-bit addresses available for memory. In most microcomputer applications this is more than adequate. One version of the LSI-11 is available that uses only the upper 2K for peripheral devices, leaving another 2K available for memory. In general, the number of addresses used by peripherals are negligible compared with the total memory used in a microcomputer for most applications.

Input/Output-Mapped I/O

This technique uses specific signals that specify that a particular I/O is to go to a peripheral device and not memory. This means that pins on the microprocessor have to be reserved for I/O signals and separate instructions are used to input or output to a peripheral device. For instance, the word "store" could be used to put data into a memory unit or a pheripheral device. There would have to be two different forms of this word, though, to distinguish between a store in a memory unit and a store in a peripheral device. In a memory-mapped system the same word would be used to store a number into either a memory unit or a peripheral device.

Because of this, comparing two microprocessors on the basis of the number of instructions can be misleading. A microcomputer with fewer instructions and memory-mapped I/O might have a more effective instruction set than a similar microprocessor with input/output-mapped I/O. The major disadvantage of input/output-mapped I/O is that pins on the chip have to be reserved for I/O signals. As mentioned before, pins are at a premium. It is usually not worthwhile to waste them for these types of signals. Very few microprocessors use such an approach. The 8080A is one of the few that does employ input/output-mapped I/O.

To isolate the various devices attached to the bus, tristate logic is used. By tristating the bus, it is possible to do DMA on a single-bus system. Since most microprocessors are not capable of providing enough current (called driving) to run all the devices attached to the bus, the bus usually has buffers or drivers attached to boost the current. Three basic types are used:

1. Transmitters, which increase the signal from the CPU to the bus.
2. Receivers, which amplify signals on the bus going to the CPU.
3. Transceivers, which do both of the above processes.

Busses that contain these drivers are called buffered busses.

Example 5.1:

The figure below is a typical buffered data line. Explain what happens when (a) a high is on the $\overline{\text{RE}}$ (read enable) line, and (b) a low is on the $\overline{\text{RE}}$.

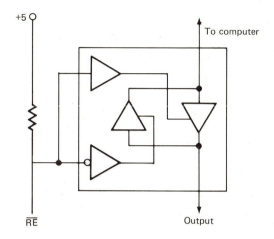

Answer: Two tristate buffers control the flow of signals on the bus line. When a (a) high is on the $\overline{\text{RE}}$, the upper buffer enables the tristate buffer on the data line so the computer can send a signal to a peripheral device (write state). When a (b) low is on the $\overline{\text{RE}}$, the lower buffer is enabled which now enables the other tristate buffer so a signal can only move from an external device to the computer (read state).

Not all busses have separate lines for addresses and data. The bus for the LSI-11/2 uses the address lines as data lines. Addresses and data appear at different times on the address lines, with the address coming during the first part of a cycle and the data during the latter part of a cycle. Addresses and data are said to be time-sliced on the bus. Because of this, such a bus transaction takes slightly longer than it would take for a bus with separate address and data lines. The advantage is lower cost. The sharing or multiplexing of lines or pins is common for 16-bit microprocessors.

As examples of busses, let us look at the busses associated with the LSI-11 microcomputer and the MC6800 microprocessor. Table 5.1 lists the lines associated with the LSI-11 bus known as the Q-bus.

This bus has the capability of using 18-bit addresses. Since $2^{18} = 262,144$ (256K), the computer can address up to 256K bytes or 128K words. With this

TABLE 5.1. *LSI-11, Q-Bus (Copyright © 1979, Digital Equipment Corporation. All rights reserved.)*

Name	No. of Lines	Function
Address/data	18	BDAL ⟨17:00⟩
Data transfer control	6	BBS7,BDIN,BDOUT,BRPLY BSYNC,BWTBT
DMA	3	BDMG,BDMR,BSACK
Interrupt control	6	BEVNT,BIAK,BIRQ4,BIRQ5 BIRQ6,BIRQ7
System control	5	BDCOK,BHALT,BINIT,BPOK BREF

system 8K bytes of address space are also reserved for I/O devices, leaving 248K bytes for main memory. Again the upper 4K words, 248K to 256K, are reserved for I/O devices. For a more complete description of the LSI-11 bus and the way addresses are used see Digital's "Microcomputer Processor Handbook" (reference 6).

The bus used with the MC6800 is much smaller than the LSI-11 bus and is easier to follow. Table 5.2 gives the lines in the 6800 bus.

Since this is a memory-mapped system, the 16 address lines are used to identify all memory and peripheral devices on the bus. The eight data lines carry the data to and from the CPU to memory or peripheral devices. The 12 control lines function as follows:

1. Clock signal: carries $\phi 2$.
2. Valid memory address (VMA): tells a peripheral device there is a valid address on the address bus.
3. Read/Write Line (R/$\overline{W}$): puts a chip in a read or write state.
4. Interrupt request ($\overline{IRQ}$): used by an external device to interrupt the CPU.
5. Data bus enable (DBE): signals the peripheral output buffers to enable them.
6. Ground
7. +5 volts
8. Halt: allows control of program execution by an outside source.
9. Three-state control (TSC): used for short DMA transfers.
10. Reset: used to initialize the CPU after it has been shut down.
11. Nonmaskable interrupt ($\overline{NMI}$): allows an immediate interrupt.
12. Bus available (BA): tells if address bus is full.

Every microprocessor has its own characteristic bus system, which is, in general, not compatible with another microprocessor's system. In order for manufacturers to make memory or peripheral devices that could be used with more than one microprocessor, a standard bus had to be developed. Quite a few such busses are now available.

For computers built around the 6800, or 6809, there is the SS 50 bus developed by the Southwest Technical Products Corporation. This company so dominated the 6800 field for microcomputers in the beginning that all manufacturers made their products compatible to this bus. There are numerous manufacturers that make products and systems for the bus.

The two most important busses are the S-100 and IEEE-488-1978 bus.

TABLE 5.2. *Bus in 6800.*

Name of Bus	No. of Lines	Function
Address	16	Unidirectional from CPU to devices and memory
Data	8	Bidirectional
Control	12	Carries clock signals, power (see text for description)

S-100 Bus

This was originally intended to be the standard bus used in the hobby and small business applications computers based on the 8080 or Z80 microprocessor. It was developed by MITs that made the Altair microcomputer based on the 8080A. At one time more than 100 different manufacturers made products compatible with this bus. The 6502 and even some 6800 microprocessor-based systems are used with this bus.

The bus gets its name from the fact that there are 100 lines in the bus. The following were the lines in the original bus;

$$
\begin{array}{rl}
8 & \text{data in} \\
8 & \text{data out} \\
16 & \text{address} \\
3 & \text{power supply} \\
8 & \text{interrupt} \\
\underline{39} & \underline{\text{control}} \\
82 &
\end{array}
$$

The other 18 lines were reserved for future use. These 18 undefined lines created a major problem in the early usage of this bus, because different manufacturers would use them for different purposes. Thus two products compatible with the S-100 bus might not work with one another because of the different uses of one or more of these undefined lines. In recent years manufacturers have been cooperating to eliminate the problem. The solution is the standard being developed by the Institute of Electrical and Electronics Engineers (IEEE) known tentatively as the S-100-696 standard. The new standard defines 24 address lines to allow for addresses much larger than 64K. As with the old S-100, the new standard has the $+8$-volt line adjacent to the -16-volt line. Since there is a possibility that these pins will touch when the bus is removed, power should always be turned off before doing so.

IEEE-488-1978 Bus (GPIB)

This bus, also known as the general-purpose interface bus (GPIB), was developed by Hewlett-Packard to handle the problems associated with the interfacing of various different testing devices or instruments to the different microprocessors. As such, Hewlett-Packard refers to it as the HPIB bus. The bus is actually a complete system that defines all the circuits, cables, and types and nature of signals sent to and from the computer. In this bus there are 16 transmission lines consisting of:

- Eight data lines — asynchronous and bidirectional
- Three control lines — handshake
- Five general management lines

Asynchronous and handshake protocol are defined later. In addition, there are two power lines. Interface units are built by manufacturers that allow this bus to be interfaced with a microprocessor. For the 6800, Motorola makes a chip numbered MC68488. This is a general-purpose interface adapter that handles the signals needed to meet the GPIB standards. An excellent reference on this bus is reference 7.

EXERCISE 5-1

1. Define bus in your own words.
2. True or false?
   a. All busses allow signals to move in any direction. _____
   b. Address lines and data lines are always separate wires in a bus. _____
   c. The two types of bus configurations are single-bus and three-bus. _____
3. DMA means:
   a. The transfer of data from memory to a peripheral device.
   b. The transfer of data from the CPU to memory.
   c. The transfer of data from a peripheral device to memory.
   d. The transfer of data from a peripheral device to memory through the CPU.
4. True or false?
   a. Only a three-bus configuration can do DMA. _____
   b. Because a three-bus configuration has more instructions, it is a more useful system. _____
   c. There are fewer addresses available for memory in a single-bus system than a three-bus system. _____
5. a. Define, in your words, S-100 bus.
   b. What is the maximum number of locations that can be addressed with the new standard?
6. The GPIB symbols uses for IEEE 488-1978 bus stands for _____ .

CHIP SELECTS

The various components that make up a microcomputer—for example, the microprocessor, memory, and peripheral device interfaces—are all present on chips connected together via the bus.

To address each chip in a microcomputer using the address lines (or bus), the pins of each DIP holding a chip are divided into chip-select pins and address pins. For our 6800 microcomputer, memory can be thought of as being divided into units of $256_{10} \times 8$ bits each. In a 16-bit address the first 8 bits could be word address bits and the upper 8 bits chip-select bits (Figure 5.3).

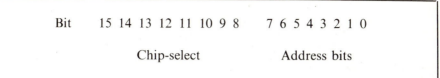

FIGURE 5.3. *Chip-select bits and address bits for a* 256 $_{10}$ *memory unit chip.*

Since 8 bits will cover any address from 00_{10} to 255_{10}, or a total of 256 addresses, we can address any memory unit using these 8 bits. The upper 8 bits then select which particular chip will be addressed.

Figure 5.4 is a schematic illustration of a typical attachment of memory units to the address bus.

In this diagram we assume each unit has one chip select (CSO), which is active high. This type of attachment to the address bus where individual address lines on the bus are attached to an individual chip select is called linear selection. In Figure 5.4, a 1 on address lines 0 through 7 plus a 1 on

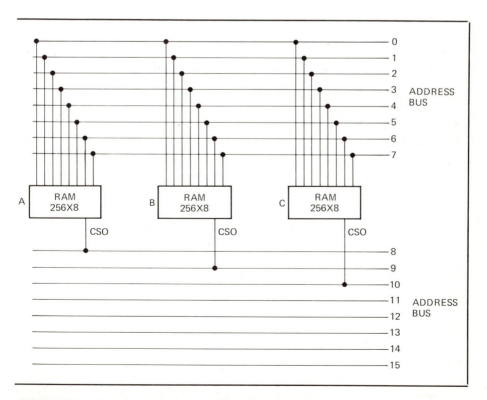

FIGURE 5.4. *Addressing memory units—linear selection.*

address lines 8, 9, or 10 would enable one of the RAMs. A 01XX (e.g., $01FF_{16}$) would enable RAM A while a $02XX_{16}$ (e.g., 028F) would enable RAM B. The notation 00XX is common in the field and implies that the value of the last two digits is immaterial. Any number there would give an acceptable value.

Note that this type of addressing can lead to problems. If the address 0000001111111111 or 03FF is put on the address bus, both RAMs A and B are enabled. This could create problems on a read command if the two RAMs have different numbers stored in them. Furthermore, any address in which the address lines 0–8 and 11, 12, etc., is high would enable RAM A. Many of the addresses are wasted.

To remove some of the above problems, more than one chip select is used on the RAM. The advantage of linear selection is that the cost is low. Not much hardware is needed to select the proper memory unit. To fully decode all 64K addresses, decoders are needed. Some systems will use a combination of linear selection and address decoders to give partial address decoding. This enables them to add as many units as desired at a minimum cost.

Example 5.2:

Assume each IC in Figure 5.4 has two chip selects. Draw a diagram of a circuit that will give each chip a unique address when lines 8, 9, and 10 are used to enable the chips.

> *Answer*:

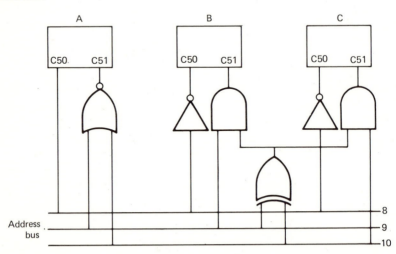

In this circuit, chip A will be enabled with a high on 8 and lows on 9 and 10. Chip B is enabled with a high on 9 and lows on 8 and 10, while chip C is enabled with a high on 10 and lows on 8 and 9. If any two lines are high, no chip is enabled.

In the ET-3400 (Heath Corporation trademark) version of the 6800, if the upper 8 bits are 00_{16}, the first 256_{10} bytes of RAM are addressed. If 01_{16} is put in the upper 8 bits, then the next 256_{10} bytes of RAM are addressed.

Bit	15	14	13	12	11	10		9	8	7	6	5	4	3	2	1	0
	c	c	c	c	c	c		a	a	a	a	a	a	a	a	a	a
			Chip-select								Address bits						

FIGURE 5.5. *Chip-select and address bits for a* 1024_{10} *memory unit.*

The number of lines used for address bits and the number used for chip-select bits will depend upon the architecture of the microcomputer. If a 1024_{10} × 8-bit memory chip is used, then 10 bits are necessary to read all 1024 units (Figure 5.5).

In the ET-3400 version of the 6800, the monitor (a program used to control the computer) is stored in a 1024_{10} cell ROM whose chip-select bits are put in their proper logic state by the hexadecimal numbers FC, FD, FE and FF. (See Figure 5.6.)

When bits 10 through 15 are 1's, the ROM is selected. When bits 8 and 9 are 0, 256_{10} addresses are decoded. When 8 is 1 and 9 is 0, a different 256 addresses are decoded. When 9 is a 1 and 8 is a 0, a third group of 256 addresses are decoded, while when both 8 and 9 are 1's, the last 256 addresses are decoded. Thus a total of $4 \times 256_{10} = 1024_{10}$ different memory units can be addressed.

In terms of hexadecimal numbers, the ROM is occupying memory locations from $FC00_{16}$ to $FFFF_{16}$. These are the upper 1024_{10} words that exist in the computer's addressable memory locations.

Example 5.3:

Given a 1024 × 8-bit ROM, how many address lines must be used for address pins and how many address lines are available for chip selects with a 16-line address bus?

	F			C				Address Bits	
	1	1	1	1	1	1	00	aaaa	aaaa
	F			D					
	1	1	1	1	1	1	01	aaaa	aaaa
	F			E					
	1	1	1	1	1	1	10	aaaa	aaaa
	F			F					
	1	1	1	1	1	1	11	aaaa	aaaa
Bit	15	14	13	12	11	10	98	7654	3210

FIGURE 5.6. *Bit arrangement for FC, FD, FE, and FF chip selects in ET-3400 ROM.*

Answer: Since $1024 = 2^{10}$, ten address lines must be used to identify a particular 8 bits of ROM. This leaves six lines available to use with chip selects.

EXERCISE 5-2

1. Explain, in your own words, what is meant by a 128×1 memory chip.
2. The chip select for a RAM is $01XX_{16}$. If the RAM is 256×4 bits, what addresses in hexadecimal and in decimal does the RAM occupy?
3. If the chip select for a RAM is 000010_2 for the highest address lines, and the RAM holds 1024×8 bits, what addresses does the RAM occupy in memory?

METHODS OF DATA TRANSMISSION

Data are transferred from one part of the microcomputer to another in the form of electrical pulses representing 0's and 1's as discussed in Chapter 2. Two different methods are used to transmit the data — *parallel* transmission and *serial* transmission.

Parallel Transmission

In parallel transmission a series of bits, usually a word or byte, is transmitted, at the same time, over different wires. In the 6800 the data bus contains eight lines, and thus 8 bits of data are transmitted at a given time. Figure 5.7 is a schematic representation of such transfers.

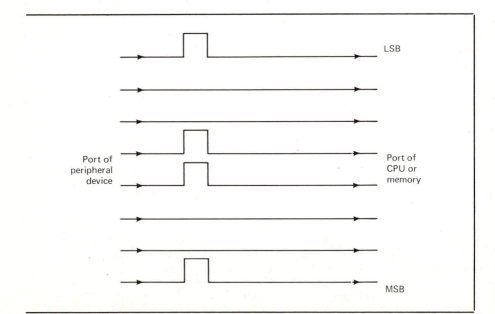

FIGURE 5.7. *Parallel transmission of data.*

The data are transmitted simultaneously from the eight pins of the port of the peripheral device to the eight pins of the port in memory of the CPU. In the example presented in Figure 5.7, the word transmitted is 10011001_2. In the LSI-11, as with other 16-bit microcomputers, data are transferred along 16 wires, and thus 16 bits of data can be transferred at a time.

Parallel transmission is fast, but expensive, since so many wires are involved. It is used within the mainframe of the computer and with a few peripheral devices such as the pushbutton switches. Data transmission between many peripherals, such as teletypewriters and cassette recorders, is done using serial transmission.

Serial Transmission

In this mode of transmission, data are sent over a single wire, 1 bit at a time, in serial format. Figure 5.8 is a schematic representation of this. Here the LSB is transmitted first, so the number transmitted in Figure 5.8 is 00100110_2.

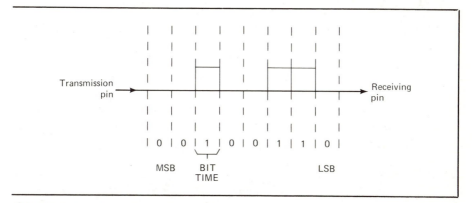

FIGURE 5.8. Serial transmission of data.

Since there may be a series of 1's or 0's following each other, it is necessary to have a coding scheme of some type so that the computer can determine how many 1's or 0's are being transmitted. The standard method uses a I/O clock, which divides the signals on the wire into bits according to time. This is called *bit time*. The serial clock signal should not be confused with the CPU clock signal. Bit times are of the order of milliseconds as compared with a microsecond for the period of a 1-MHz CPU clock.

Serial transmission rates are measured in terms of the number of bits transferred per second. This is called the *baud rate*. If data are transmitted at 110 bits per second, the baud rate is 110. Baud rates for various devices range from 50 to 9600. At a baud rate of 9600, the bit time is

$$\frac{1\ 000\ 000\ \mu s/sec}{9600\ bits/sec} = 104\ \mu s$$

Serial transmission is slower than parallel, but is less expensive since only one wire is needed. Any device that is a distance away from the computer will transmit in serial format. Serial transmission is discussed in greater detail in the next section.

EXERCISE 5-3

1. For each of the following statements check whether it applies to parallel or serial transmission.

	Parallel	*Serial*
a. Faster method of transmission.		
b. One bit at a time.		
c. Used by peripheral devices some distance from the computer.		
d. First bit transferred is the LSB.		
e. Uses many wires in the bus.		

2. The following signal is transmitted along a serial wire. What is the value of the number transmitted?

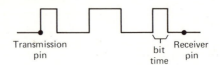

Transmission pin   bit time   Receiver pin

3. A peripheral device sends signals at a baud rate of 400. What is the bit time?

INTERFACING PERIPHERALS

There are two basic ways of building microcomputers from chips. If the various chips that make up the microcomputer (microprocessor, memory, and interfacing to peripheral devices) are attached to the bus as discussed in the section on chip selects, we have what is called a chip microcomputer. This is the approach used in the Apple II, PET, and TRS-80 microcomputers.

The alternative is to put the chips together on a "board" and attach the board to the bus. This is called a board microcomputer, and is the method used in the ATARI and LSI-11 microcomputers. Interfacing peripherals to a microcomputer will thus vary depending upon whether it is a chip or board microcomputer.

Since the different peripheral devices operate at various baud rates and are much slower than the CPU, they are not connected directly to the CPU. Each device is connected to the bus through an *interface* as shown in Figure 5.2. The interface has a register called a buffer, to store the data temporarily before being placed on the bus or after removal from the bus, some form of synchronization circuitry, and another register that allows the computer to exercise control over the interface and thus the peripheral device. Since there are two methods of transmitting data, there are two general types of interfaces — parallel and serial. Because each manufacturer has its own interface design, the following discussion will be centered on the interface units associated with the LSI-11 and 6800 as typical examples.

Parallel Data Input/Output

In memory-mapped systems data coming and going to peripherals are treated the same way as data coming and going from memory. Each type is assigned an address of its own. The addresses used by the LSI-11 and the 6800 for the peripherals are different.

LSI -11 Parallel Board

To keep things simple, we will restrict our discussion to the 64K addressable form of the LSI-11. In the LSI-11 all peripheral addresses range from $160\ 000_8$ to $177\ 776_8$. Interfacing is done through what is called a parallel I/O interface card (DRV-11). This card contains all the hardware, including the control circuits for parallel transmission.

It was shown previously that with 16 address lines it is possible to address 64K bytes of memory or 32K 16-bit words. In the LSI-11 this 32K is divided into eight banks (0 through 7) of 4K. Addresses $160\ 000_8$ to $177\ 776_8$ occupy the highest bank, or bank 7. Note that, in this case, the highest 3 bits, 15, 14, and 13, are always set equal to 1. (See Figure 5.9.) As a reminder, the X means any acceptable digit, 0 or 1 in binary, or 0 through 7 inclusive in octal.

If bit 12 is a 0, the address is $16XXXX_8$, whereas if bit 12 is a 1, the address is $17XXXX_8$. The card contains three important registers.

Address	Name	Function
16XXX0	Control/status	Can be read or written into; allows CPU to control the peripheral or check the status of the peripheral.
16XXX2	Output buffer	16-bit buffer register; data can be sent here by the CPU and read back. This port has a "memory."
16XXX4	Data input	16 bits of data are transmitted here by the peripheral to the CPU. There is no "memory" function built into this input port.

The address of the control status register is hard-wired on the board, while the other two registers are automatically set two and four addresses above that of the control status register.

To activate the interface board, a signal called *bank select 7* is generated by the CPU. This sets bits 15, 14, and 13 to 1. A decoder circuitry in the device examines bits 12, 11, 10, 9, 8, 7, 6, 5, 4, and 3.

Binary value	1 1 1 X	X X X	X X X	X X X X X
Bit number	15 14 13 12	11 10 9	8 7 6	5 4 3 2 1 0
Octal equivalent	6 or 7	X	X	X X

FIGURE 5.9. *Bit assignment for addressing peripherals in LSI-11.*

Only one of the peripherals will respond to this particular set of bits. It is thus possible to have 2^{10} or 1024_{10} different peripherals on the bus. Each peripheral has a decoder circuit that will examine bits 2, 1, and 0 to see what function (i.e., register) is to be activated. Since the bus is time-sliced, other signals must be generated by the CPU to ensure data are flowing on the bus properly. A D-IN (data-in) signal allows data to flow onto the bus while a D-out (data-out) allows data to flow from the bus to the peripheral. The control/status register is used by the CPU to control the actions of the peripheral device.

6800 PIA

In the 6800 the equivalent to the parallel board interface is a chip known as a *peripheral interface adapter* (PIA). Figure 5.10 gives the pin assignment for the PIA. The PIA is essentially two parallel boards in one. It can be used to attach two different peripherals to the CPU. The address of the PIA is set by the programmer when wiring the chip up. There are two 8-bit data busses and four interrupt/control lines used to connect the peripheral devices to the PIA. The eight data lines from the peripheral are attached to either section *A* (PA0-PA7) or section *B* (PB0-PB7) of the PIA. Inside the PIA are two data registers, two data direction registers, and two control registers. These registers function as follows:

1. Data registers. These are 8-bit registers that hold a word before being input to the computer or store a word outputted from the computer before it is transmitted to the peripheral device.
2. Data direction registers. These are 8-bit registers that determine whether the data on a given line are an input or output. If the bit for a line is set to "0," the data are an input, and if set to "1," the data are treated as output.
3. Control registers. These are also 8-bit registers that allow the CPU to control the operation of each peripheral device. They also handle interrupt signals and select whether the data direction register or data register is being referred to by the CPU. Figure 5.11 shows the format of this register.

Bit 2 determines whether the data or data direction register is being referenced. Bits 0, 1, 2, 3, 4, and 5 are <u>read/write</u> bits. This means they can be read

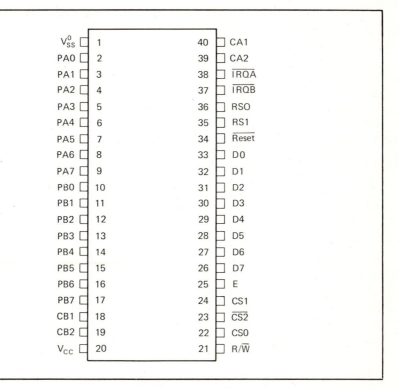

V_{SS}^0 ☐ 1	40 ☐ CA1	
PA0 ☐ 2	39 ☐ CA2	
PA1 ☐ 3	38 ☐ $\overline{IRQA}$	
PA2 ☐ 4	37 ☐ $\overline{IRQB}$	
PA3 ☐ 5	36 ☐ RS0	
PA4 ☐ 6	35 ☐ RS1	
PA5 ☐ 7	34 ☐ $\overline{Reset}$	
PA6 ☐ 8	33 ☐ D0	
PA7 ☐ 9	32 ☐ D1	
PB0 ☐ 10	31 ☐ D2	
PB1 ☐ 11	30 ☐ D3	
PB2 ☐ 12	29 ☐ D4	
PB3 ☐ 13	28 ☐ D5	
PB4 ☐ 14	27 ☐ D6	
PB5 ☐ 15	26 ☐ D7	
PB6 ☐ 16	25 ☐ E	
PB7 ☐ 17	24 ☐ CS1	
CB1 ☐ 18	23 ☐ $\overline{CS2}$	
CB2 ☐ 19	22 ☐ CS0	
V_{CC} ☐ 20	21 ☐ $R/\overline{W}$	

FIGURE 5.10. *Pin assignment in PIA* (MC 6820). (*Courtesy Motorola Semiconductor Products, Inc.*)

or changed by the CPU. Bits 6 and 7 are read-only bits. The CPU can read these bits but cannot change them. These bits (6 and 7) allow a peripheral device to interrupt the CPU. By using various combinations of the register select pins (RS0, RS1) and bit 2 of the control register, the three different types of registers in the PIA can be selected. The pins CA1, CA2, CB1, and CB2 are control lines used to generate the interrupt signal. This signal is sent to the CPU from either of two interrupt request pins ($\overline{IRQA}$, $\overline{IRQB}$). The E pin is an enable pin. This is the only timing pin on the chip. Its signal is determined normally from the $\phi2$ clock pulse. The eight data lines (D0–D7) connect the

bit	7	6	5	4	3	2	1	0
	IRQ 1	IRQ 2		control bits		Data direction register	Control	

FIGURE 5.11. *A control register in the 6800,* (*Courtesy Motorola Semiconductor Products, Inc.*)

chip to the data bus of the CPU. The function of the rest of the pins should be clear from their symbols.

In summary, all parallel interfaces have two or more registers: a register to store the data when going to or from the CPU and a control/status register that tells the CPU just what the peripheral device is doing at a particular time. Data are transmitted in parallel format between the CPU and the interface.

Serial Data Input/Output

In the previous paragraphs it was shown that the CPU sends data out in a parallel manner 8 bits at a time in the 6800 and 16 bits at a time in the LSI-11. The serial interface, besides doing all the functions of a parallel interface, must also be able to take a parallel set of data from the CPU and convert it into serial format. In addition, it has to be able to accept serial bits from the peripheral device and convert them into parallel format. Both of these functions are carried out by a special register in the serial board called a *shift register*. The theory behind this register was discussed in Chapter 3. Serial data enter the register through a one-pin port and leave as parallel data through another port. Parallel data enter from the data bus and leave as serial data through the single-pin port. This is represented schematically in Figure 5.12.

In general, every serial board has two such shift registers; one receives serial data from the peripheral and converts the data to parallel, and the other receives the parallel data from the CPU and converts the data to a serial format.

The most common form of peripheral that uses serial transmission is the teletypewriter (TTY). The teletypewriter generates a serial data string whenever a key is depressed. Conversely, it can print a character if the proper serial data string is sent to the TTY. A TTY, and devices like it, can operate in three different ways:

1. Simplex. In this form the TTY can send data to the computer but the computer cannot send data to the TTY.

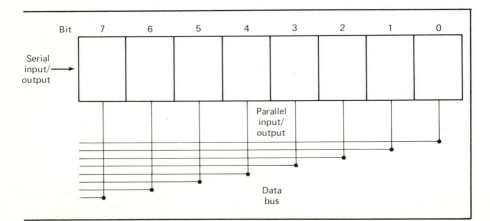

FIGURE 5.12. *Schematic diagram of a shift register.*

2. Half-duplex. Both the TTY and the computer can send data to one another though only one can transmit the data at any given time.
3. Full-duplex. Both TTY and computer can transmit data to one another independently of each other.

There are 128 characters on the various keys of a TTY. To encode these, only 7 bits are needed. Table 5.3 gives the 7-bit ASCII (American Standard Code for Information Interchange) for the different characters.

When a key is struck, the 7-bit ASCII code plus an additional bit called a parity bit is transmitted by the TTY. The parity bit is used by a receiver to check for errors in a transmitted signal. Two different types of parity bits

TABLE 5.3. *Seven-Bit ASCII Code.*

Hex Code	Character	Hex Code	Character	Hex Code	Character	Hex Code	Character
00	NUL	20	SP	40	@	60	
01	SOH	21	!	41	A	61	a
02	STX	22	"	42	B	61	b
03	ETX	23	#	43	C	63	c
04	EOT	24	$	44	D	64	d
05	ENQ	25	%	45	E	65	e
06	ACK	26	&	46	F	66	f
07	BEL	27	'	47	G	67	g
08	BS	28	(	48	H	68	h
09	HT	29	)	49	I	69	i
0A	LF	2A	*	4A	J	6A	j
0B	VT	2B	+	4B	K	6B	k
0C	FF	2C	,	4C	L	6C	l
0D	CR	2D	–	4D	M	6D	m
0E	SO	2E	.	4E	N	6E	n
0F	S1	2F	/	4F	O	6F	o
10	DLE	30	0	50	P	70	p
11	DC1	31	1	51	Q	71	q
12	DC2	32	2	52	R	72	r
13	DC3	33	3	53	S	73	s
14	DC4	34	4	54	T	74	t
15	NAK	35	5	55	U	75	u
16	SYN	36	6	56	V	76	v
17	ETB	37	7	57	W	77	w
18	CAN	38	8	58	X	78	x
19	EM	39	9	59	Y	79	y
1A	SUB	3A	:	5A	Z	7A	z
1B	ESC	3B	;	5B	[	7B	{
1C	FS	3C	<	5C	\	7C	/
1D	GS	3D	=	5D	]	7D	}
1E	RS	3E	>	5E	↑	7E	≈
1F	US	3F	?	5F	–	7F	DEL

Character	7-Bit String	Number of Ones	Parity Bit	Signal Sent
A	1000001	2; even	0	01000001

FIGURE 5.13. *Adjusting the parity bit in a serial string for even parity.*

normally are generated. A particular TTY is wired to generate one of these two types of bits. The receiver has to be programmed to accept the same type of parity bit.

The most significant bit of an 8-bit serial string is used as the parity bit. If this bit is set so that the total number of 1's in the 8-bit string is an even number, it is called *even* parity; if the number of 1's in the string is odd, it is called *odd* parity. Figure 5.13 shows this.

The computer can be set to ignore the parity bit. Some TTYs always set the bit equal to a 1, which is called mark parity, and others to a 0, called space parity. Figure 5.14 is an example of what the serial string would look like for the characters B and C in all four possible parity states.

This is one of the communications protocol that is used to ensure the correct reception of serial data by a receiver. Serial data communications can be divided into two classes: synchronous and asynchronous.

Synchronous data must be transmitted continuously with the data conforming exactly to the bit time associated with the serial clock signal. To be certain the receiver knows that data are coming, the set of data bits is preceded by one or two special characters called *Sync* characters. As soon as the receiver sees the Sync character(s) it starts interpreting the data bits. If the device does not have data available to send, it will either transmit these Sync characters until the next legitimate character is ready to be sent or send a waiting signal. This could happen on a TTY when a person types at a variable speed.

In the case of a TTY asynchronous protocol is the normal means of communication between the computer and the TTY. To ensure that the receiver translates the bits properly, a *start bit*, a 0, is placed at the beginning of a character and 1 or 2 *end bits* (or stop bits), which are 1's, at the end of the character. A typical serial transmission using asynchronous protocol is given in Figure 5.15.

Character	Even Parity	Odd Parity	Mark Parity	Space Parity
B	01000010	11000010	11000010	01000010
C	11000011	01000011	11000011	01000011

FIGURE 5.14. *Eight-bit serial string with different parities.*

1 1	P	XXXXXXX	0
Stop bits	Parity bits	Data	Start bit

FIGURE 5.15. *Asynchronous serial transmission.*

When the key is depressed, the start bit (0) tells the receiver a bit string is coming. In the case of Figure 5.15 this string contains 8 bits including the parity bit. This number can be varied by programming the computer to accept less than 8 bits. If this is done, the higher bits are ignored. Once the receiver sees the 0, it sets up a counter. When the counter has been decremented to 0, the data are made available to the bus as a parallel word. The purpose of the 2 stop bits (1) is to allow time for the receiver to place the word on the bus. The level of the receiving line is usually held at a 1 (high) until it receives the next start bit. To send 7 bits of data using asynchronous serial transmission, a total of 11 bits is usually transmitted. If synchronous is used, only the 7 data bits need be sent and every so often a Sync character sent as an error check. Because of this difference, synchronous transmission is much faster than asynchronous.

In using asynchronous serial transmission, 11 bits are transmitted to send one ASCII character. At a baud rate of 110, the bit time is 9.09 ms as previously shown. The time to transmit one character is thus 11×9.09 ms or 0.1 second. Thus, at a baud rate of 110, ten characters can be sent per second (CPS). The symbol CPS is often encountered in discussions of printers.

For an interesting discussion of synchronous and asynchronous communication, see reference 7.

Let us examine the parallel interface units in the LSI-11 and a 6800-based microcomputer.

The LSI-11 Serial Board

Since the serial board both receives and transmits data, it must contain a receiver buffer register and receiver control/status register (CSR) as well as a transmitter buffer register and transmitter control/status register. As with the parallel board, the receiver CSR is hard-wired to a particular address in bank 7, usually ending in zero. See Figure 5.16.

The receiver buffer register is two addresses above this, while the transmitter CSR and buffer register are four and six addresses above the receiver CSR respectively.

Since serial data are normally transmitted in 8-bit strings or less, the receiver and transmitter buffer registers are 8-bit registers, respectively, while the CSR registers are 16-bit registers. Only the first 8 bits are shown in Figure 5.16. Bit 7 of the CSR is a busy or done signal. When the bit is a 1, the corresponding buffer register is ready to interact with the computer. When the

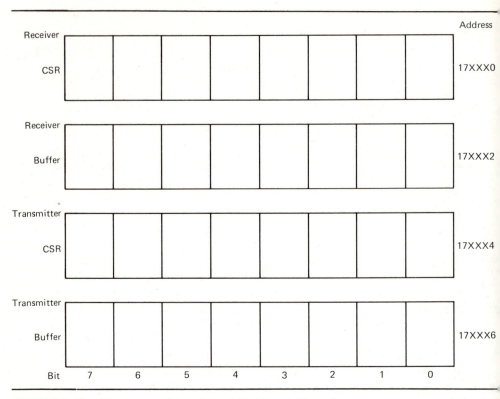

FIGURE 5.16. *The four registers in an LSI-11 serial board.*

bit is a 0 the buffer register is busy. That is, when bit 7 of both CSRs is a 1, the receiver buffer register is ready to place data on the bus and the transmitter buffer register is ready to accept data from the bus. When bit 7 of both CSRs is a 0, the receiver buffer register is in the process of receiving data from the terminal. This bit can be used in programming to control the transfer of data to and from a terminal. It can be examined to see if it is positive or negative since it is the MSB of the low-order byte.

The 6800 ACIA

The chip MC6850, known as an *asynchronous communications interface adapter* (ACIA), is used with the 6800 to interface serial devices to the computer. Figure 5.17 gives the pin assignments in the ACIA (MC6850).

This device is an example of a universal asynchronous receiver transmitter (UART). As with the LSI-11, up to 8 bits of data can be transmitted and received via this interface. Data are transmitted from a peripheral device to the ACIA through the receive data pin (RSDATA, pin 2). The ACIA contains four registers:

1. Status register (SR)
2. Receiver data register (RDR)

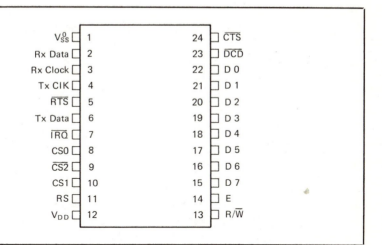

FIGURE 5.17. *Pin assignments for the ACIA (MC 6850). (Courtesy Motorola Semiconductor Products, Inc.)*

3. Transmit data register (TDR)
4. Control register (CR)

The first two are read-only registers, and the last two are write-only registers. A total of 15 lines runs from the CPU to this chip; eight bidirectional data lines, three chip-select lines, one register-select line, one interrupt request line, one enable line, and one read/write line.

By putting the chip selects in their proper state (CS0 and CS1 high while $\overline{\text{CS2}}$ is low) the ACIA is addressed. A combination of the register-select and read/write line determines which register is selected.

As can be seen in Table 5.4, when both lines are low, the control register is selected. This register determines the baud rate, word length to be transmitted or received, the parity, and the number of stop bits. When the register select is low and the R/$\overline{\text{W}}$ high, the status register is selected. This tells the CPU whether the ACIA is ready to receive a data string or transmit a string or the status of the peripheral attached to the ACIA. The transmit data regis-

TABLE 5.4. *State of RS and Read/Write Control Lines to Select the Registers in an ACIA.*

Register Select	Read/Write	ACIA Register Selected
0	0	Control
0	1	Status
1	0	Transmit data
1	1	Receive data

ter is a parallel to serial shift register and the receive data register is a serial to parallel shift register, and each is accessed as shown in Table 5.4.

To ensure that errors are as few as possible in transmitting or receiving data, the ACIA uses an external clock that is faster than the baud rate. In the ACIA clock frequencies of x1, x16, or x64 the baud rate can be used. This is symbolized as $\div 1$, $\div 16$, or $\div 64$ state. Other UARTs use a x32 clock frequency.

Let us examine how this works as the ACIA receives data. We will assume an external clock of x16 the baud rate is being used. This means 16 clock pulses will occur during the bit time; thus the bit time is divided into 16 parts and hence the $\div 16$ representation.

Before data are received, the peripheral device is in a mark state (i.e., a high is on the line). The start bit is initiated by the high-to-low transition. When this transition is detected, a counter, which keeps track of the clock pulses, counts eight of the pulses (one half of 16) and examines it again on the ninth pulse. This puts the signal in the middle of the bit time. If the bit is still low, the device assumes that it is a valid start bit. It then continues to read the bits after every 16 clock pulses, again reading the middle of each bit time until all bits have been read. The middle of the bit time is chosen since the signal should be clean there, and little chance of an error in reading will occur. This is summarized in Figure 5.18.

With a x64 clock frequency, the start bit would be examined halfway through (after 32 clock pulses or on the 33rd clock pulse), and then after every 64 clock pulses.

In general, a serial interface contains four registers—one used in receiving data, one for transmitted data, and two for control/status. The transmit data register is a write-only register, while the receive data register is a read-only

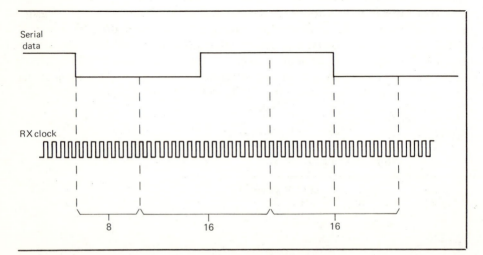

FIGURE 5.18. *A x16 clock signal used to read serial data.*

register. For those interested specifically in the 6800 microprocessor, the PIA, and ACIA, reference 9 is excellent, and reference 8 is a very good general reference on interfacing.

The current trend in microcomputers is to put as many parts of the computer as possible on a single chip. Chips are available with the CPU and main memory on the same chip. Motorola, as do other computer companies, has a chip 6802 that contains both the CPU and the clock on the one chip. It is possible now to buy a complete computer on a single chip.

EXERCISE 5-4

1. True or false?
    a. An interface is a register that temporarily stores data as it goes from a peripheral to the computer. _____
    b. Interfacings are interchangeable from one computer system to another. _____
    c. In single-bus systems peripherals are treated like memory. _____
    d. Sixteen address lines will address a maximum of 64K bytes of memory. _____
2. Define, in your own words, the registers in a LSI-11 parallel board.
3. Explain why it is possible to address 1024_{10} different peripherals in the LSI-11.
4. A read bit (*true* or *false*)
    a. Can be read by the CPU and written by the peripheral. _____
    b. Can be read by the peripheral and written by the CPU. _____
    c. Can be read and written by the CPU. _____
    d. Can be read and written by a peripheral. _____
5. *True* or *false*?
    a. Every serial board must have a shift register. _____
    b. All serial data consist of 8 bits including the parity bit. _____
    c. The same shift register can be used for either serial-to-parallel or parallel-to-serial conversion. _____
6. Which of the following is not an asynchronous serial string?
    a. 11011110010
       MSB   LSB
    b. 11000000000
    c. 11000000001
    d. 11100000000
7. Define communications protocol.
8. Which of the following signals will activate a peripheral in an LSI-11?
    a. $1\ 101\ 000\ 010\ 000\ 111_2$
    b. $1\ 000\ 000\ 010\ 000\ 010_2$
    c. $0\ 000\ 110\ 010\ 000\ 010_2$
    d. $1\ 110\ 110\ 010\ 000\ 010_2$

9. Which of the following acts as the asynchronous serial interface in the 6800?
   a. ACIA   b. PIA   c. MPU   d. Serial board
10. Describe the difference(s) between a "board" computer and a "chip" computer.

REVIEW QUESTIONS

1. A peripheral device sends signals at a baud rate of 400. What is the bit time?
   a. 2500 ms   b. 250 μs c. 2500 μs
   d. 250 ms
2. Which of the following statements is *not* true for serial transmission of data?
   a. Data is transmitted 1 bit at a time.
   b. It is a faster method of transmitting data.
   c. The first data bit transmitted is the start bit.
   d. It is used by peripheral devices some distance from the computer.
3. The 7-bit ASCII code for the letters B and C are as follows:
   B   1000010
   C   1000011
   If these letters are transmitted as the following 8-bit string
   B   01000010
   C   11000011
   which type of parity is being used?
   a. Even   b. Odd   c. Mark   d. Space
4. Serial boards or chips have a register that can convert a parallel word to serial or a serial word to parallel. This is called a
   a. Data direction register
   b. Shift register
   c. Control/status register
   d. Input/output buffer
5. Another name for chips like the ACIA is
   a. USRT   b. Peripheral interface   c. PIA   d. UART
6. The part of the bus used to send information in either direction between two parts of the computer is the
   a. Central bus   b. Data bus   c. Address bus   d. All of these
7. Explain in your own words what each of the following means.
   a. Chip selects
   b. Partial decoding
8. Draw a diagram similar to Example 5.2 such that each IC will have a unique address if each chip has only one chip select.
9. Texas Instruments uses a ROM in its TMS 990/189 single-board computer that occupies addresses 3000 to 3FFF. Since this is a 16-bit computer, what size is the ROM?

10. How many cycles per second can be sent at a baud rate of 9600 using asynchronous serial transmission?
11. What is meant by half-duplex? By full-duplex serial transmission?
12. What is the difference between asynchronous and synchronous serial transmission?
13. Given the following serial string, identify the binary number transmitted and the parity used. One start bit and 2 stop bits are used.

REFERENCES

1. Introduction to Minicomputers, *Bus Structure*. Digital Equipment Corp., Maynard, Mass., 1977.
2. Adam Osborne, *An Introduction to Microcomputers*, Volume 1. *Basic Concepts*. Osborne & Associates, Berkeley, Calif., 1977, Chapter 5.
3. Adam Osborne, *An Introduction to Microcomputers*, Volume II, *Some Real Products*. Osborne & Associates, Berkely, Calif., 1977, Chapter 8.
4. *Microcomputer Handbook*. Digital Equipment Corp., Maynard, Mass., 1977, Chapters 4.9 and 4.10.
5. *Heathkit Manual for the Microprocessor Trainee*, Model ET-3400. Heath Co., Benton Harbor, Mich., 1977, pp. 108–109.
6. *Microcomputer Processor Handbook*. Digital Equipment Corp., Maynard, Mass., 1980, Chapters 8 and 9.
7. Frank Toth, Serial Communications and Interface Circuits in Microprocessor Systems, *Interface Age 6* (4), 82 (Apr.), 1981.
8. Bruce A. Artwick, *Microcomputer Interfacing*. Prentice-Hall, Englewood Cliffs, N. J., 1980, Chapters 4 and 7.
9. Ron Bishop, *Basic Microprocessors and the 6800*. Hayden Book Co., Rochelle Park, N. J., 1979, Chapter 9.

GLOSSARY

ACIA (Asynchronous Communications interface Adapter)	Device used in 6800 as an interface to convert serial data to parallel on input and parallel data to serial on output.
Address bus	Terminology used in microcomputers to mean address lines.
Address Lines	Wires in a bus that carry the address and chip select signals

ASCII	A 7-bit binary code for the characters on a TTY. Stands for American Standard Code for Information Interchange.
Asynchronous protocol	Data transmitted by a peripheral device are identified by a start bit and a stop bit.
Bank select 7	A control signal in the LSI-11 that sets bits 15, 14, and 13 to a 1 to address a peripheral device.
Baud rate	Bits transmitted per second.
Bidirectional bus	A bus that allows signals to move along it in either direction.
Bit time	Time between bits in a serial transmission.
Bus	Flat, flexible cable with connectors on each end, used to connect one part of a computer to another.
Bus buffer (or driver)	A device used to increase the current in a bus.
Three-bus configuration	System with three separate busses each containing address, data, and control lines.
Chip selects	Pins on a chip used to address the chip.
Communications protocol	A rule used when peripherals communicate with the CPU.
Control bus	Terminology used in microcomputers to mean control lines.
Control lines	Wires in a bus that carry the control signals.
Control/status register	Register in an LSI-11 serial or parallel board that controls inputs and outputs and senses the status of a peripheral device.
CPS	Characters per second. Transmission rate based on baud rate — 110 baud corresponds to 10 CPS.
Data bus	Terminology used in microcomputers to mean data lines.
Data direction register	An 8-bit register in the 6800 PIA that determines if data are an input or output.
Data lines	Wires in a bus that carry the data.
DMA (direct memory access)	Peripheral can enter data directly in main memory without passing through the CPU.
End (stop) bit	One of two 1's used at the end of an asynchronous transmission to allow time for the computer to get ready for the next data string.
Interface	Device used to connect a peripheral to bus.
Parallel transmission	Data are sent along many wires at the same time.
Parity bit	MSB in a data string used by the computer to check for errors in transmission.

PIA (peripheral interface adapter)	Chip in 6800 that contains two parallel boards.
Port	Pins on a chip or board where the bus attaches.
Read-only	A bit(s) that can be read by the CPU but not changed.
Read/write	A bit(s) that can be read and changed by the CPU.
Serial interface	Interface between the computer and a peripheral device that transmits serial data. The interface does parallel-to-serial and serial-to-parallel conversions.
Serial transmission	Data are sent along one wire in series format.
Shift register	Register in serial interface that carries out parallel-to-serial and serial-to-parallel conversion of data.
Single-bus configuration	System with only one bus connecting memory, CPU, and I/O.
Start bit	A zero used before an asynchronous transmission to initiate the acceptance of the data string by a computer.
Sync character	Special character used to inform the computer a data string is starting.
Synchronous protocol	Data transmitted in a unit of time headed by sync characters.
TTY (teletype-writer)	Typewriter-like device used to communicate with a computer.
UART	Universal asynchronous receiver, transmitter; a device used to input or output serial information to or from a computer.
Unidirectional bus	A bus that allows signals to move along it in one direction only.
Write only	A bit(s) that can be changed by the CPU but not read.

ANSWERS TO EXERCISE 5-1

1. Include the words "group of wires" and "typically flat flexible cable with connectors at each end."
2. a. False   b. False   c. True
3. c or a
4. a. False   b. False   c. True
5. a. Include words "Bus containing 100 lines developed for 8080A-based microcomputers."
   b. 16,777,216 bytes
6. General-purpose interface bus

ANSWERS TO EXERCISE 5-2

1. Include the words "128 addressable areas" in chip's memory, each capable of holding "1 bit" of data.

2.

	Hexadecimal	Decimal
Begins	0100	256
Ends	01FF	511

3. The 16-bit address bus is broken into the following parts: 0–9 address bits, 10–15 chip-select bits:

Begins	0	0	0	0	1	0		0	0	0	0	0	0	0	0	0
Bit No.	15	14	13	12	11	10		9	8	7	6	5	4	3	2	1	0
Ends	0	0	0	0	1	0		1	1	1	1	1	1	1	1	1	1

	Hexadecimal	Decimal
Starting address	0800	2048
Ending address	0BFF	3071

ANSWERS TO EXERCISE 5-3

1. a. Parallel
    b. Serial
    c. Serial
    d. Serial
    e. Parallel
2. 10011001_2
3. $\dfrac{10000\ 000}{400} = 2500\ \mu s$

ANSWERS TO EXERCISE 5-4

1. a. False (more than a register)
    b. False
    c. True
    d. True
2. Mention three basic registers:
    a. Control/status   gives directions to CPU and peripheral
    b. Output buffer   CPU to peripheral
    c. Data input   peripheral to CPU
3. Bits 12, 11, 10, 9, 8, 7, 6, 5, 4, and 3 are used to address peripherals when bits 15, 14, and 13 are a 1. This gives $2^{10} = 1024$ different addresses or peripherals that can be addressed.
4. a. True   b. False   c. False   d. False (cannot be read)
5. a. True   b. False   c. False (may be less than 8 bits)
6. c. LSB must be a zero.
7. A series of rules defining the manner in which a peripheral communicates with the CPU.

8. d. Bank select 7 signal means bits 15, 14, and 13 are 1's.
9. a.
10. "Board" computer: Components are boards containing chips and hard-wires. System is put together by combining the boards. "Chip" computer: Components are "chips" normally on DIPs. Wires between the pins of the DIPs connect components.

ANSWERS TO REVIEW QUESTIONS

1. c
2. b
3. a
4. b
5. d
6. b
7. a. These are pins on the chip used to address the chip. When put in their proper state, they enable the chip.
   b. Insufficient hardware is used in a system to give each chip a unique address; that is, the same chip may be addressed by two or more addresses.
8.

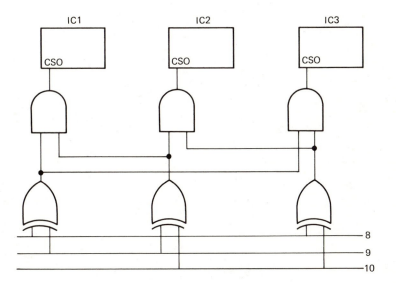

9. 4096 × 16
10. 874
11. Half-duplex: A peripheral device can send information to the computer and the computer can send information to the peripheral device, but not at the same time.

Full-duplex: Both of the above operations can be done independently of each other.

12. Asynchronous data: serial data with start and stop bits.
Synchronous data: serial data with no start or stop bits. Occasionally a sync character is transmitted.

13. 110101000_{LSB} : even parity is used.

CHAPTER 6

INPUT/ OUTPUT II- DEVICES

LEARNING ACTIVITIES

Study lecture material on devices.
Read resource material at end of unit.
Complete exercises.
Self-check answers to exercises.
Consult instructor for assistance as necessary.

OBJECTIVE

By completing these requirements, you should be able to achieve the following for this unit when formally evaluated.

Given a list of the following devices, identify each in terms of its normal use with computers, and its advantages and disadvantages.

a. Hexadecimal keyboard
b. LEDs, seven-segment and dot matrix
c. TTYs
d. Paper tape readers and punches
e. Cassette recorders
f. Video screens
g. Stepper motors
h. Floppy disks

EVALUATION

Your ability to demonstrate achievement on these objectives will be assessed after all instruction on this unit by:

• Multiple-choice items
• Identification items

INTRODUCTION

In Chapter 5 we learned how devices input data to a computer or receive data from a computer. Here we will look at the devices in greater detail to see some of their advantages and disadvantages.

HEXADECIMAL KEYBOARD

If a microprocessor is used for a specific dedicated purpose it is controlled by a program stored in a ROM. If you wish to change the program, you change the ROM. When you are using a microprocessor or microcomputer with RAM, there must be some means of entering the program into the RAM. One of the more common and least expensive means of entering data into a computer is via a keyboard. Figure 6.1 is a diagram of the keyboard used in the Heath ET-3400, MC6800-based microcomputer.

This keyboard contains 17 keys through which information can be sent to the computer. Keys 1 through F are dual-purpose keys. Only one of their uses is shown in Figure 6.1. The 0 and the RESET key are single-purpose keys. In other systems there may be more keys, with none acting as a dual-purpose key. The keys are arranged in a matrix format. In Figure 6.1 this format corre-

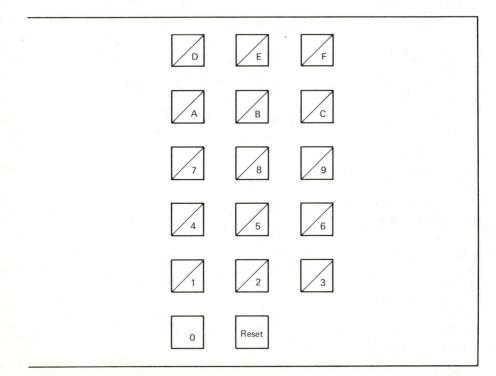

FIGURE 6.1. *Example of a hexadecimal keyboard.*

sponds to three columns of six rows. Many other arrangements are possible. The keys themselves may be either pressure-activated or touch-activated switches.

Once the switch is activated, the computer must have a means of detecting the proper key. Two basic types of keyboards are available — encoded and noncoded. Encoded keyboards have additional hardware in the keyboard that detects which key has been activated and the hardware holds this information until the next key is activated. Nonencoded keyboards are read by a software routine. This is another example of a hardware/software trade-off. The hardware is usually faster but more expensive.

To determine which key is being pressed using a software routine, a "keyboard scanning routine" has to be written. This is stored in a part of the ROM known as the monitor. In this procedure each column is assigned an address in memory. When that address is activated, each row in the column is checked to see if a key is depressed. If no key in a column is active, the next column is checked. This is continued until the microcomputer (μC) determines which key has been activated. Once the key has been determined, it is checked by another monitor routine for 20 ms or so to eliminate contact bounce. Writing routines to do a keyboard scan is fairly difficult. The routine must take into consideration problems that might be encountered, such as two keys being pressed at the same time (called rollover).

With the advent of cheaper parallel interface chips such as the MC6820 PIA, another method known as the "line reversal technique" can be used. If a 4 × 4 matrix keyboard is used, one PIA can handle the routine. In this case the first 4 bits of the data register are tied to the columns and the upper 4 bits of the data register are tied to the rows. The data direction register assigns 4 bits as inputs and the other 4 as outputs. When a key is depressed, a 0 will appear on the output line of the appropriate column or row. The direction of the eight rows is then reversed, and again a 0 will occur at the appropriate spot. By examining the combination of 1's and 0's stored, it is possible to determine which key was depressed. For example, if the number now stored in the data register is 0111 1101, this could mean the key in the fourth row, second column, if the higher nibble was used to hold the row value and the lower nibble the column value. This number would direct the μC to a look-up table in memory to find the value of the key depressed.

LED DISPLAYS

Light-emitting diodes (LEDs) are often used with microprocessors (μPs) or μCs. The intensity of the LED is determined by the amount of current flowing through it. At TTL levels, the LED is lit whenever an input of 0.6 volt or greater turns on the transistor associated with the LED. Single LEDs are often used to show the status of a device (on or off). LEDs are also combined to form display units. The two most common display units are the seven-segment LED and the dot-matrix LED.

The Seven-Segment LED

Figure 6.2 is an illustration of a seven-segment LED. It is composed of seven diodes that make up segments a through f, and an eighth diode for the decimal point h.

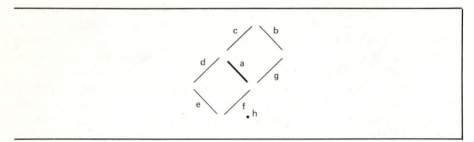

FIGURE 6.2. *Seven-segment LED with decimal point.*

Each of the seven-segments and the decimal point have their own address in memory. When a 1 is stored at this address, the segment lights. (There are some seven-segment LEDs that are lit by having a 0 stored at the proper address.) In some microcomputers, once these LEDs are lit, they stay on until turned off by another signal. These are said to be latched. Others use non-latched diodes and thus a signal has to be constantly sent to the LEDs to keep them lit. This is called refreshing. Common chips used with these are the BCD to seven-segment decoder/driver or HEX to seven-segment decoder/driver. These chips take a binary coded decimal number or a hexadecimal number, respectively, and output the correct signal to the seven-segment LED to light the decimal or hexadecimal number on the LED.

Because of their low cost, seven-segment LEDs are often used. Their major disadvantage is their inability to display all the letters of the alphabet in their normal format. By using a convention, it is possible to *represent* the 26 letters of the alphabet. Figure 6.3 is an example of such a representation used by Texas Instruments in its Model TM990/189 16-bit microcomputer. (See reference 1 for an interesting discussion of this problem.)

FIGURE 6.3. *A scheme to represent the 26 letters of the alphabet on seven-segment LEDs. (Courtesy Texas Instruments Incorporated; Copyrighted, 1979.)*

With conventions like this it is possible for the computer to "talk" to the user using English words and sentences. The seven-segment LED is the more common output device used for hand calculators.

Dot-Matrix LEDs

The dot-matrix LED comes in two standard sizes: a 5 × 7 and a 7 × 9 matrix. Figure 6.4 is an illustration of a dot-matrix LED.

By lighting the proper set of dots all the letters of the alphabet can be clearly read on a dot-matrix LED. In addition, other standard symbols such as arrows, dollar signs, and question marks, can also be displayed. This is a major advantage over the seven-segment LED, which is restricted in its

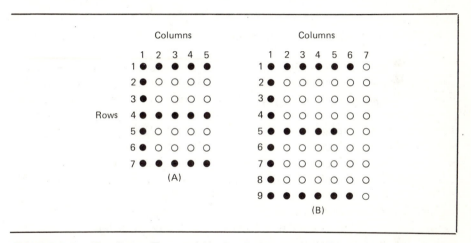

FIGURE 6.4. *The letter E on a (A) 5 × 7 dot-matrix LED and (B) 7 × 9 dot-matrix LED.*

output. A chip known as a character generator or character ROM can be used to display any desired character.

Some hand calculators are now using dot-matrix LEDs in place of seven-segment LEDs to enable better communication between the user and the calculator for long calculations. The small pocket computers use the dot-matrix format for their output, utilizing either LEDs or a similar device called a liquid crystal display (LCD). Although the cost of this device and its character ROM is greater than that of the seven-segment LED, its versatility makes up for the difference in price.

EXERCISE 6-1 Keyboard entry and LEDs

1. Explain, in your own words, the following.
   a. Rollover
   b. Line-reversal technique

2. Use the character representation in Figure 6.3 to draw the following words in their seven-segment LED format.
    a. Science
    b. Accumulator
    c. Computer
3. Explain, in your own words, the meaning of a character generator.

TELETYPEWRITERS

Teletypewriters (TTY) are the most common peripheral used to interface with a computer. There are two ways in which signals are sent to a computer from a TTY:

20-mA (milliampere) current loop
EIA RS232C (Electronics Industry Association)

With a 20-mA current loop, all TTL signals are converted into a current, with 0 amperes corresponding to a 0 and 20 mA corresponding to a 1. The data are transmitted in an asynchronous manner using these current levels along a cable connecting the TTY to the interface unit (serial board or chip) of the computer. This cable is known as a bit-serial bus. Since only 1 bit is transmitted at a time along this bus, it differs considerably from the parallel busses previously discussed. An important part of these transmissions are the "interrupt request" by the serial board (or TTY) and the "interrupt acknowledge" by the computer in which the peripheral device and computer "talk" to one another to tell the other a signal is coming or has been properly received. Such signals are part of the standards used in bus communications. (The GPIB parallel bus had three wires to handle these signals.) These are called handshake signals since there is a similarity between handshaking and the type of communication taking place between the peripheral device and the computer. A series of signals might be sent as follows:

TTY: I have some data for you (interrupt request).

Computer: O.K. I am ready to accept the data (interrupt acknowledge).

Computer: O.K. I have received the data (data in).

The last signal would clear the TTY and enable it to prepare to send another signal to the computer.

The RS232C standard is a procedure developed by the Electronic Industries Association. This procedure includes a complete description of the electrical signals and physical specifications needed to transmit serial data in this format. Using RS232C (RS232), data may be sent at baud rates of 50, 75, 110, 300, 600, 1200, 2400, 4800, 9600, or 19,200. To send a signal, pulses of -12

volts to represent a "1" or +12 volts to represent a "0" are sent along the bus. RS232 is one of the more popular methods of transmitting data as this is the convention used in most time-shared telephone systems.

Care must be taken to make sure the +12 volts or −12 volts needed to run a TTY never enter the computer because this excess voltage would destroy the chips. There are different ways in which the computer can be isolated from these voltages. The most common is to use photoelectric diodes that act as optical isolators (opto-isolators). These convert the signal from the TTY to the 0-volt or 5-volt signal that the chips can handle.

When attaching any peripheral device to the computer, you should be careful of spurious voltages reaching the computer from the device. Other types of isolation devices used are isolation amplifiers, which restrict the voltage that can be passed to the computer, and fusable resisters, which burn out if an excess voltage enters them.

PAPER TAPE READERS AND PUNCHES

One of the least expensive storage medium that is available with TTYs is the paper tape reader and punch. This is also one of the slowest methods of introducing programs or information to a computer. Figure 6.5 is a diagram of the standard eight-hole paper tape.

The sprocket holes are used to drive the paper tape over a sensing device, often a photoelectric cell. This cell reads the various combinations of punched holes and translates this into a signal the computer understands. High-speed paper tape readers are available.

The cost of this device is low, but it has many disadvantages. Dirt in the holes or ragged edges may lead to misreadings. And the paper can be easily torn or bent to give wrong readings.

The paper tape itself cannot be as conveniently stored as other devices, and in terms of the slow readers, the process of reading tapes takes a discouragingly long time. With the introduction of cassette players and tapes, paper tape as a storage medium has almost disappeared, except for back-up storage.

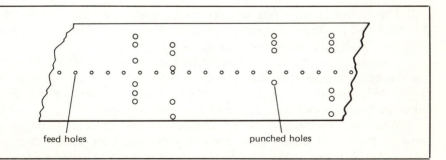

feed holes   punched holes

FIGURE 6.5. *Eight-hole paper tape.*

EXERCISE 6-2 TTYs and paper tape

1. Identify each of the following.
    a. 20-mA current loop
    b. RS232C
    c. Opto-isolators
    d. Handshaking
2. List advantages and disadvantages of using paper tape.
3. What is meant by a bit-serial bus?

CASSETTE INTERFACING

One of the most popular means of storing a fairly large quantity of data for use with micros is cassette tape storage. This is the least expensive form of magnetic tape storage available. Digital information is stored on the tape using one audiofrequency to represent a 1 and another frequency to represent a 0. Not all systems use the same combination of frequencies, and thus tapes are not interchangeable even if the languages are.

One of the more popular formats for recording data on cassette tape is known as "Kansas City Standard." This standard uses 4 cycles of 1200 hertz to represent a "0" and 8 cycles of 2400 hertz to represent a "1." This is illustrated in Figure 6.6. Note that one frequency is twice the other. Manufacturers of computer systems that do not use Kansas City Standard may use other frequencies, or even combinations of frequencies, to represent the binary numbers.

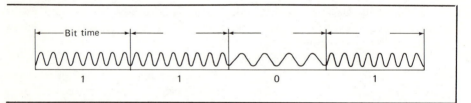

FIGURE 6.6. *Kansas City Standard audio signal.*

The normal transfer rate between the computer and the cassette for the KC Standard is 300 baud. Some systems, using other standards or a variation of the KC Standard, can transfer at rates up to 1500 baud.

Cassette recorders can be bought as cheaply as $25, while other tapes capable of storing 100,000 bytes of information range from $1 to 2.50 in price. The same investment in paper tape would hold only 10 percent of this data. In addition, tapes can be erased and used over and over again.

When information is stored on tapes, it is stored in blocks. There are gaps between the blocks known as interrecord gaps, which are needed due to the stop and start times associated with the recorder. It is good practice to record the program twice in succession as an error check. Referred to as a redundant recording, this will help to minimize problems as the chance that both copies of the program will contain errors is small. If one copy is bad, the other is available. Some companies that sell programs on tape triply record these programs.

Figure 6.7 is an illustration of programs recorded on an audio tape.

Each program can be subdivided into parts:

1. A leader
2. An identification code or other signal used to identify the particular program
3. Actual data
4. Checksum: value used in error detection

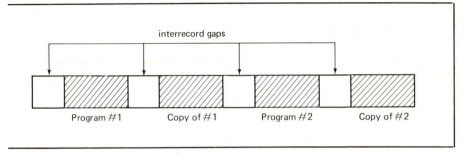

FIGURE 6.7. *Recording on an audio cassette.*

In a very simple system, not all of the above need be used. When you first put a tape in the cassette player it should be advanced before attempting to record. Most cassette tapes have a leader on which you cannot record. If you attempt to, the program will not be stored and the computer will not tell you of this error. You may think you have a good copy on the tape when, in fact, the beginning of your program is missing. When you turn the cassette player on to record a program, there is a short period of time during which the player accelerates to its normal speed. To accommodate this time there is a small section of the tape on which no program is recorded. This is the program leader. Most computer systems allow you to store your program on the tape under a name, which usually serves as the identification code for the program. The checksum is one type of error detection available. It is normally a byte of data added to the end of the program. The value of the data is determined by the information in the program. One way to form a checksum is to add all the data in the program together and the least significant 8 bits would be the checksum. If, after loading the program, the computer does not agree with the checksum, the computer will signal you that an error has been detected in reading the tape.

One major problem in using tapes is the alignment of the tape from one program to another. If you have just finished with the fifth program on the tape and want to use the second program, you must run the tape almost back to its beginning. There is no easy way to go directly to the beginning of any individual program.

Magnetic tapes in cassettes are an example of a sequential-access device. In this type of device the computer must start at the beginning and search through all programs until it comes to the proper program. A bulk storage device that overcomes this is the floppy disk.

FLOPPY DISKS AND WINCHESTER DISKS

A floppy disk or diskette is a magnetic storage device that looks like a 45-rpm phonograph record without grooves. There are two basic types; the regular is an 8-inch disk, and the minifloppy, which is $5\frac{1}{4}$ inches, holds one third the amount of material that the regular size holds. Because the floppy disk is so flexible, it comes in a protective cardboard envelope; Figure 6.8.

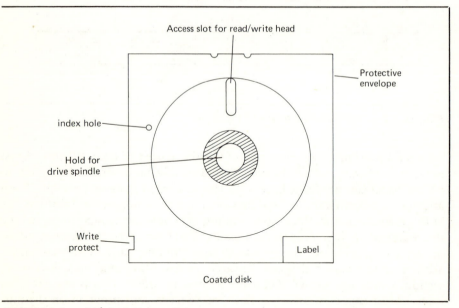

FIGURE 6.8. *A $5\frac{1}{4}$ inch floppy disk.*

The regular 8-inch floppy disk is divided into 77 tracks, numbered 0 to 76, and each track is divided into sectors; Figure 6.9. The number of sectors in a track is dependent upon the technique used in making the disk. There are two techniques for formatting disks — *hard-sectoring* and *soft-sectoring.*

Using hard-sectoring, 32 holes are punched into the disk, defining 32 sectors, each containing 128 bytes. The total storage here is (128 × 32 × 77) or 315,362 bytes. In soft-sectoring only one hole is punched into the disk, which identifies sector zero. If an IBM format is used, then there are 26 sectors containing 128 bytes in each track for a total of (128 × 26 × 77) 256,256 bytes available on a disk. Since each sector contains the same number of bytes no

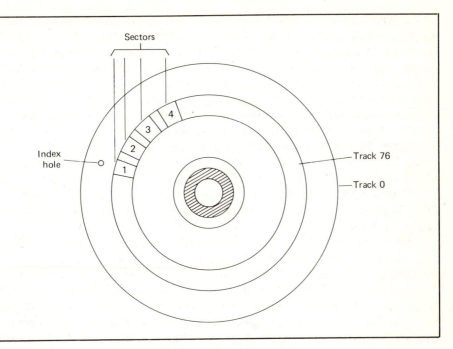

FIGURE 6.9. *Tracks and sectors on a floppy disk.*

matter which track it is on, there is more wasted space on the longer (or outer) tracks.

On a soft-sectored disk each sector has a header containing an identification code. Soft-sectored disks hold less information than hard-sectored disks, but the identification code present in the sector makes data transfers more reliable with soft sectors than with hard sectors.

Most home systems use the 5¼-inch diskettes sometimes referred to as minifloppies. There are 35 tracks in a minifloppy. These also come in hard-sectored or soft-sectored format. With the hard-sectored disk, two formats are used: 16 sectors containing 128 bytes each or ten sectors containing 256 bytes each. The first gives 71,680 (35 × 16 × 128) bytes storage while the second allows 89,600 (35 × 10 × 256) bytes. With the soft-sectored format, the number of sectors may be left to the manufacturer or the programmer. Some computers use "double-density" floppy disks. These hold 256 bytes in a sector, thus doubling the number of bytes that can be stored on a disk.

Before a disk can be used, it must be initialized (or formatted) for the particular system on which it will be used. This gives the disk an identification code and prepares the disk in a manner that enables the computer to use it. At least one track of the disk is reserved as a directory that keeps track of the programs on the disk. Let us look at the diskette system found in two popular home computers.

A typical system is that found in the Apple II. Each diskette contains 35 tracks, with 13 sectors in each track for a total of 455 sectors. Some of these are reserved to carry out the transfer of information from the disk to the computer. In the Apple II one of the tracks is a catalog that contains a list of all the programs stored on the disk and on the tracks and sectors of which the program is stored. When the program is called, the disk goes to the catalog, gets this information, and then goes to the proper place on the diskette. It continues this until the complete program is loaded into the computer's memory. Communication between the computer and the disk is carried out in any system by a program called a "disk operating system" (DOS). Many computers have different versions of their DOS. In DOS 3.2 for the Apple II four tracks are reserved for holding the directory and other information, leaving 403 sectors each containing 128 bytes available for the user. The newer 3.3 DOS by Apple is a little more efficient and each disk can thus hold a little more information.

Another popular home system is the PET computer by Commodore Business Machines. This company makes four different disk drives that can be attached to its computers. In drive 4040 a double-density diskette containing 35 tracks is used. The number of sectors varies depending upon the track. Each diskette holds a total of 683 sectors. One of the tracks (number 18) contains the identification of the disk and a directory. The directory functions similarly to the catalog in the Apple systems. The disk thus holds around 170,000 bytes of information.

Floppy disks are random-access storage devices. The transfer time for the minifloppy is slower, by a factor of around 3, than for floppy disks. Regular disk systems cost between $1000 and $2000 while the minifloppies run from $600 to $1000 for a single-disk drive.

A newer disk system that has just become available for small computer systems are the Winchester disk drives, which are available as 8-inch and $5\frac{1}{4}$-inch drives. The Winchester differs from the floppy in that there is no removable disk in the Winchester. It is a fixed disk in a completely sealed system to keep out air and dirt. This drive holds over 2 Mbytes (megabytes) of information compared with about 1 kbyte for a single-density $5\frac{1}{4}$-inch minifloppy. Though the cost is two to three times more than a minifloppy, you get 10 to 15 times the amount of storage on a disk.

VIDEO DISPLAYS

With the advent of the home microcomputer, the TV typewriter (TVT) or video screen has become popular as an input/output device. Various chips are available that will allow a user to connect a home television set as a video display with the computer. Television is an example of one method of displaying an image on a video screen. Since it is the most popular display screen used with small computers, we will restrict our discussion to it.

The television screen is an example of a *raster scan* device. Here the display is created by having a beam of electrons move horizontally across the picture tube from left to right (Figure 6.10).

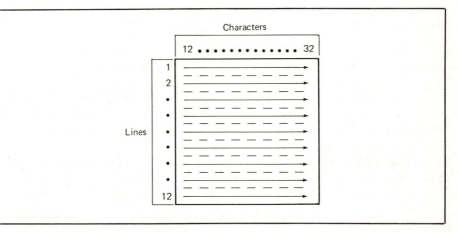

FIGURE 6.10. *Raster scan display.*

A phosphor coating on the display tube glows for a short period of time (10–100 ms) after being struck by the beam of the electrons. The beam is blanked and returned to the left side of the screen while being lowered slightly to prepare for the next trace.

A standard TV set made in North America has a picture composed of 525 scan lines. The scan lines are divided into two fields of $262\frac{1}{2}$ lines. This is represented in Figure 6.10 by the straight and dotted lines. Two types of scanning are possible. In direct, or noninterlaced, scanning only one field is used. A picture is made from the 262 lines. With an interlaced scan, the screen is scanned twice, so all 525 are used. Because of the curvature of the screen only approximately 484 lines are visible, and thus usable to develop an image. Since the screen is not latched, it must be refreshed at 60 Hz (hertz) to prevent flicker. A typical format divides the video screen into a number of lines — 12, 13, 16, and 25 are most common — with so many characters per line, usually 32, 40, or 64, although many others are possible. With word processors, 80 characters per line are preferred. Room must be left between the rows in order to make the characters readable. The characters are generated using the dot-matrix pattern previously discussed.

The screen is divided into thousands of areas called picture elements (pixels). The resolution of the screen is expressed as the product of the number of horizontal pixels times the number of vertical pixels. Since the screen must be refreshed to display an image, the value of each pixel must be stored in memory. The greater the resolution, the more memory is needed to store an image.

A system has a "curser," a means of identifying where the next character from the keyboard will be displayed. Some will allow a blinking curser. In addition, some have scrolling capabilities. Scrolling is the ability to move data around the screen without actually moving the data first in refresh memory.

STEPPER MOTORS

Though these do not fall into the same class as the previous devices, the use of stepper motors in the scientific and hobby field has become so common that a word about them is appropriate.

A stepper motor is a motor that is capable of rotating in either direction in well-defined steps. Typical sizes are 200, 180, 144, 72, 24, and 12 steps per revolution. The motor can be stopped or started at any of these steps or backed up.

Most motors are constructed for two-, three-, or four-phase operations. The motor has four windings. By applying pulses of current in a given sequence, the motor will step. There are three sequences: (1) low power, which advances the motor one step; (2) normal sequence; (3) half-step sequence. By reversing the sequence, the motor can be made to move backward.

The advantage of such a motor is that the computer can keep track of exactly where the motor is at any given time. This is the technique used in infrared and ultraviolet spectrometers that are μP controlled. It is also used in disks to keep track of where the disk is with respect to the head used to read the disk.

EXERCISE 6-3 Cassette recorders, disks, video terminals, and stepper motors

1. Explain how binary 1's or 0's are stored on cassette tape.
2. Why are programs on a cassette written for one computer often not usable for another computer even though both use the same language?
3. What is meant by Kansas City Standard?
4. What is redundant recording?
5. Explain the difference between a sequential-access and a random-access storage device.
6. What are the two sizes of floppy disks?
7. What is the difference between hard-sectoring and soft-sectoring?
8. What is a TVT?
9. What is the difference between noninterlaced and interlaced video screens?
10. What are stepper motors?

REVIEW QUESTIONS

1. Which of the following storage devices have the fastest access time?
   a. Minifloppy disk   b. Floppy disk   c. Cassette   d. Paper tape
2. Which of the following is not a method by which the computer can read a hexadecimal keyboard?

    a. Using an encoded keyboard   c. Using a keyboard scanning routine

    b. Line-reversal technique   d. Using a nonencoded keyboard

3. LEDs are currently used
   a. To represent the state of a device
   b. As outputs on hand calculators
   c. As outputs on some microcomputers
   d. All of the above

4. Which is not true for the dot-matrix LED?
   a. It comes in two standard sizes, 5×7 and 7×9.
   b. It can output any symbol in its conventional form.
   c. It should be used in place of the seven-segment LED since it costs about the same and is easily programmed for output.
   d. It needs a character generator chip for convenient output of the symbols.

5. Which of the following is not true for a TTY?
   a. Signals can be sent asynchronously using a 20-mA current loop.
   b. A TTY need not be isolated from the computer when 20-mA current loops are being used, as the voltages generated here are too small to harm the computer.
   c. Signals can be sent asynchronously using EIA RS232C voltage levels.
   d. Since RS232C voltages levels are $+12$ and -12, isolation of a TTY from a computer is a must.

6. A TTY is connected to its interface unit using
   a. A bit-serial bus
   b. A parallel bus
   c. The GPIB bus
   d. Any one of the above three

7. Which of the following is not true for diskettes?
   a. Hard-sectoring is more reliable, but has fewer sectors available.
   b. Soft-sectoring is more reliable, but has fewer sectors available.
   c. They are random access storage devices.
   d. They are available in two sizes, 8 inches and $5\frac{1}{4}$-inches.

8. What is a pixel? A scan line?

9. What is a checksum?

10. What is the difference between an encoded and nonencoded keyboard?

11. Why must you take care to "isolate" devices attached to a computer? What methods of isolation are commonly used?

12. What is meant by a "double-density" disk?

REFERENCES

1. Daniel Chester, A Digital Alphanumeric Display, *Byte*, 4 (4), p. 218 (Apr. 1979).

2. Paul Giacomo, A Stepper Motor Primer Part I, *Byte*, 4 (2), p. 90 (Feb. 1979).

3. Paul Giacomo, A Stepper Motor Primer Part II. *Byte*, 4 (3), p. 142 (Mar. 1979).
4. Austin Lesea and Rodnay Zaks, *Microprocessor Interfacing Techniques*, 2nd ed. Sybex, Berkeley, Calif., Chapter IV.
5. Phyllis Cole and Brian Howard, *A Manual for Using the Apple Disk II, with DOS Version 3.2.* Apple Computer Co., Cupertino, Calif., p. 135.
6. *Individual Learning Program in Microprocessors.* Heath Corp., Benton Harbor, Mich. 1979.
7. *User's Manual for CBM 5 1/4-inch Dual Floppy Disk Drives*, Commodore Business Machines, 1980.

GLOSSARY

Bit-serial bus	A group of wires used to transmit serial signals to a computer.
Character generator	A chip used to generate any symbol on a dot-matrix LED.
Checksum	A system used to check for errors in transferring information from an external device to the computer. One type of checksum is to add all the bytes together and store the least significant byte of the sum as an additional byte at the end of the program.
Dot-matrix LED	A device composed of five columns and seven rows of LEDs or 7 × 9 LEDs used to generate any symbol.
Encoded keyboard	A keyboard hard-wired so the computer can read which key has been depressed.
Floppy disk	A random-access storage device that looks like a 45-rpm record.
Handshaking	A series of signals sent between the computer and a peripheral device to ensure data are transmitted properly.
Hard-sectoring	A method of dividing up tracks on a floppy disk into sectors; 32 holes identify each of the 32 sectors.
Hexadecimal keyboard	Keyboard consisting of pushbuttons that enable the user to enter hexadecimal numbers.
Interlaced	A video screen in which all 525 scan lines are used. First one field (262) is scanned and then the second field is scanned to fill in the total image.
Kansas City Standard	A common form of recording data on cassette tape. Using 4 cycles of 1200 Hz for 0 and 8 cycles of 2400 Hz for 1.
LED	Light-emitting diode.
Line-reversal technique	A program routine using a PIA or its equivalent to "read" a keyboard.
Nonencoded keyboard	Keyboard that depends upon a "software" routine for the computer to read which key is depressed.

Opto-isolator	Device used to isolate peripheral devices from the computer and to prevent excess voltages from reaching the chip in a computer.
Paper tape recorder	Device used to read the holes punched in paper tape. May be low speed or high speed.
Pixel	A picture element. Smallest part of the screen that is used to draw a part of a picture.
Raster scan	Video device that displays an image on a raster (or screen) by motion of a beam of electrons across its face.
RS232C	A method used to transmit binary numbers; -12 volts represent a binary 1, while $+12$ volts represent a binary 0.
Seven-segment LED	A device composed of seven LEDs to draw letters or numbers plus another LED for a decimal point.
Soft-sectoring	A method of dividing up tracks on a floppy disk into sectors. This disk contains only one hole for sector alignment.
Stepper motor	A motor whose angle of rotation can be controlled in specific steps.
20-mA current loop	A method used to transmit binary numbers on a TTY with 0 mA representing a binary 0 and 20 mA representing a binary 1.
TVT	Television typewriter; teletypewriter with a video screen.

ANSWERS TO EXERCISE 6-1

1. a. Pressing two keys at the same time on a keyboard.
    b. Procedure using a chip similar to a PIA in which the row and column of the key depressed is stored as an 8-bit number in the chip. The value of the key is found in a look-up table.

2.

    a) ⌐⌐ ⌐ ⌐ ⌐⌐

    b) ⌐⌐⌐ ⌐ ⌐⌐ ⌐⌐ ⌐⌐⌐ ⌐⌐

    c) ⌐ ⌐ ⌐ ⌐ ⌐

3. Chip used to create a letter on an LED or similar device.

ANSWERS TO EXERCISE 6-2

1. a. Method of transmitting data—0 mA = 0, 20 mA = 1.
    b. Transmitting standard developed by EIA; -12 V = 1; $+12$ V = 0.
    c. Device used to isolate a peripheral from the computer; uses photoelectric diode.
    d. Protocol used when a computer "talks" to a peripheral.

2. Advantages: easy to use, inexpensive, a part of many TTYs.
   Disadvantages: slow, inconvenient to store or handle, easily damaged.
3. Bus used to transmit a serial string.

ANSWERS TO EXERCISE 6-3

1. By combining audiofrequencies, a 0 is one frequency, a 1 is another.
2. They use different frequencies or combinations to represent 1's or 0's.
3. See Glossary.
4. Making two or more copies of a program on a cassette.
5. Sequential access: Must start at the beginning and go through whole tape to point where data of interest starts.
   Random access: May obtain data from any place on the device.
6. 8 inches, $5\frac{1}{4}$-inches.
7. Hard-sectoring — 32 holes.
   Soft-sectoring — one hole on disk.
8. Television typewriter.
9. Noninterlaced uses half the lines on a screen (262); interlaced uses all 525.
10. Motors that have precisely defined angles of rotation.

ANSWERS TO REVIEW QUESTIONS

1. b
2. d (all of the answers are true to some extent)
3. d
4. c
5. b
6. a
7. a
8. A picture element; the horizontal movement of the electron beam across the face of a video tube.
9. A method of checking for errors on input to the computer.
10. Encoded: Hard-wired to prevent contact bounce.
    Nonencoded: Must be debounced by a software program.
11. A device may send a voltage to the computer that is too high and thus burn out the chips, opto-isolators, and isolation amplifiers.
12. A disk that stores 256 bytes of information per sector instead of the normal 128.

CHAPTER 7

COMPUTER PROGRAMMING

LEARNING ACTIVITIES

Study lecture material on programming.
Read resource materials listed at end of unit.
Complete exercises.
Self-check answers to exercises.
Consult instructor for assistance as necessary.

OBJECTIVES

By completing these requirements, you should be able to achieve the following for this unit when formally evaluated.

Objective 1

Given a list of words and statements, choose whether each applies to machine language, assembly language, or both, as used in a typical microcomputer.

Objective 2

Given the words compiler, interpreter, absolute assembler, and relocatable assembler, define each as used in a computer.

Objective 3

Given a list of statements, choose which of the following software packages each applies to according to standard computer usage: text editor, monitor, ODT or memory map.

Objective 4

Given a list of addressing modes and the five steps used to write a program, define each according to standard computer usage.

Objective 5

Given the following addressing modes used in a microprocessor, identify them according to their operating specifications.

a. Implied (or inherent)
b. Immediate
c. Direct
d. Extended
e. Index
f. Accumulator
g. Relative
h. Autoincrement
i. Autodecrement

EVALUATION

Your ability to demonstrate achievement on these objectives will be assessed after all instruction on this unit by:

- Multiple-choice items
- Identification items
- Matching items

MACHINE LANGUAGE

By now it should be clear that microprocessors operate by manipulating the binary numbers 1 and 0. In certain combinations these bits represent an instruction, and in other combinations or under other conditions, they are a number that represents data or an address.

A group of instructions that tells the microprocessor what to do is called a *program.* The programs that can be written in a microprocessor are called *software* — to differentiate between the wires and gates that determine electrical flows in a computer, which are known as *hardware.*

In recent years another term that has come into common use in the field is *firmware.* A software program, stored in a ROM or similar device, that cannot be changed easily is called firmware.

Remember, an 8-bit microprocessor handles 8-bit words. Each instruction could then be made up of a combination of 8-bits. These instructions constitute what is referred to as the *machine code.* An instruction word can be broken into two major parts — an operation field and an operand field.

In Figure 7.1 an 8-bit instruction word has been broken into a 3-bit operation field and a 5-bit operand field. An operation field contains a binary code called an *OP code.* The OP code tells the microprocessor exactly what operation is to be done, for example, ADD, MOVE, HALT. With 3 bits, there are

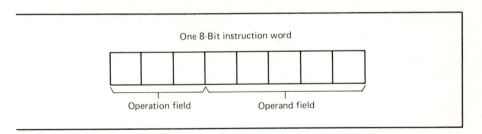

FIGURE 7.1. *Typical instruction word.*

2^3 possible combinations of these bits or eight different instructions that can be stored as an OP code. Most microprocessors use more instructions than that. This is accomplished by using two consecutive words to generate the operation field and the operand field. The first 8 bits are the OP code. This allows $2^8 = 256$ possible instructions.

The operand field holds the information (operand) that is being operated on by the OP code. This, therefore, may be a number (data) or an address. For the 5-bit operand field in Figure 7.1, 2^5 or 32_{10} memory locations can be directly addressed in the operand field, while for the 8-bit operand field in the 6800 or other μPs, you can directly address 2^8 or 256_{10} memory locations. Some instructions use three words, with the last two giving a 16-bit address.

EXERCISE 7 -1   Machine language

1. Which combination of the following field(s) are found in a typical machine word?
    1. Label field   2. Operand field
    3. Data field   4. Operation field
        a. 1 and 2
        b. 2 and 4
        c. 1, 2, and 4
        d. 1, 2, 3, and 4
2. An OP code
    a. Stores data.
    b. Instructs the CPU.
    c. Translates a mnemonic.
    d. Is contained in the operand field.
3. The operand field might contain
    1. An address   2. Data
    3. An instruction   4. An OP code
        a. 1 and 2
        b. 3 and 4
        c. 2 only
        d. 1, 2, 3, and 4

4. If an operand field contains 6 bits, it can directly address _____ memory locations.
   a. 12
   b. 36
   c. 216
   d. 64

MONITORS

When you receive a computer, its memory is completely empty. Before you can use the computer you must store some instructions in that memory. These instructions allow you to carry out simple communications with the computer. Such a set of instructions is known as a *bootstrap loader*. With these instructions in memory, more complex instructions (or programs) can then be loaded.

In the case of microcomputers a different approach is normally used. Most microcomputers have permanently stored in memory, in a ROM, a software program that enables you to:

1. Load a program through a teletypewriter or other terminal using octal or hexadecimal code and deposit this code into successive memory locations.
2. Examine any memory location or general purpose register (GPR).
3. Change the contents of a memory location or GPR.

Such a program is called a *monitor*. These usually occupy between 512 and 2048 bytes of memory.

An example of a monitor is the one found in the LSI-11 microcomputer and is called ODT^R for *On*-line *D*ebugging *T*echnique (or *O*ctal *D*ebugging *T*echnique). Suppose you want to place the number 20_8 in one of the GPR's in the LSI-11. A machine code that would do this is 0001010111000000_2. To load this through a teletypewriter, the command must be converted to octal. This code then becomes 012700_8, which is typed into a specific location in memory.

Figure 7.2 gives an example of what these commands would look like on a teletypewriter (TTY).

When the computer and TTY are turned on, the monitor prints out an ampersand. This is the monitor-ready signal. The operator types the location

	Location	Octal Code	
@	1000/000000	012700	LF
	1002/000000	000020	CR
@			

FIGURE 7.2. *Monitor instructions for the LSI-11.*

1000 to tell the computer what memory cell to start at, and then a slash. The computer will type out the contents presently stored in the memory unit. The operator now types what is to be stored in that memory unit followed by a line feed (LF). This generates a carriage return and causes the monitor automatically to go to the next memory location (1002 in the LSI-11) and to type out the contents of this location. The operator then types a 20_8 to be stored here followed by the carriage return (CR). This generates a line feed and the ampersand tells the operator the monitor is ready.

When working with a monitor you are working in machine code, usually in its octal or hexadecimal equivalent. When toggle switches were common, octal was usually used, but now that pushbutton switches are replacing the toggle, hexadecimal has become more popular.

EXERCISE 7-2 Monitors

1. A monitor
   1. Enables you to load a program into computer using a TTY.
   2. Is an example of software.
   3. Allows you to examine and/or change any memory location or GPR
      a. 2
      b. 1 and 3
      c. 1 and 2
      d. 1, 2, and 3
2. ODT is a
   a. Monitor
   b. Piece of hardware
   c. GPR
   d. PROM
3. ODT uses the octal equivalent of
   a. Assembly language
   b. Machine code
   c. Object code
   d. PL/1

ASSEMBLY LANGUAGES

To know the value of all 8 bits in every (256) 8-bit instruction would be an imposing task for a programmer. To simplify this task, each OP code is assigned a three- or four-letter abbreviation called an *instruction mnemonic* or a *mnemonic op code*. Each microprocessor has its own characteristic set of instruction mnemonics. For example, in the 6800 the machine language code for an addition is 10001011_2. The OP code is 8B. The instruction mnemonic is ADD. In the 6800 there are 72 such instruction mnemonics, while in the 8080A there are 74 and in the Z-80 there are 124. Programs written using instruction mnemonics are written in what is called assembly language.

Since a microprocessor recognizes only 1's and 0's, there must be a software program stored somewhere in the computer that will translate the assembly language into machine code. Such a program is called an *assembler*.

It should be remembered at this point that when a person runs a program, using assembly language, there are two different programs stored in the computer: the program the operator wrote, and a program, usually supplied by the company that sold the microprocessor, that translates the operator's program into machine language.

A program written in assembly language is called a *source program*, and one written in machine language is called an *object program*.

Assembly language programs are easier to use because:

1. The instruction mnemonics used are easier to learn.
2. It is faster to write programs using assembly language.
3. The assembler assigns memory locations for variables and constants.
4. It is easier to outline in a format that others can follow.

In order for an assembler to translate assembly language into machine binary code, the assembler must scan (read) the program. Each scan is called a *pass*. Not every instruction mnemonic is translated during a given pass. Usually it takes an assembler two or more passes before the source program is translated into an object program. The first pass is used to make a list of the different symbols and labels employed called a *symbol table*, and to define addresses where necessary. There is a check for errors at the end of this pass, for example: Were words used that the assembler does not recognize? During the second pass, these instructions and data are converted into binary code. A second pass cannot occur unless the first pass is error-free. Such an assembler is called an *absolute assembler*.

There is another type of assembler that converts assembly language into an *object code*. This cannot be read by the computer. An object code must go through another program called a *linker* in order for it to be translated into an object program. This type of assembler is called a *relocatable* assembler. The linker (or linkage editor) has the advantage of being able to take two parts of a program, written at different times, and combine them to form a single program.

If there is sufficient memory, another software program can be stored that enables you to write, correct, and modify programs written in assembly language. This software is called a *text editor*. After completion, the editor's output is a source program, written in assembly language. To use this program, it must pass through an assembler.

EXERCISE 7-3 Assembly languages

1. The language that uses mnemonic OP codes is
   a. Machine code
   b. ALGOL
   c. Assembly language
   d. Machine language

2. Mnemonic OP codes are
   a. Instructions
   b. Used to eliminate excessive memorization
   c. Used in assembly language
   d. All of the above
3. Assembly language is an example of
   a. Software
   b. Hardware
   c. High-level language
   d. Flowcharts
4. The use of assembly language necessitates a(an)
   a. Compiler
   b. Interpreter
   c. Assembler
   d. RAM
5. A(an) _____ translates source programs into object programs.
   a. Absolute assembler
   b. Compiler
   c. Relocatable assembler
   d. Interpreter
6. Object code is generated by
   a. An absolute assembler
   b. A computer
   c. A relocatable assembler
   d. A linkage editor
7. A linker (linkage editor)
   1. Translates object code into machine code.
   2. Combines parts of a program.
   3. Is an example of software.
      a. 1
      b. 2
      c. 1 and 2
      d. 1, 2, and 3
8. The first pass of an absolute assembler
   1. Creates symbol table.
   2. Checks for errors.
   3. Translates assembly language into binary code.
      a. 1 and 2
      b. 2 and 3
      c. 1 and 3
      d. 1, 2, and 3
9. Which of the following statements referring to text editors is false?
   a. A text editor is a software program.
   b. Its output is a source program written in assembly language.
   c. A text editor is used to write, correct, or modify assembly language.
   d. A text editor can be used to load a monitor into memory.

ADDRESSING MODES

In order to address a large number of memory units, various different addressing modes are found in different microprocessors. With 8-bit microprocessors, 256 memory locations can be directly addressed, if all 8 bits are used as an address. Because of this memory can be divided into blocks of 256_{10} (FF_{16}) locations called *pages*. Table 7.1 gives an example of the pages found in 64K of memory.

TABLE 7.1. *Pages in an 8-Bit Micro-computer.*

Page	Memory Location in Hexadecimal
00	0000–00FF
01	0100–01FF
02	0200–02FF
⋮	⋮ ⋮
09	0900–09FF
0A	0A00–0AFF
⋮	⋮ ⋮
FD	FD00–FDFF
FE	FE00–FEFF
FF	FF00–FFFF

An examination of the number and types of addressing modes available gives an indication of how powerful the microprocessor is. In general, the greater the number of addressing modes in an instruction set, the more powerful the instruction set. The more powerful the instruction set, the faster and more efficient it is.

Let us look at the addressing modes available in the 6800. We will consider these in more detail in Chapter 8.

Implied or Inherent Mode

These are all 1-byte instructions. They can be further classified into two types, those that need an address and those that do not.

Example :

TAB   Transfer contents of accumulator A to accumulator B.
PSHA   Take the data from accumulator A and place the data in a memory
        address determined by a number in the stack pointer.

The TAB does not need an address. The address needed for the second instruction (PSHA) is contained in another register in the microprocessor.

Immediate Mode

These are mainly 2-byte instructions, with some instructions needing 3 bytes. The first byte is the instruction. In this mode the operand is contained in the memory location following the instruction.

Example :

Memory Address	OP Code	Mnemonic
0100	8B	ADDA#
0101	02	$02

The OP code 8B is an add immediate instruction. The # sign means immediate addressing mode. The computer is to take the number in the next address (02) and add it to any value already stored in accumulator A. The 3-byte instructions are encountered whenever either of the two 16-bit registers in the 6800 are used.

Direct Addressing

In this addressing mode, all instructions are 2-byte instructions. The first byte is the instruction and the second byte is an address in page zero. This is thus a page zero addressing mode.

Example :

Memory Address	OP Code	Mnemonic
0200	9B	ADDA
0201	02	$02

In this example, 9B is an add instruction using direct mode. The next number is the address to which the computer must jump. At this address the computer will obtain the data to be added to accumulator A. Since this is a page zero addressing mode, the address is 0002_{16}.

Extended Addressing

This mode uses 3 bytes. The first is the instruction OP code while the last 2 bytes are combined to form a 16-bit address. This enables the computer to address up to 64K memory units.

Example :

Memory Address	OP Code	Mnemonic
0000	BB	ADDA
0001	OA	$OAFF
0002	FF	

In forming the 16-bit address from the last 2 bytes, the second byte (OA) forms the more significant byte and the third byte (FF) the least significant byte of the 16-bit address. Some microprocessors use the opposite convention to this in their extended addressing mode.

Indexed Addressing

The 6800 has a 16-bit register called an index register. This register can also be used to direct the computer to all possible memory units. Instructions using this addressing mode are 2-byte instructions. The first byte is the instruction and the second byte is a number. The number in the second byte is added to the lower byte of the number stored in the index register to get an address in memory. The computer goes to this address to get the data.

Example :

Memory Address	OP Code	Mnemonic
0000	AB	ADDA,X
0001	02	$02
Index register	0400	

In the above example the index register has the number 0400 stored in it. When the instruction add to accumulator A using index mode (AB) is encountered, the computer will take the second byte of the instruction (02) and add it to the index register as an unsigned number. The result (0402) is the address to which the computer must go, to get the data to be added to accumulator A. Index addressing is one of the most powerful addressing modes available in the 6800. In fact, it is one of the more powerful addressing modes available in any microprocessor or microcomputer.

Relative Addressing

This mode is used to enable the computer to branch from one memory address to another. These are 2-byte instructions with the first byte being the instruction and the second byte an offset address. This address is added to the value of the program counter (PC) to get the distance the computer must move. The second byte is treated as a signed two's complement number. Thus it could have values ranging from −128 to +127. Since the PC is one instruction ahead, the computer can branch backward 128 memory units from the next instruction or forward 127 memory units from the next instruction. This is the same as saying it can branch backward 126 steps or forward 129 steps from the branch instruction, since all branch instructions are 2 bytes long.

Example :

Memory Address	OP Code	Mnemonic
0100	20	BRA
0101	FD	$FD

In this example the OP code 20 is a branch-always command. The FD means −3 steps. The PC is at 102 so the computer would branch back to memory address OOFF.

Accumulator Addressing

These are 1-byte instructions involving either accumulator. No address is necessary. Examples would be clear accumulator A, arithmetic shifts, or logic shifts on either accumulator.

Other microprocessors or microcomputers may have other forms of addressing. The LSI-11, for instance, has a form in which the number following the instruction is added to the PC to get either a direct or indirect address, which are called relative and relative deferred modes respectively. The advantage of these modes is that a program can be moved to a different memory location without changing these instructions since the desired address is usually a fixed distance from the PC. Figure 7.3 gives an illustration of the format used in the 16-bit LSI-11 microcomputer.

This computer has an autoincrement or autodecrement mode. Using this mode, the address stored in a register is either automatically increased or decreased whenever the address is retrieved by an operand.

The autoincrement or autodecrement mode can greatly increase the efficiency of a search through a table stored in memory.

The LSI-11 has many other addressing modes. The indirect addressing mode mentioned above is also referred to as an "address of an address." You go to the address to get the address of the operand. This mode is useful in carrying out searches of addresses. A summary of the LSI-11 addressing modes is found in the glossary.

The MC6809 is a hybrid 8-bit to 16-bit microprocessor. Its programming is similar to that for 8-bit microprocessors but it has some of the more powerful instructions available to 16-bit microprocessors. It has the autoincrement and autodecrement mode. In addition it has a hardware register called a direct

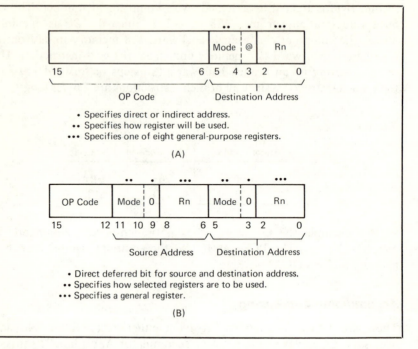

FIGURE 7.3. *Single-operand instruction (A) and double-operand instruction (B) in an LSI-11. (Courtesy Digital Equipment Corporation; copyright © 1979. All rights reserved.)*

page register. The 8 bits stored in this register correspond to the higher byte of the address when direct addressing is used. This now enables the computer to jump to any address in its 64K of memory.

This microprocessor, in addition to the short branches available to 6800 users, has long relative branches. These are branch commands with a 16-bit signed offset. The computer can now branch to anywhere in the 64K memory of the computer. Though there are only 59 basic instructions with the 6809, when you include all possible addressing modes of each instruction you now have 1464 instructions.

Other microprocessors may have additional or slightly different meanings of these addressing modes. For instance, some microprocessors have branch commands in which the second or third byte (for short or long branches) gives the address to which the computer must go.

EXERCISE 7-4 Addressing modes

1. When an operand field contains the address of the operand, the computer is using _____ .
   a. Direct addressing
   b. Indirect addressing

    c. Page addressing

    d. The immediate mode

2. The operand of an instruction using the immediate mode

    a. Is always on page 0.

    b. Is found at the address following the instruction.

    c. Is found at the address the PC points to.

    d. Is located at the address indicated on the index register.

3. The two words following an instruction contain an address. This is an example of

    a. Relative addressing

    b. Indexed addressing

    c. Extended addressing

    d. Direct addressing

4. Assume the use of an LSI-11 microcomputer. The number following an instruction is added to the PC to give an indirect address. This is an example of the

    a. Relative mode

    b. Relative deferred mode

    c. Immediate mode

    d. Extended mode

5. In extended addressing, all instructions are:

    a. 1 byte   b. 2 bytes   c. 3 bytes

    d. 1, 2, or 3 bytes

6. In extended addressing, the number following the instruction is

    a. Data

    b. An address

    c. An address of an address

    d. Any of these

7. Which of the following is not true for direct addressing?

    a. All are 2-byte instructions.

    b. It is a page 0 form of addressing.

    c. It can be used to address any place in memory.

    d. The second byte is an address.

8. Immediate mode instructions are described as follows:

    a. They are 2- or 3-byte instructions.

    b. Bytes 2 and 3 contain data.

    c. Bytes 2 and 3 contain an address.

    d. Bytes 2 and 3 contain an address of an address.

9. Index addressing instructions are described as follows:

    a. They are 2- or 3-byte instructions.

    b. All are 3-byte instructions.

    c. The second byte is a number that is added to the number in the index register to get an address.

    d. The second byte is a number that is added to the number in the index register to get the data.

10. Which of the following is not true for relative addressing in the 6800?
    a. It is used to branch forward or backward from the program counter.
    b. It is a 2-byte instruction.
    c. The second byte is a signed hexadecimal number.
    d. The second byte is an address to which the computer must branch.

PROGRAMMING AND DEBUGGING TECHNIQUES

Writing computer programs should not be approached in a haphazard way. In order to make maximum use of the limited storage area, the programmer should go through a sequence of steps to ensure the program is as efficient as possible. One example of these steps is as follows:

1. *Define the problem.* At this point, determine exactly what type of information (input) will be available and what specific results (output) you

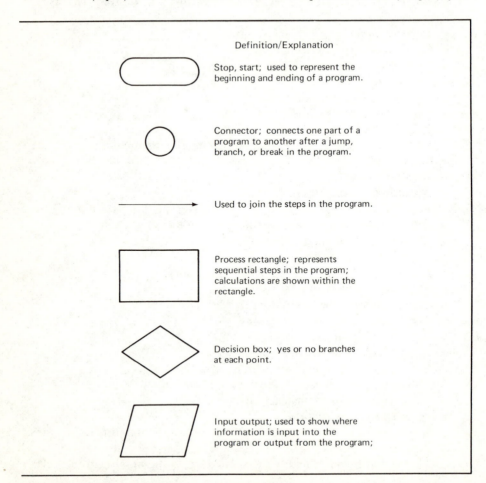

FIGURE 7.4. *Typical symbols used in flowcharting.*

want. For instance, if you are monitoring the temperature of a process with time, the input to the computer will be a signal corresponding to the temperature. For output, you would have to decide (1) how often you want the temperature read out, (2) in what units, (3) whether you want the highest temperature recorded, (4) whether you want the lowest temperature recorded, and so on.

2. *Determine the method of solution.* There is often more than one way of solving a problem. Decide which way is best for your problem. In computer terminology this is deciding which *algorithm* to use. An algorithm is a detailed step-by-step process needed to solve a problem.

3. *Flowchart the problem.* Using the standard flowchart symbols (Figure 7.4), diagram the algorithm.

An example of a flowchart to convert readings of temperature from °F to °C is given in Figure 7.5. If the flowchart is written in sufficient detail, it serves two purposes: (a) it enables the programmer to write a more efficient program, and (b) it can be used as documentation by the

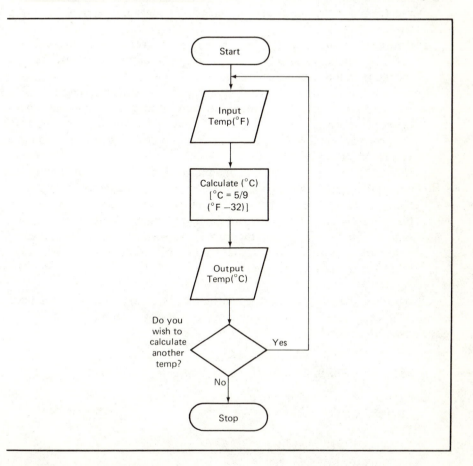

FIGURE 7.5. *Flowchart example.*

programmer along with the program for other people interested in using the program.

4. *Coding.* Translate the problem into whatever language you are going to use. If more than one language is available, decide which language would be most appropriate.

5. *Testing and debugging.* Test the program using known quantities to make sure the correct results are output. If errors occur, any or all of the following techniques may be used.

   a. Check your program to make sure you have written it properly.

   b. If it is a small program, ODT or a similar monitor can be used to make sure the program has been stored properly.

   c. For larger programs, a DUMP routine may be written in which all values stored are typed or printed out. There are two different types of DUMP routines. One would print out the entire program as it is stored in memory (in machine language). The other type available on some microcomputers as a software instruction will print out the value of all variables used in the program when the program has ended or been stopped.

   d. Check a certain variable as the program progresses to make sure this variable is being changed properly. This is usually done by printing out the value of the variable each time it is referenced.

   e. A trace routine may be written. Using this, the values stored in various registers are recorded or printed out step by step as the computer goes through a program.

   f. Commericial analyzers are available for microprocessors that enable you to do steps d or e.

   g. Besides the DUMP routine, many microcomputers have other software commands available to help in debugging. A trace command gives a listing of which line in a program is being executed at any given time. A disassembler takes a program in machine language and outputs an assembly language copy of the program. Since assembly language is easier to read than machine language, this could make it easier to detect an error in the program.

Program debugging is a costly and time-consuming process. It has been estimated that as much as 80 percent of the cost of running a computer is associated with software.

EXERCISE 7-5 Programming and debugging techniques

1. The proper steps in writing an efficient program are
   1. Flowcharting
   2. Debugging
   3. Constructing an algorithm
   4. Defining the problem
   5. Coding

The proper order for these steps is
a. 4, 3, 1, 5, 2
b. 4, 1, 3, 2, 5
c. 4, 5, 3, 1, 2
d. 4, 2, 3, 1, 5

Match each of the following flowchart symbols to its proper function.

2. _____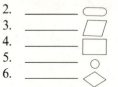
3. _____
4. _____
5. _____
6. _____

a. Decision box to cause branching when a particular condition is met.
b. Connector to join steps in proper order.
c. Represents sequential steps in a process.
d. I/O box.
e. Start and stop symbol.

7. One would use _____ to be sure a program has been stored properly.
a. An assembler
b. ODT
c. A DUMP
d. A flowchart

8. A(an) _____ will display all values stored.
a. Dump routine
b. Monitor
c. Linkage editor
d. Trace routine

SAMPLE PROGRAMS

The following program illustrates a typical program on an LSI-11 (Figure 7.6).

This program adds the numbers stored in memory locations 1002 and 1006. The result is stored in GPR R1. In a program the first column gives the

Memory Address	Octal Code	Instruction Mnemonics	Comments
1000	012700	MOV #100, R0	LOAD 100 INTO GPR R0
1002	100		
1004	012701	MOV #7, R1	LOAD 7 INTO GPR R1
1006	7		
1008	060001	ADD R0, R1	ADD THE TWO NUMBERS
1010	000000	HALT	

FIGURE 7.6. *A program to add two numbers on an LSI-11 microcomputer.*

address in memory where the instruction is stored. The second column is the octal equivalent of the OP code (hexadecimal equivalent for the 6800). The third column is the assembly language mnemonic used, and the last column gives any comments that might be useful. In the LSI-11, a 16-bit microcomputer, each memory location differs by two, while in the 6800 and other 8-bit microprocessors, they differ by one.

A similar program written for a 6800 would be as follows (Figure 7.7).

In the assembly language used by the 6800 the # sign means the immediate addressing mode is used, whereas the $ means that a hexadecimal number follows.

Memory Address	Hexadecimal Code	Instruction Mnemonic	Comment
0001	86	LDA A # $10	Store the hexadecimal
0002	10		#10 in accumulation A
0003	8B	ADD A # $07	Add hexadecimal
0004	07		#7 to accumulation A
0005	97	STA A # $08	Store the results in
0006	08		0008 memory address
0007	3E	WAI	HALT

FIGURE 7.7. *A program to add two numbers on a 6800.*

MEMORY MAPS

Before attempting to store a program in memory, be certain you are acquainted with any restrictions that may exist on the various memory locations. Some locations in memory are reserved by the manufacturer for specific functions. Figure 7.8 shows two typical *memory maps*. Memory maps show what part of memory is available for users' programs. Some microprocessors reserve the lower byte addresses for RWM (ROM), others put it somewhere in the middle, and still others use higher byte addresses. Be certain you know how your microprocessor makes these allocations.

HIGH-LEVEL LANGUAGE

Microcomputers and more microprocessors are being built that can handle higher level languages as well as assembly language. A higher level language is one written in a language closer to English than machine language. When high-level languages are translated into machine code, every instruction corresponds to more than one machine code. Basic, Fortran, Cobol, and PL/I are examples of high-level languages. They have the decided advantage of being much easier to learn and use. Their disadvantages are that they occupy much more room in memory and their computing speed is often much slower.

As with assembly language, there must be a software package stored in

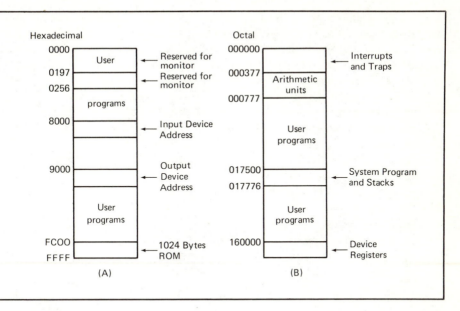

FIGURE 7.8. *Memory maps for (A) 6800 and (B) LSI-11.*

memory that will translate the higher level language into machine language. There are two major types of translators: compilers and interpreters.

Compilers

A compiler uses two distinct steps to run a program. The first is the translation of the high-level language instructions called macroinstructions into machine code; the second is the execution of the programming. Fortran and Cobol are compiler-based high-level languages.

Interpreters

An interpreter carries out the translation and execution step simultaneously. Basic and Focal (Digital Equipment Corporation trademark) are interpreter-based languages. Interpreter-based languages are generally more convenient to work with since the translator is always present and complex calculations can be handled with simple commands. Rapid turnaround (editing, debugging, and running) is a trademark of interpreters. Their disadvantage is they are much slower than compilers since each line is compiled and executed step by step. In general, interpreters also occupy a larger space than compilers, thus leaving less room for the user's programs.

EXERCISE 7-6   Memory maps and high-level languages

1. A _____ shows what part of memory is available for users' programs.
   a. ROM
   b. RAM

c. PROM

d. Memory map

2. The instructions of a high-level language are
   a. Macroinstructions
   b. Microinstructions
   c. Mnemonic instructions
   d. Deferred instructions

3. The major disadvantage of high-level languages is that
   a. They are harder to learn.
   b. The required translator occupies much of the available memory.
   c. Documentation is less specific.
   d. Flowcharts and algorithms cannot be used.

4. Interpreters
   1. Translate and execute simultaneously.
   2. Translate in one step and execute in the next.
   3. Require more memory space than compilers.
   4. Require less memory space than compilers.
      a. 1 and 3
      b. 2 and 4
      c. 2 and 3
      d. 1 and 4

5. Compilers and interpreters are examples of
   a. Hardware programs
   b. Software languages
   c. High-level language interpreters
   d. Identical software programs

REVIEW QUESTIONS

Match each term on the left to the statement on the right that best describes it.

1. Assembly language   a. Contains data or address.
2. Machine language   b. Employs mnemonic OP codes.
3. Operand field   c. Step-by-step procedure.
4. Mnemonic OP code   d. Diagram of procedure.
5. Flowchart   e. Coded in binary.
6. Algorithm   f. Suggests the meaning of the instruction.

Mark each of the following statements true or false

7. Assembly language programs are easier to write than machine language programs.

8. An absolute assembler translates assembly language into object code.

9. The output of a relocatable assembler is binary code.

10. A software program called the linkage editor translates object code into an object program.

11. Using direct addressing, the operand field of an instruction contains the address of the operand.

12. A page is a physical partition of memory.

Match the statements on the left to the words they best describe on the right. Each letter may be used only once.

13. This program, stored in a ROM, enables a programmer to load a program and examine and/or change the contents of any memory location.

    a. Linkage editor
    b. Monitor
    c. ODT
    d. Test editor

14. Name of the monitor found in LSI-11 microcomputer.
15. Combines separate parts of a program.
16. This software program enables a programmer to write, correct, and modify program.
17. Which of the following statements referring to high-level languages is incorrect?
    a. Program is written using macroinstructions.
    b. Has many-to-one correspondence with machine language instructions.
    c. Requires extra hardware to translate into binary code.
    d. Allows computer programs to read much like English and/or algebra.
18. An interpreter
    a. Translates and executes an instruction simultaneously.
    b. Translates and executes in two distinct steps.
    c. Is stored in a PROM.
    d. Is stored in a GPR.
19. The major advantage of an interpreter over a compiler is that it
    a. Occupies less memory space.
    b. Has rapid turnaround.
    c. Works faster.
    d. Can perform complex calculations.
20. Which of the following is NOT an example of software?
    a. Flowchart
    b. Monitor
    c. ODT
    d. Absolute assembler
    e. Compiler
    f. Interpreter
    g. Source program
    h. Algorithm
    i. Instruction decoder
    j. Object code
    k. Symbol table
21. Explain what is meant by a "high-level language"?
22. What is the difference between an object program and a source program?
23. In the PDP-8 by Digital Equipment Corporation direct addressing is done using 7-bit addresses. Give the starting and ending addresses of the first three pages in this computer.
24. List some of the advantages and disadvantages of compilers and interpreters.
25. Identify each of the following.
    a. Hardware

    b. Software

    c. Firmware

26.
0000	01	0005	01
0001	05	0006	2C
0002	80	0007	FC
0003	05	0008	3E
0004	9B		

    In the above program, identify by line number the

    a. Immediate addressing mode instruction

    b. Direct addressing mode instruction

    c. Relative addressing mode instruction

27. Draw a flowchart for the following problem: Add two numbers together; if the result is positive, branch back to the second number and add it again. Continue branching back and adding until the result is negative, then halt.

28. Explain why the direct addressing mode is only 2 bytes long in the 6800.

29. Refer to Figure 7.3. How many different instructions are possible in the single-operand format used in the LSI-11?

30. What is the difference between an absolute assembler and a relocatable assembler?

REFERENCES

1. *Microcomputer Handbook.* Digital Equipment Corp., Maynard, Mass., 1977, Section II, Chapter 2.

2. *Individual Learning Program in Microprocessors.* Heath Corp., Benton Harbor, Mich., 1977, Units 4, 5, and 6.

3. *M6800 Microcomputer System Design Data.* Motorola, Inc., 1976, pp. 2–38.

4. Sam Perone and David Jones, *Digital Computers in Scientific Instrumentation.* McGraw-Hill Book Co., New York, 1973, Chapters 9, 10, and 13.

5. John S. Murphy, *Basis of Digital Computers.* Vol. 3, Hayden Book Co., Rochelle Park, N. J., 1970.

6. Lance A. Leventhal, *6800 Assembly Language Programming.* Osborne & Associates, Inc., Berkeley, Calif., 1978 (now a division of McGraw-Hill).

7. *Microcomputer Processor Handbook.* Digital Equipment Corp., Maynard, Mass., 1979, Chapter 6.

GLOSSARY

Absolute assembler	Program that translates assembly language into machine language.
Accumulator addressing	In 6800 these are 1-byte instructions that specify one of the two accumulators.

Addressing with PC in LSI-11	Immediate — actual operand follows instruction. Absolute — address of operand follows instruction. Relative — value following instruction is added to PC to produce the address of the operand. Relative deferred — Value following instruction is added to PC to produce the address of the operand.
Algorithm	Detailed step-by-step procedure to solve a problem.
Assembly language	A low-level computer language written symbolically.
Compiler	Translator that translates high-level language program into machine code and executes the program in two distinct steps.
Debugging	The process of searching for and correcting errors in a program.
Deferred addressing in LSI-11	Four modes are used: Register deferred — Specified register contains address of operand. Autoincrement deferred — Contents of specified register contains address of the address of the operand. Then register is incremented by 2. Autodecrement deferred — Specified register is decremented by 2. This is used as the address of the address of the operand. Index deferred — Value following instruction is added to the contents of specified register. This sum is then the address of the address of the operand.
Direct addressing in LSI-11	Four modes are used: Register — Specified register contains operand. Autoincrement — Specified register points to operand. Register then incremented to point to following operand. Autodecrement — Specified register is decremented first, then points to operand. Index — Value following instruction is added to contents of specified register to compute address of operand.
Direct addressing in 6800	These are 2-byte instructions in which the second byte contains address of operand. Can only address lower 256 (2^8) bytes of memory.
Extended addressing	In 6800 these are 3-byte instructions. The second and third bytes contain the higher and lower bytes of the desired memory location. This addressing mode can address 65, 536 (2^{16}) memory locations.
Flowchart	The diagramatic representation of an algorithm.
Hardware	Concrete structures of a computer system including mechanical, electric, and electronic devices.

High-level language	A computer language with a many-to-one correspondence between each instruction and actual computer operations.
Implied addressing (inherent)	In 6800 these are 1-byte instructions in which the instruction gives the address.
Indexed addressing	In 6800 these are 2-byte instructions. The value contained in the second byte is added to the contents of the index register. This value is then the address of the operand.
Indirect addressing in LSI-11	See Deferred addressing.
Inherent addressing	See Implied addressing.
Interpreter	Translator that translates and executes one high-level language instruction at a time.
Linkage editor	See Linker.
Linker	Program that combines separate parts of a program into one single program. Also translates object code into machine code.
Low-level language	A computer language with a direct correspondence between each instruction and actual computer operations.
Machine language	Actual language computer understands; coded in binary.
Macroinstruction	Single special assembly language instruction that represents a sequence of steps; used to simplify the writing of source programs. Also the form of all high-level language instructions.
Software	All programs, flowcharts, and associated documentation of a computer system.
Source program	Program written in assembly language.
Subroutine	Semi-independent sequence of instructions referenced by a main program (or another subroutine).
Symbol table	Table of corresponding symbolic and actual addresses constructed by assembler during translation.
Symbolic address	A word used to mark and refer to specific instructions in an assembly language program.
Syntax	The rules of a computer language.
Text editor	Program that allows user to write, correct, and modify a source program.
Translator	A program that translates a program into another language. Compilers, interpreters, and assemblers are all translators.

ANSWERS TO EXERCISE 7-1

1. b
2. b
3. a
4. d

ANSWERS TO EXERCISE 7-2

1. d
2. a
3. b

ANSWERS TO EXERCISE 7-3

1. c
2. d
3. a
4. c
5. a
6. c
7. d
8. a
9. d

ANSWERS TO EXERCISE 7-4

1. a
2. b
3. c
4. b
5. c
6. b
7. b
8. a, b
9. c
10. d

ANSWERS TO EXERCISE 7-5

1. a
2. e
3. d
4. c

5. b
6. a
7. b
8. a

ANSWERS TO EXERCISE 7-6

1. d
2. a
3. b
4. a
5. b

ANSWERS TO REVIEW QUESTIONS

1. b
2. e
3. a
4. f
5. d
6. c
7. True
8. False
9. False
10. True
11. True
12. False
13. b
14. c
15. a
16. d
17. c
18. a
19. b
20. i
21. A language closer to English than machine language, that is, it "looks" like English.
22. Object program: machine language program
    Source program: assembly language program
23.

Page	Memory Locations
0	$0-177_8$
1	$200-377_8$
2	$400-577_8$

24.

	Advantage	*Disadvantage*
Compiler	Faster to execute long programs or programs used over and over again; uses less memory	Less convenient to work with; slower turnaround time
Interpreter	Rapid turnaround time; more convenient to work with	Slower in operation; uses more memory

25. a. Actual wiring and electrical connections.
    b. Programs stored in memory as electrical signals.
    c. Semipermanent or permanent software programs.

26. a. 0002
    b. 0004
    c. 0006

27.

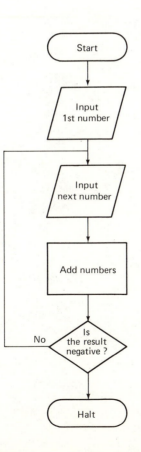

28. This is a page zero addressing mode. The high byte is automatically set to 00.

29. 2^{10} or 1024
30. Absolute assembler: Translates assembly language into an object program.
    Relocatable assembler: Translates assembly language into an object code, which, in turn, needs to be further translated by a linker into an object program.

CHAPTER 8

PROGRAMMING THE 6800

LEARNING ACTIVITIES

Study lecture material on the 6800.
Read resource materials listed at end of unit.
Complete exercises.
Self-check answers to exercises.
Consult instructor for assistance as necessary.

OBJECTIVES

By completing these requirements, you should be able to achieve the following objectives for this unit when formally evaluated.

Objective 1

Given a diagram, identify the register structure in the 6800 microprocessor according to Motorola specifications.

Objective 2

Write simple programs using the machine language of the Motorola 6800 as defined by its operating specifications.

Objective 3

Given one of the following terms, identify the term according to its standard definition:

a. Stack
b. Push-down stack
c. FIFO stack
d. FILO stack
e. Cascade stack
f. Memory stack

Objective 4

Given programs written for a MC6800, determine the time it takes to run a program according to Motorola operating specifications.

EVALUATION

Your ability to demonstrate achievement of these objectives will be assessed after all instruction on this unit by:

- Multiple-choice items
- Writing short programs
- Evaluating programs

INTRODUCTION

In Chapter 7 we learned that instructions are sent to a microprocessor in the form of OP codes. The OP codes that a microprocessor responds to, and how the microprocessor responds, are determined by the manner in which the arithmetic and logic circuits in the CPU are put together. This hardware is normally fixed by the manufacturer. The exceptions are those microprocessors containing PLAs or FPLAs. Programming languages thus vary considerably from one microprocessor to another, unless languages are deliberately copied, for example, the 8080 and Z-80. Even in the case of the 8080 and Z-80 there are some commands written for the Z-80 that are not recognized by the 8080. Since it is not possible to study all the languages, we will instead look at one particular language, that of the MC6800, in detail. In the process certain techniques will be developed that can be used with other languages.

THE 6800 MPU

The addressable register structure of the 6800 is given in Figure 8.1. This microprocessor has two 8-bit accumulators (A and B), a 16-bit index register, a 16-bit stack pointer, and a 16-bit program counter. It also contains another 8-bit register in which 6 of the bits are used as status flags. This is called the condition code register.

The two accumulators and the program counter function as explained in Chapter 4. The 16-bit index register is an additional hardware register that can be manipulated by the programmer. The programmer can store any 16-bit unsigned number in this register and use this as a starting address. With this register it is possible to directly address any address in the 64K memory. The 16-bit stack pointer is another addressable hardware register. Again the programmer can store a number in this register and use it as the beginning address of another instruction. The purpose of these two registers is explained in more detail later in this chapter.

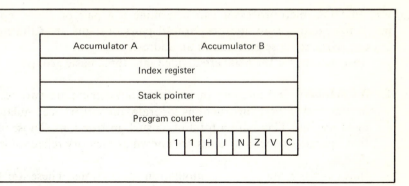

FIGURE 8.1. *The registers in an MC6800.*

The condition code register was also mentioned in Chapter 4. Let us look at this register in greater detail. This is an 8-bit register in which only the first 6 bits are used. Bits 6 and 7 are always set to a 1. The other bits are assigned as follows:

Bit 0:   This is the carry bit (C). This bit is set to a 1 any time there is a carry from either accumulator. This occurs whenever bit 7 is a 1 and a 1 is added to bit 7.

Bit 1:   This is called an overflow bit (V). A special circuit follows bit 7 of either accumulator. If there is an overflow into or out of bit 7, the V flag is set. Thus this flag gets set whenever there is a carry or if an overflow from bit 6 to bit 7 occurs. This last is important since a carry from bit 6 to bit 7 changes the sign of the number.

Bit 2:   This is the 0 bit (Z). If all 8 bits of the accumulator become 0 during an operation, this bit is set to a 1.

Bit 3:   This is the negative bit (N). This also monitors bit 7 of the accumulator. If bit 7 goes from 0 to 1 during an operation, this bit is set to a 1.

Bit 4:   This is an interrupt request bit (I). This bit is set to a 1 whenever a peripheral device requests service of the microprocessor.

Bit 5:   This is known as the half-carry bit (H). This bit is set whenever a carry occurs from bit 3 to bit 4. The half-carry is used with binary coded decimal instructions since it monitors a carry from one BCD number to another.

It is important to remember that the status of the condition code register is determined by the last operation on *either* accumulator.

INSTRUCTIONS FOR THE 6800

All information is transmitted to the microprocessor in pairs of hexadecimal digits. Certain pairs of these digits are instructions whereas others represent data or addresses. These must be entered into the microprocessor in such a way that the microprocessor can determine if a pair of digits represents an instruction, data, or an address. Not all pairs of digits are valid instructions, but any pair can represent data or an address.

Instructions for the 6800 are divided into three basic groups.

1. Accumulator and memory instructions. Since there are two accumulators in the 6800, these instructions operate on either accumulator or any memory unit. There are a total of 65 such instructions. Those instructions that operate on memory units are known as memory reference instructions (MRI).
2. Index register and stack manipulation instructions. These are 11 instructions that operate on the index register or stack pointer.
3. Jump and branch instructions. This set includes 23 instructions that allow the programmer to branch forward or backward from the present position or jump to a new section of memory. They also include the interrupt instructions.

Appendix A is a list of all the instructions and the number of bytes each instruction contains and Appendix B lists the same instructions in order of increasing OP code number. The latter is useful in decoding a program. Appendix B also gives the time it takes for each instruction to be executed. With the standard 1-MHz clock on the 6800, each cycle takes 1 μs.

ACCUMULATOR AND MEMORY REFERENCE INSTRUCTIONS

These are instructions that allow the programmer to transfer data between memory units and either accumulator or to carry out arithmetic or logic operations on the accumulators. There are 40 basic instructions, summarized in Table 8.1. A complete listing is found in Appendix A.

The second column of Table 8.1 lists the Boolean or arithmetic operation carried out by the instruction. In this table M stands for memory unit, ACC for either accumulator, · is a Boolean AND, and $\oplus$ is an exclusive OR. The arrow ($\rightarrow$) means the result is transferred to wherever the arrow points. A + sign is used to represent either an addition or an inclusive OR. A dash ($-$) means subtract.

The operation of many of the memory reference instructions should be obvious from the name of the instruction; for example, add, clear, decrement, load, or subtract. Others such as the rotate and shift commands and the push or pull commands need more explanation.

When you consider the number of different addressing modes available for each instruction, the total number of these instructions now becomes 140. That is, there are 140 different OP codes needed to cover all memory and accumulator instructions. Let us look at some typical programs.

The first program, listed in Table 8.2, is the addition of two numbers, with the result being stored in memory. In this program the hexadecimal number 05

TABLE 8.1. *Summary of Accumulator and Memory Instructions.*

Instruction	Boolean/Arithmetic Operation
ADD	Acc. + M → Acc.
ADD accumulators	A + B → A
ADD with carry	Acc. + C + M → Acc.
AND	Acc. · M → A
BIT TEST	Acc. · M
CLEAR	00 → M, or Acc.
COMPARE	Acc. − M
Compare accumulators	A − B
ONE's complement	$\overline{M}$ → M or $\overline{Acc.}$ → Acc.
TWO's complement	00 − M → M or 00 − Acc. → Acc.
DECIMAL ADJUST	converts to BCD Format
DECREMENT	M − 1 → M or Acc. − 1 → Acc.
EXCLUSIVE OR	Acc. ⊕ M → Acc.
Increment	M + 1 → M or Acc. + 1 → Acc.
LOAD ACCUMULATOR	M → Acc.
Inclusive OR	Acc. + M → Acc.
PUSH DATA	Acc. → M (SP Address)
PULL DATA	M → Acc. (SP + 1 Address)
Rotate left	See chapter material
Rotate right	See chapter material
Arithmetic and logic shifts	See chapter material
Store Accumulator	Acc. → M
SUBTRACT	Acc. − M → Acc.
SUBTRACT Accumulator	A − B → A
SUBTRACT with Carry	Acc. − M − C → Acc.
Transfer Accumulator	Acc. A → B or Acc. B → A
TEST (ZERO or MINUS)	M − 00 or Acc. − 00

TABLE 8.2. *Addition of Two Numbers.*

Memory Address	OP Code	(LABEL)	Mnemonic	Mnemonic Operand	Comment
0000	86	START	LDAA	# $05	LOAD ACC A
0001	05				with Hex 05
0002	8B		ADDA	# $04	ADD to ACC A
0003	04				hex 04
0004	97		STAA	# $07	Store the result
0005	07				in memory
					location 0007.
0006	3E		WAI		HALT
0007	—				

is loaded into accumulator A using the immediate addressing mode. A load instruction is used since this clears the accumulator of any previous number before it stores the 05 in the accumulator. Instruction 8B then adds hexadecimal 04 to the number stored in accumulator A, again using the immediate addressing mode. The next instruction is a direct addressing mode instruction. This stores the number in accumulator A at the address that follows the instruction. Hexadecimal 9 will thus be stored in memory address 0007. With the store instruction, whatever number had previously been located in memory address 0007 was erased. Because of the difference in operation of the load and subtract or add instruction, if you wish to add a series of numbers or subtract numbers, the load instruction should be first used to initialize the accumulator. If you tried to add or subtract from an accumulator, and there was an unexpected number already stored in the accumulator, a wrong result would obviously occur.

Example 8.1

Let us examine the program in Table 8.2 to see how some of the registers in the microprocessor change as the program is executed.

Original State

At the beginning of the program the first address in memory (0000) is loaded into the program counter. The XX notation means the number stored in the register is immaterial.

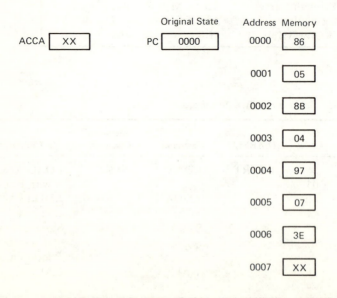

Fetch Cycle

During the first fetch cycle the computer goes to the address stored in the program counter and takes the instruction there. This instruction (86) is placed in the data register and decoded as a load ACCA immediate instruction. The program counter is incremented by 1.

Fetch Cycle

ACCA | XX   PC | 0001

Execute Cycle

During the execute cycle the computer goes to address 0001 to take the data stored there (05) and place it in the data register. The control and logic circuits have already decoded the instruction, so this data is then loaded into accumulator A. At the end of this cycle the ACCA and PC have the following values:

Execute Cycle

ACCA | 05   PC | 0002

The control and logic circuits have decoded the instruction 86 as a 2-byte instruction. Once the second byte (05) is loaded into the accumulator, the computer is ready for another fetch cycle. This means the number (8B) in the next address (0002) must be a valid instruction. If this were not the case, an error in the program would occur and in most cases the computer would stop. This procedure is continued until the program has been completely executed.

Appendix B gives the number of clock cycles needed to execute each instruction. For the program in Table 8.2, this is summarized in Table 8.3. It takes a total of 17 clock cycles to complete the program. Since the 6800 uses a 1-MHz clock, each clock cycle is 1 μs. It would thus take 17 μs to complete this program. This is an example of what is known as *benchmarking*. A benchmark is a program used to compare the speed of one microprocessor or microcomputer with another. In this technique a program is written for a microprocessor and the time taken to execute the program is either calculated or observed. The identical program is written for another microprocessor and the times are compared. It should be noted that these programs need not be ef-

TABLE 8.3. *Number of Clock Cycles Needed for Addition Program (Table 8.2).*

OP Code	Cycle Time
86	2
8B	2
97	4
3E	9
Total	17

ficiently written. To be fair, though, they must be programmed as similar as possible from one machine to the other.

This same program written using the direct addressing mode is given in Table 8.4.

Note that this program now starts at address 0003. If you should run the program starting at address 0000 and one of the numbers chosen to be added corresponds to an instruction OP code, an error will occur. Remember the fetch – execute cycle the microprocessor goes through. When it reaches an instruction, the instruction is decoded and the microprocessor then assumes that

TABLE 8.4. *Addition of Two Numbers Using Direct Addressing.*

Memory Address	OP Code	(LABEL)	Mnemonic	Mnemonic Operand	Comment
0000	05		$05	—	Hex. 05
0001	04		$04	—	Hex. 04
0002	—		—	—	—
0003	96	START	LDAA	$00	LOAD ACC A
0004	00				with # in Address 00
0005	9B		ADDA	$01	ADD TO ACC A #
0006	01				in address 01
0007	97		STAA	$02	Store Acc A in
0008	02				address 02
0009	3E		WAI		HALT

a certain number of bytes that follow the instruction are data or an address. If this is programmed incorrectly, then the computer will "bomb out," that is, fail to operate properly.

In the program in Table 8.4 the first instruction at address 0003 says to go to address 0000, take the data there, and load the data into accumulator *A*. The next instruction (9B) says take the data at address 0001 and add the data to accumulator *A*. The store instruction now stores the result at memory address 0002.

Example 8.2

Let us follow the changes in the registers as this program is executed.

Before First Instruction

ACCA [XX]   0003 [96] ◄── PC

0004 [00]

After First Instruction

ACCA [05]   0000 [05]

0001 [04]

0002 [00]

0003 [96]

0004 [00]

0005   ◄── PC

After Second Instruction

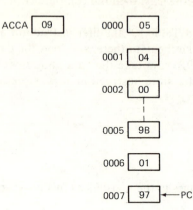

After Third Instruction

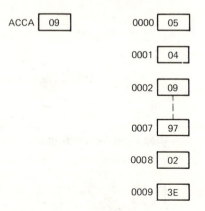

The add with carry and subtract with carry instructions listed in Table 8.1 are used in multiple-precision arithmetic. Here, in order to handle more significant figures, two or more memory units are used to store a number. For a double-precision routine, one memory unit would hold the higher byte, while the other memory unit would hold the lower byte. Here 16 bits are used to represent the number. When there is a carry from the highest bit of the lower byte to the lowest bit of the higher byte during addition, the add with carry handles this operation. The subtract with carry takes care of a similar situation during subtraction (i.e., a borrow from the higher byte).

If you wished to add two numbers in BCD format such as 9 and 4, the computer would normally treat these as hexadecimal numbers and output the result D. The DAA is used immediately after such a BCD addition. This checks for invalid results and corrects the result to a BCD number. In the above case 13 would be output. The DAA instruction cannot be used after subtraction. It only works after addition.

There are five instructions that allow us to move the data bits in an accumulator or memory address to a different position in the accumulator or memory address. They are as follows:

Instruction	Mnemonic		Description
Rotate left	ROL ROLA ROLB	M A B	$C \quad M_7 \qquad M_0$
Rotate right	ROR RORA RORB	M A B	$C \quad M_7 \qquad M_0$
Shift left — arithmetic	ASL ASLA ASLB	M A B	$C \quad M_7 \qquad M_0 \quad 0$
Shift right — arithmetic	ASR ASRA ASRB	M A B	$M_7 \qquad\qquad C$
Shift right — logic	LSR LSRA LSRB	M A B	$0 \to M_7 \qquad M_0 \quad C$

Each operation can be carried out on accumulator A, accumulator B, or a memory address (M). When a rotate left (ROL) instruction is executed, the most significant bit (M_7) is transferred to the carry register, the carry bit is transferred to the least significant bit (M_0), and all the other bits are transferred to the next highest bit. The arithmetic shift left (ASL) is similar except that the carry bit is lost and a 0 is transferred into the least significant bit.

The ROL instruction is useful in determining the parity of a byte. By rotating a byte eight times, the original byte is restored. If the number of times the carry bit is set to 1 during these rotations is counted, the parity of the word or byte can be determined. The shift-left arithmetic can be used to pack two binary coded decimal numbers (BCD) into 1 byte. Four shifts left put the first decimal number into the higher 4 bits and add the lower 4 bits to it to get two decimal numbers on 1 byte.

Example 8.3

Suppose the number 24_{10} were stored in ACCA and an arithmetic shift right were executed. What would be the value of the number now stored in ACCA?

   Answer: Originally the value in ACCA was 00011000_2. After the arithmetic shift right, the number becomes 00001100_2. This is 12_{10}.

Example 8.4

What would the number in Example 8.3 become after two arithmetic shift rights were executed?

Answer: After the second shift the number is 00000110_2. This is 6_{10}. Note that this operation is a divide-by-2 operation. After every shift the number is one half its previous value. An arithmetic shift left is thus a multiply-by-2 operation.

In order to use these instructions in a program, we need to understand the operation of the branch and jump instructions.

BRANCH AND JUMP INSTRUCTIONS

There are 22 instructions that fall under this group. They are given in Table 8.5. Every branch instruction, except the branch always, is controlled by one or more of the bits in the condition code register. Whenever the computer encounters a branch instruction, it checks the test condition by examining the proper bits (flags) in the condition code register. If the test checks properly, the computer branches to the appropriate step in the program.

For instance, the branch, if equal to 0 (BEQ OP code 27), is an instruction that causes a branch to occur if the Z flag is equal to 1. In the following program such an instruction is encountered.

Memory Address	OP Code	Mnemonic
FD	—	—
FE	—	—
FF	—	—
100	27	BEQ #$FC
101	FC	
102	—	—

When the computer gets to address 100, it checks the Z flag. If the Z flag is 0, the program continues on. If the flag is 1, it means the last operation on an accumulator left the value of the accumulator equal to zero. The computer will branch to an address given by the FC. FC in two's complement means minus 4. The program counter is at address 102 when the FC is encountered, so the computer will branch back four addresses from the 102 and will end up at address FE.

Example 8.5

Suppose you have a branch always instruction at address 0200 in a program. The address you wish to branch to is 01F9. What is the value of the second byte of the branch always instruction?

Answer: When the branch instruction is executed, the program counter

TABLE 8.5. *Branch and Jump Instructions.*

Branch Command	Mnemonic	OP code	Memory Cycles	Test
Branch always	BRA	20	4	none
Branch if carry clear	BCC	24	4	$C = 0$
Branch if carry set	BCS	25	4	$C = 1$
Branch if = zero	BEQ	27	4	$Z = 1$
Branch if ≥ zero	BGE	2C	4	$N \oplus V = 0$ $\oplus$ = (Exclusive OR)
Branch if > zero	BGT	2E	4	$Z + (N \oplus V) = 0$ + = Inclusive OR
Branch if higher	BHI	22	4	$C + Z = 0$
Branch if ≤ zero	BLE	2F	4	$Z + (N \oplus V) = 1$
Branch if lower or same	BLS	23	4	$C + Z = 1$
Branch if less than zero	BLT	2D	4	$N + V = 1$
Branch if minus	BMI	2B	4	$N = 1$
Branch if not equal zero	BNE	26	4	$Z = 0$
Branch if overflow clear	BVC	28	4	$V = 0$
Branch if overflow set	BVS	29	4	$V = 1$
Branch if plus	BPL	2A	4	$N = 0$
Branch to subroutine	BSR	80	8	Special operation
Jump	JMPXXXX	6E, 7E	4, 3	May go anywhere in memory (unconditional GOTO)
Jump to subroutine	JSRXXXX	AD, BD	8, 9	A temporary jump to anywhere in memory
Return from subroutine	RTS	39	5	Sends the computer back to the original program after a BRS or JSR
Software interrupt	SWI	3F	12	$I = 1$
Return from interrupt	RTI	3B	10	Tell the computer the interrupt is over
Wait for interrupt	WAI	3E	9	Used when you want the computer to wait for an external interrupt. Can also be used as a HALT.

is at address 0202. Address 01F9 is 9 address backward (-9). The second byte must be -9 or F7. To verify this start at address 0202 and count this as 0. Count through the addresses until you reach 01F9. Address 0201 is -1, 0200 is -2, 01FF is -3, and so on.

Note in Table 8.5 that there are two different jump instructions. One is an unconditional jump, and the other is a jump to subroutine. With the unconditional jump, the program jumps to the address that follows the jump command and continues on from the new address. With the jump to subroutine, the program jumps to the address given, does a short program, and then returns to the next address following the jump to subroutine.

The branch and jump to subroutine instructions are illustrated in the program given in Table 8.6.

This program takes two hexadecimal numbers and multiplies them together with the result stored in accumulator A. If the result exceeds 8 bits, the wrong answer will be given. Multiplication here is carried out using repetitive addition. Here 4×2 is found by adding 2 to itself four times. At address 0005 is found a decrement B instruction. This instruction subtracts 1 from accumulator B (ACCB) whenever it is encountered. At address 000B the computer compares the number stored in accumulator B with zero. If the number is not equal to zero, the branch instruction that follows causes the computer to branch back to address 0008 (MULT).

When accumulator B is zero, the number 2 has been added four times, so instead of branching the computer goes to address 000F. This is a jump to subroutine using extended addressing. The 2 bytes that follow are the 16-bit address—FE20 in this case. Note that byte 2 is the higher address byte, while byte 3 is the lower address byte.

After completing the subroutine (which displays the answer on seven-segment LEDs in an ET3400), the computer returns to address 0012, the next address in the program. This instruction halts the program.

Jump-to subroutines are used any time a particular part of a program is to be used over and over again. A common subroutine is a short delay routine. A delay routine would be used, for instance, where you wanted to print a message on a screen for a period of time, and then turn the message off. The following program would generate a 0.5- to 1-second delay.

Memory Address	OP Code			Memory Address	OP Code
0009	BD			001B	CE
000A	00			001C	FF
000B	1B	Delay		001D	FF
000C	—	Subroutine		001E	09
—	—			001F	26
				0020	FD
				0021	39

The BD 001B instruction is a jump to subroutine at address 001B. At this address, the index register is loaded with the number FFFF. The 09 decrements the index register and the 26 checks to see if the value is 0. If not, the computer branches back to address 001E and decrements again. This con-

TABLE 8.6. *A Program To Multiply Two Numbers.*

Address	OP Code		Mnemonic	Mnemonic Operand	Comment
0000	02		$02		Hex. #02
0001	04		$04		Hex. #04
0002	00		$00		used to store result
0003	D6	START	LOAD	$01	LOAD ACC B with data in 0001
0004	01				
0005	5A		DECB		DECREMENT ACC B
0006	96		LDAA	$00	LOAD ACC A with data in 0000
0007	00				
0008	9B	MULT	ADDA	$00	ADD ACC A with contents of 0000
0009	00				
000A	5A		DECB		DECREMENT ACC B
000B	C1		CMPB	#$00	Compare ACC B with 0
000C	00				
000D	2E		BGT	#$F9	Branch to MULT if B > 0
000E	F9				
000F	BD		JSR	$FE20	JUMP to subroutine at FE20
0010	FE				
0011	20				
0012	3E		WAI		HALT

tinues until the index register is 0, then the OP code 39, which is a return from subroutine instruction, causes the computer to go to address 000C. The instructions for the index register are covered later in this chapter.

A more efficient way to multiply is found in the program in Table 8.7.

Let us look at the way we multiply.

Multiplication

Base 10	Base 2	
13	0101	multiplicand
12	0110	multiplier
26	0000000	
13	000101	
156	00101	
	0000	
	0011110	

To multiply in base 10, the multiplicand is multiplied by the least significant digit. This result is rotated to the right. The multiplicand is then multi-

TABLE 8.7. *Multiplication Using Shifts.*

Address	OP Code		Comment
0000	05		Multiplicand
0001	02		Multiplier
0002	4F	START	Clear ACC A
0003	0C		Clear carry (not Necessary)
0004	D6		LOAD ACC B with multiplicand
0005	00		
0006	74	MULT	Logic shift right
0007	00		LSB goes into carry bit
0008	01		
0009	24		Branch if carry is clear to 000C
000A	01		
000B	1B		Add Acc's if carry is one
000C	58		Arithmetic shift left AccB
000D	7D		TEST memory address
000E	00		0001
000F	01		
0010	2E		Branch to MULT if great
0011	F4		than zero
0012	BD		JUMP to subroutine at FE20
0013	FE		
0014	20		
0015	3E		WAIT (HALT)

plied by the next significant digit and the result is added to the original. By rotating the first result to the right, the 3 from the second multiplicand lines up under the 2 of the first multiplication. We can carry out a similar procedure in base 2. The procedure is as follows:

1. Check the LSB of the multiplier. If it is a 1, add the multiplicand to any result you might have.
2. Rotate the multiplicand to the left (this is the same as rotating the result to the right as described above).
3. Rotate the multiplier to the right to get a new LSB.
4. Have you checked all bits? If not go back to step 1.

Both a logic shift and an arithmetic shift are used in the program. Each transfers a bit into the carry register. The order in which these instructions are executed is very important as we want to multiply only when a 1 is shifted into the carry bit from the multiplier. Figure 8.2 is a flowchart of this program.

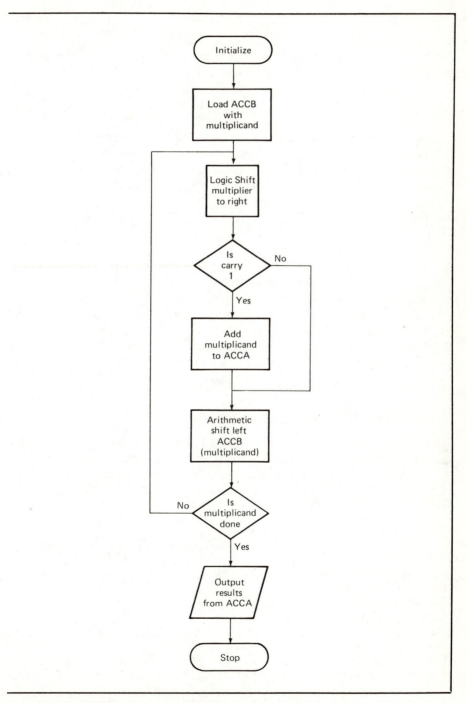

FIGURE 8.2. Flowchart for multiplication program.

EXERCISE 8-1

1. Identify the flags in the condition code register.
2. a. How long does it take the computer to execute the program given in Table 8.4 using a MC6800?
   b. If an MC68B00 is used in place of the MC6800, what is the time it would take to do the same program? The MC68B00 uses a 2-MHz clock in place of the 1-MHz clock used in the MC6800.
3. Write the addition program (from Table 8.4) using extended addressing. Store your three variables in addresses 0100, 0101, and 0102.
4. In the following, the OP code 20 at memory address 0110 is a branch always instruction. After the computer has completed this instruction it will branch to memory address _____ .
   0110   20
   0111   02
   a. 0113 b. 0114 c. 0115 d. 0002
5. Explain in general how you determine to which memory address a branch instruction will cause a program to go.
6. The first byte of an instruction is known as a(an)
   a. Reference instruction b. Instruction decoder
   c. Op code d. All of these
7. Refer to Figure 8.2 for the following question. At address 0004 is a load ACCB instruction. What number is stored in accumulator B by this instruction?

INDEX REGISTER AND STACK POINTER

This last set of instructions uses the two additional 16-bit hardware registers in the microprocessor. There are 11 basic instructions summarized in Table 8.8. There are a total of 24 instructions when all addressing modes are considered.

TABLE 8.8. *Summary of Index Register and Stack Pointer Instructions.*

Instruction	Boolean/Arithmetic Operation
Compare Index Register	$X_H - M, X_L - (M + 1)$
Decrement Index Register	$X - 1 \rightarrow X$
Decrement Stack Pointer	$SP - 1 \rightarrow SP$
Increment Index Register	$X + 1 \rightarrow X$
Increment Stack Pointer	$SP + 1 \rightarrow SP$
Load Index Register	$M \rightarrow X_H, M + 1 \rightarrow X_L$
Load Stack Pointer	$M \rightarrow SP_H, M + 1 \rightarrow SP_L$
Store Index Register	$X_H \rightarrow M, X_L \rightarrow M + 1$
Store Stack Pointer	$SP_H \rightarrow M, SP_L \rightarrow M + 1$
Index Register $\rightarrow$ Stack Pointer	$X - 1 \rightarrow SP$
Stack Pointer $\rightarrow$ Index Register	$SP + 1 \rightarrow X$

These instructions used with these two registers are similar to the accumulator instructions. Because these registers are 16-bit registers, there are some slight differences.

- Compare index register. This instruction allows us to compare the 16-bit number in the index register with 2 consecutive bytes in memory. The higher byte is compared with M and the lower byte with M + 1. Neither the register nor the memory addresses are altered. Changes may occur in the condition code register.
- Load index register and load stack pointer. Here 2 consecutive bytes in memory are transferred to the higher and lower byte of the appropriate register. The first byte is the higher byte and the second is the lower byte.
- Store index register and store stack pointer. This operation is just the reverse of the load instruction. Increment and decrement stack pointer or index register. The increment and decrement instructions work the same as the accumulator instructions. The change is always 1.
- Transfer instructions. There are two transfer instructions that allow you to transfer the data from the stack pointer to the index register or vice versa. Index register → stack pointer or stack pointer → index register. It is important to note the number is changed in the process. The stack pointer is loaded with one less than the number in the index register, while the index register is loaded with one more than the number stored in the stack pointer. Both instructions are used where tables of data are needed.

STACK OPERATIONS

In many applications, especially scientific, a series of data must be stored and later retrieved. This is especially true in data base management. The area where these data are temporarily stored so they can be retrieved is called a "stack."

There are two basic types of stacks. Some microprocessors have available a small number of special registers (usually 8–16) in which data can be temporarily stored. These registers are referred to as a cascade stack (Figure 8.3). With this type of stack, all data transfers take place between the top of the stack and the accumulator.

The advantage of using a cascade stack is that the instructions to add data to a stack or remove the data from the stack are single-byte instructions. No addresses are needed. Data are transferred to and from the stack using the push or pull instruction listed in accumulator and memory instructions.

As data are transferred to the stack the first byte goes to the top of the stack. When the next set of data is sent to the stack, the first byte is pushed down to the next register in the stack. This is why it is referred to as a pushdown stack. Data removed from the stack are always taken from the top of the stack. This means the second byte will be removed before the first byte. Another name for this type of stack is a first in/last out (FILO) stack.

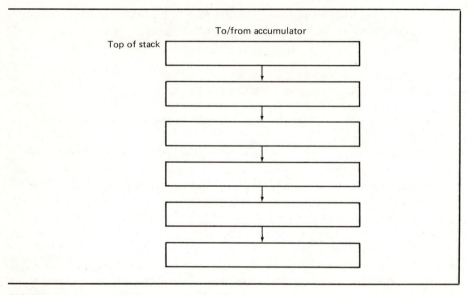

FIGURE 8.3. *A cascade or push-down stack.*

Note that a cascade stack is limited in its use. If the stack contains eight registers, only 8 bytes can be placed in the stack. If a ninth byte is sent to the stack, the first byte is pushed out the bottom of the stack and is lost. This type of stack is also a destructive type of stack. Once the data are removed, they are also lost. The advantage of such a stack is that a stack pointer is not needed.

Another type of stack is a memory stack. In the 6800 any section of memory (RAM) can be defined as a stack. The advantage of this is that the data are permanently stored, and more than one stack can be created. A separate register called a stack pointer is used to store the address of the top of the stack. When a program is being written, the programmer must reserve a section of memory to be used as a stack.

Stacks are used during interrupts and branch-to subroutines. In a branch-to subroutine the value of the program counter is stored in the stack before going to the subroutine; after the subroutine is completed and a return from subroutine (RTS) is encountered by the CPU, the CPU gets the address of the next instruction from the top of the stack. If a second subroutine is used while going through a subroutine, the top of the stack has the return address of the second subroutine. This is why nested subroutines must be used in programming.

From the earlier examples, it should be obvious that it is not necessary to have a stack pointer to use data stored in a section of memory, but with a stack pointer and the push or pull instruction, it is much more efficient than the program previously written when a large amount of data are being used.

As with a cascade stack, a push instruction is used to place data in a memory stack while the pull instruction removes data from the memory stack.

A big difference here from a cascade stack is that a pull instruction is not destructive. Data are read from the stack without changing the value stored in memory. A summary of these instructions is as follows:

Instruction	OP Code	Mnemonic	Description
Push	36	PSHA	$A \to M_{sp}$ $Sp - 1 \to SP$
	37	PSHB	$B \to M_{sp}$ $Sp - 1 \to SP$
Pull	32	PULA	$M_{sp} \to A$ $SP + 1 \to SP$
	33	PULB	$M_{sp} \to B$ $SP + 1 \to SP$

When a push instruction is used, data are transferred from an accumulator to a memory address and the stack pointer is decremented by 1. This is summarized in the description given above. When a pull instruction is used, the stack pointer is increased by 1 and then data are taken from a memory address and placed in the proper accumulator. Note that this is still a pushdown stack but the address of the top of the stack moves rather than each byte stored in the stack. If data are to be removed, the last byte entered is the first byte removed.

An example of this type of programming is as follows:

Memory Address	OP Code	Mnemonic
0100	32	PULA
0101	26	BNE #$FD
0102	FD	
⋮	⋮	
0200	00	
0201	FC	$FC
0202	FC	$FC
0202	FC	$FC
0203	00	$00
Stack pointer	0200	

In the above program the instruction at address 0100 says to take a byte of data from the stack and load it into accumulator A. The stack pointer was originally at 0200. When the PULA instruction is encountered, the stack pointer is incremented by 1 to 0201. The computer goes to this address to get the data (FC) that are to be put in accumulator A. The OP code 26 causes the computer to branch back to address 0100 until the number 00 is retrieved from the stack.

PROGRAMMING

From the instructions covered you should be able to write simple programs using immediate, direct, or extended addressing modes. The operation of all the instructions has not been illustrated in this chapter, but the instructions not covered can be deduced by examination of the tables or Appendix A or B. To learn to program well at this level requires at least another semester dedicated to just programming.

It is important to note that the nature of the instructions available for the 6800—for example, two's complement, logic and arithmetic shifts, stack pointer, and index addressing—is what enables this microprocessor to be used in a microcomputer. Without these instructions the microprocessor would be useful mainly as a controller. The greater the number of these instructions and addressing modes, the better it will work in support of higher languages.

THE MC6809

Appendix C has a listing of the OP codes and hexadecimal values used by Motorola's enhanced version of a microprocessor known as an MC6809.

This has an instruction set that is compatible at the source level with the MC6800. An examination of the instruction mnemonics will show the similarity to the 6800 set. Some of the additional instructions available that make this a hybrid 8-bit, 16-bit microprocessor are the 16-bit accumulator and memory instructions. These take accumulators A and B and combine them into a 16-bit accumulator called accumulator D. This enables the computer to operate on 16-bit words.

Another change that makes the 6809 a more powerful microprocessor than the 6800 is its direct page register. This enables the microprocessor to have long branches as well as short branches. Note that long branches mnemonics are similar to the short, except that the long branches begin with *L*; for example, BEQ and LBEQ for branch if equal to 0. The long branches allow branching to anywhere in memory.

Another change is the presence of two stacks in the 6809; a hardware stack as well as the memory stack is available in the 6800. These are given the symbols *U*, for user, and *S*, for hardware, in the mnemonics.

The last addition to be discussed here is the presence of two index registers called *X* and *Y*. These both operate the same as the single-index register in the 6800.

EXERCISE 8-2

1. In the 6800 a stack pointer is used to address a memory stack. Which of the following is not true of the stack pointer?
   a. It is a 16-bit register.
   b. It is automatically incremented or decremented after a PUSH or PULL instruction.

   c. The stack pointer can only be used to address a stack on pages greater than 0.

   d. The stack pointer always points to the top of the stack.

2. Explain what a stack is.

3. What is the difference between a FIFO and FILO stack?

4. How does a JMP instruction differ from a JSR?

5. What are PUSH and PULL instructions used for?

REVIEW QUESTIONS

1. In this addressing mode the second byte is a page 0 address.
   a. Indirect
   b. Direct
   c. Immediate
   d. Extended

2. If a minus command causes a branch, which of the following flags are set on the condition code register?
   a. $C = 0, V = 1$
   b. $Z = 0, N = 0$
   c. $Z = 0, N = 1$
   d. $C = 1, Z = 0$

3. Which of the following is not a 16-bit register?
   a. Condition code
   b. Program counter
   c. Index
   d. Stack pointer

4. The second byte of a branch command in a 6800 is
   a. A direct address
   b. An OP code
   c. An address of an address
   d. A relative address

5. Which of the following is a typical stack in a 6800-based microcomputer?
   a. A cascade stack in RAM
   b. A FIFO stack in RAM
   c. A FILO stack in RAM
   d. A FIFO stack in ROM

6. Which of the following flags is set when there is a carry from bit 3?
   a. I
   b. C
   c. V
   d. H

7. Write a program using the immediate addressing mode that will add the first four decimal numbers together.

8. What is the status of each bit in the condition code register when 10000000 is added to 10000000?

9. Assume an accumulator had a -10_{10} stored in it. Show, after one arithmetic shift right, that the value now stored in the accumulator is -5. What is the value of the number stored after two arithmetic shift rights?

10. Suppose you have a program with a branch always at address 00F0 and you wish to end up at address 0104. What is the value of the second byte in the branch instruction?

11. Identify the difference between a cascade stack and a memory stack.

REFERENCES

1. *M6800 Microcomputer Systems Design Data*. Motorola Semiconductor Products, Inc., Phoenix, Ariz.

2. Ron Bishop, *Basic Microprocessors and the 6800*. Hayden Book Company, Inc., Rochelle Park, N.J., 1979.

3. Lance Leventhal, *6800 Assembly Language Programming*. Adam Osborne and Associates, McGraw-Hill Book Company, New York, 1978.

4. T. Rodhakrishman and M. V. Bhat, Stacks in Microprocessors, *Byte* 4 (6), p. 168 (June 1979).

5. *Introduction to Microprocessors*. Heath Corporation, Benton Harbor, Mich., 1978.

6. *Advanced Information Sheet, MC6809*. Motorola Semiconductors, Austin, Tex., 1980.

GLOSSARY

Accumulator	Register in which all arithmetic operations are carried out.
Addressing mode	A format used in machine language instructions in which the first byte is a command whereas the second or third byte, if there is one, contains address or data.
Benchmark	A program written to test a microprocessor or microcomputer. Time it takes to run the program is observed and compared with that of other micros.
Cascade stack	A special stack composed of 8–16 registers available in some microprocessors (see also FILO stack).
Condition code register	Eight-bit register in the 6800. First 6 bits are used as flags.
Direct mode addressing	Two-byte instruction; first is the instruction, and the second is a page 0 address.
Extended addressing	Three-byte instruction; first is the instruction, and the rest is a 16-bit address.
FIFO stack	First in/first out stack; first byte of data entered into stack is first removed.
Immediate addressing	Two-byte instructions except for stack pointer and index register instructions. First byte is the instruction; the rest, the data.

Implied addressing	One-byte instruction.
Index addressing	Two-byte instruction; first is the instruction, and the second is a number that is added to or subtracted from the address in the index register to get an address.
Index register	A 16-bit register in the 6800 used to address all 64K of memory.
Memory reference instruction (MRI)	First byte of an instruction that represents a command to the computer.
Memory stack	A section of memory that has been defined as a stack.
Relative addressing	Two-byte instruction; first byte is the instruction, and the second byte is a number that is added to or subtracted from the program counter to get an address.
Stack	A part of memory where data are stored.
Stack pointer	A 16-bit register in the 6800 used to transfer data to and from a stack.

ANSWERS TO EXERCISE 8-1

1. H, half-carry I, interrupt N, negative
   Z, zero V, overflow C, carry
2. 96   3
   9B   3
   97   4
   3E   9
   ___
   19 cycles
   MC6800 19 μs
   MC68B00 9.5 μs
3. 0000   B6   LDAA $0100
   0001   01
   0002   00
   0003   BB   ADDA $0101
   0004   01
   0005   01
   0006   B7   STAA $0102
   0007   01
   0008   02
   0009   3E   WAI
   — — — — — — — — — —
   0100   05
   0101   04
4. b
5. Add the number in the second byte to the value of the program counter (which is always at the next address).
6. c
7. 05

ANSWERS TO EXERCISE 8-2

1. c
2. Section of the computer used to store data.
3. FIFO; first in/first out
   FILO; first in/last out
4. JMP is permanent jump; JMS is a temporary jump.
5. To add data to a stack or remove data from a stack.

ANSWERS TO REVIEW QUESTIONS

1. b
2. c
3. a
4. d
5. c
6. d
7.
0000	86
0001	01
0002	3B
0003	02
0004	3B
0005	03
0006	3B
0007	04
0008	3E
8.
H	I	N	Z	V	C
0	0	0	1	1	1
9. $-10_{10} = 10001010$; after one shift we have 11000101, which is -5. Note this shift retains the sign bit. After two shifts, -2.
10. 18_{10} or 11_{16}
11. Cascade stack: hard-wired stack capable of storing a limited number of bytes.
    Memory stack: the ability to use any part of memory as the stack.

CHAPTER 9

INTERFACING AND DATA ACQUISITION

LEARNING ACTIVITIES

Study lecture material.
Read resource material at end of unit.
Complete exercises.
Self-check answers to exercises.
Consult instructor for assistance as necessary.

OBJECTIVES

By completing these requirements, you should be able to achieve the following objectives when formally evaluated.

Objective 1

Given the three basic methods used to transfer data from a peripheral device—polling, interrupt control, and DMA—identify each according to its standard use.

Objective 2

Given the following analog devices, identify each according to its standard use: a. one-shot; b. Schmitt trigger; c. transducer.

Objective 3

Given A/D and D/A converters, identify each type and its various forms according to standard use.

Objective 4

Given an analog signal, identify each of the following according to its standard use.

a. Nyquist frequency
b. Endogenous noise
c. Exogenous noise
d. Analog filtering
e. Digital filtering
f. Boxcar averaging
g. Ensemble averaging

EVALUATION

Your ability to demonstrate achievement on these objectives will be assessed after all instruction on this unit by:

• Multiple-choice items
• Identification items
• Matching items

INTRODUCTION

In Chapters 5 and 6 we discussed general input/output techniques. Here we continue this discussion with a special application to the analysis of data.

MULTIPLE INPUT/OUTPUT INTERFACING

Three basic methods are used to transfer data from a peripheral device:

1. Polling
2. Interrupt control
3. DMA

Polling or Programmed Input/Output

In this technique all input/output transfers are controlled by the program being executed. When the program needs data it checks the peripheral(s) (polls) for a flag. If the flag is set, the data are transferred. A handshaking routine, as described in Chapter 5, is necessary. If more than one peripheral is on line, two different methods can be used to determine which peripheral will be accessed first by the computer, that is, assigning priorities to the peripherals. The simplest is to poll through the peripherals as a function of the distance along the bus from the computer. The peripheral closest to the computer is polled first, and so on, until the last device is polled. The second way is to assign priorities to the various devices. Since a tape drive is faster than a

TTY, it is usually necessary to access a tape drive before a TTY. This is done by encoding a priority to each device in either a look-up table in a ROM or by using a priority-encoder chip. When this is done, the device with the highest priority is accessed first. Since polling is handled mainly by a software program, it is an inexpensive method of transferring data. Its major disadvantages are that it is slow, since it has to check all the peripherals before coming back to the first, and it is wasteful of the CPU's time, again since it requires the CPU to check constantly for flags.

Interrupt Control

Most microprocessors have a hardware circuitry that allows a peripheral to send a signal to the microprocessor requesting access to the computer. This signal is referred to as an interrupt request signal. The microprocessor checks the interrupt flag after every instruction. If the flag is not set, it continues on to the next instruction. If the flag is set, it will service the device that generated the interrupt.

Interrupts can be classified into two groups: (1) maskable and (2) non-maskable.

Certain routines have such a high priority that they should never be interrupted. A power failure routine is a prime example. Those systems with a battery back-up can detect a power failure and, in the time it takes for the power to shut down, a microprocessor can save the contents of all its registers and be ready to continue programming when the power comes back. These routines are called nonmaskable. Once they start, the computer will ignore an interrupt request.

Other routines are called maskable since they can be ignored under the proper conditions. In addition, the computer ignores the interrupt until it has finished with its instruction. Figure 9.1 illustrates the timing involved in an interrupt.

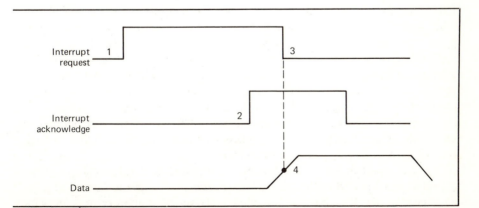

FIGURE 9.1. *Timing signals in an interrupt.*

At point 1 the peripheral asks the computer to accept or send some data; at point 2 the computer acknowledges the request of the peripheral. The midway of point 4 corresponds to point 3. At this point the data are being transferred so the interrupt request flag is cleared.

Since a program is normally in progress when an interrupt occurs, there must be a procedure to restore the computer to the place in the program after the interrupt. There are two general ways in which this can be accomplished. In some computers an interrupt request causes a microprogram, in the control unit, to store the contents of the program counter, accumulators, and status flags in a cascade stack. If the microprogram is not available, then the user will have to write a software routine called an "interrupt service routine" program, which will accomplish the same thing.

If a number of peripherals are to be serviced, then the computer must decide which device asked for the interrupt. This may be accomplished by hardware, software, or a combination of the two. Branching to the I/O address of the peripheral is called "vectoring the interrupt."

With a software routine, polling is often used. This method was described above. With a little additional hardware a second software routine, which is much faster, can be done. This procedure uses a "daisy chain" to identify the device. The interrupt acknowledge is sent to the first peripheral. If this was the peripheral that requested the interrupt, it places a signal on the bus that tells the computer it is the proper peripheral. If it was not the peripheral that asked for service, it passes the acknowledge signal to the next device on the bus. The disadvantage of this method is that the additional hardware needed by the peripherals increases the cost significantly for the microcomputer. The fastest method is what is known as "vectored interrupt." Using this procedure, the I/O device supplies both the interrupt and the direct 16-bit address the computer needs to access the peripheral. This has become possible through the use of priority-interrupt-controller (PIC) chips.

DMA

Direct memory access (DMA) is used when data transfers are needed between high-speed storage devices such as disks or magnetic tapes and the computer. This is accomplished by a hardware circuitry known as a direct-memory-access controller (DMAC). This controller takes over the address and bus lines from the microprocessor. There are various ways in which this can be accomplished. It may halt the microprocessor and send a "burst" of information to memory, or it may steal cycles from the microprocessor, or it may even stretch the clock pulses. Some of the newer micros utilize part of the instruction cycle to use the address bus while the processor is not using it, and then the data bus while this bus is not needed by the CPU.

To accomplish DMA, the busses are tristated. When the microprocessor completes its instruction, it releases the busses (or floats the busses) and goes to a hold state. This state is activated by a signal that interrupts the clock pulses coming to the microprocessor. During this state the DMAC can use the address bus and data bus to transmit I/O information.

In the 6800 the DMAC is a cycle-stealing controller. It floats the busses for a period of time of up to 500 μs since dynamic memory is used and they need to be refreshed every 2 ms or so. Figure 9.2 is an illustration of the timing in a DMA transfer. In Figure 9.2 two clock pulses are stolen from the CPU to do a DMA transfer.

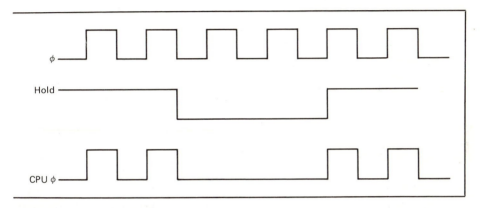

FIGURE 9.2. *Cycle stealing from a CPU.*

EXERCISE 9-1 I/O Interfacing

1. a. What is programmed input/output?
    b. What are the disadvantages of this technique?
2. Identify priority-encoder chip.
3. What is an interrupt?
4. What are maskable and nonmaskable interrupts?
5. Identify the following terms.
    a. Interrupt service routine
    b. Vectoring the interrupt
    c. Daisy chain
    d. Vectored interrupt
    e. Cycle stealing

ONE-SHOTS, SCHMITT TRIGGERS, AND TRANSDUCERS

In addition to the computer circuits previously discussed, there are two other circuits that are commonly encountered in computer systems:

1. Monostable multivibrator (one-shot)
2. Schmitt trigger

A monostable multivibrator or one-shot is an analog device used to generate accurate, reproducible time delays. It does this by stretching pulses. Figure 9.3 is a representation of the input and output signals to a one-shot.

By attaching different resistors and capacitors, delays can be generated that range from nanoseconds to seconds or minutes. One-shots are useful with the reset sequence in a micro and to generate interrupt pulses.

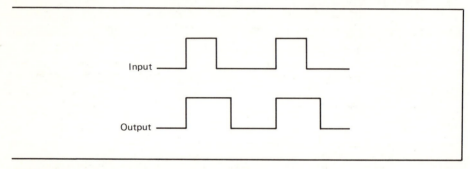

FIGURE 9.3. *Pulse stretching from a one-shot.*

A Schmitt trigger is a device used to clean up noisy signals. The device contains an input, an output, and upper and lower threshold voltage terminals. Before the output can change state, the input signal must pass through both the lower and upper threshold voltage. Figure 9.4 illustrates how this works.

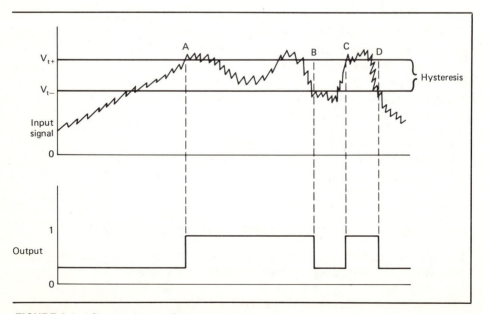

FIGURE 9.4. *Signals from a Schmitt trigger.*

In this diagram the input signal has passed through the lower and then the upper threshold value at point *A*. This causes the output to go from a low to high. (Schmitt triggers are often inverters. With the inverter type, the output would go from high to low.) Even though the signal passes below the upper threshold value between points *A* and *B*, there is no change in the output because the signal did not pass through the lower threshold value. Points *B*, *C*, and *D* show changes in the output since the signal has passed through both voltage levels. The difference in upper and lower threshold values is called the hysteresis. Schmitt triggers are used with one-shots to generate a clean reset signal.

Many of the measurements we often wish to make in the real world involve an analog signal such as pressure, temperature, or sound. In order to feed this signal into a computer, we must convert it into an electrical signal. A device that does this is called a transducer. Transducers are devices that respond to one form of energy and convert it to another. With computers we are interested in devices that convert electric energy into another form or the reverse, for example, heat or pressure into electric energy.

Transducers are divided into two types—input transducers and output transducers. An input transducer converts a nonelectrical signal into an electrical signal, which can be fed to the computer. People who work in laboratories often use input transducers, though they probably do not refer to them as such. Common examples are conductance cells used to measure the conductivity or resistance of a solution, electrodes used to measure pH or specific ion concentrations, detectors on a gas chromatograph, and temperature transducers such as thermocouples or thermistors.

Output transducers convert electric energy into nonelectrical signals. The speaker in a radio is an example of this type of transducer. It converts an electrical signal into a sound wave.

EXERCISE 9-2   One-shots, Schmitt triggers, and transducers

1. Explain, in your own words, the major purpose of a monostable multivibrator.
2. How are time delays changed on one-shots?
3. What is meant by the upper and lower threshold for a Schmitt trigger?
4. What is the hysteresis of a Schmitt trigger?
5. What is a transducer? Give examples.

D/A AND A/D TECHNIQUES

There are many applications where data are obtained from the surroundings in an analog form and must be transmitted to the computer in a digital form. In addition, it is often necessary to send a digital signal out to an analog world. The transmission of the analog data to and from the computer can be accomplished in different ways. Figure 9.5 shows the most common method

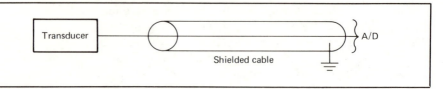

FIGURE 9.5. *Transmission of data using a shielded cable.*

employed in the laboratory. This is known as direct transmission using shielded cable. Surrounding the cable is a wire shield, which is grounded. It reduces interference from electrical signals such as fluorescent lights.

Direct transmission is highly limited. It requires that no high-intensity electric field be nearby and you run into problems when the distance is over 20 feet, especially if low signals are being sent.

A better method is the two-wire transmitter using a twisted pair of wires. Here you normally have a current of 50 mA flowing while the noise level is in the microampere region. The effect of noise on the signal is thus small. A third type involves the conversion of the signal from the transducer to a frequency (voltage-to-frequency converter). This frequency is transmitted over the wires and is converted back into a voltage (frequency-to-voltage converter) before entering the computer. This last method is used for data that have to be transmitted some distance.

Digital-to-Analog Converters

When data must be transmitted to the outside world, a device is needed to convert the digital signal from the computer into an analog signal. Such a device is called a digital-to-analog converter (DAC or D/A). Figure 9.6 is a schematic representation of this.

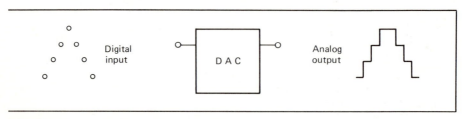

FIGURE 9.6. *Digital-to-analog conversion.*

This may be accomplished internally through a resistive ladder network. Figure 9.7 illustrates its principle. Such a network is known as a weighted resistor ladder because of the ratios of the resistances. The Rx in the first box of Figure 9.7 is a resistance much larger than the largest in the ladder (8R in this case). The resistance Rx can be replaced by the circuit shown in the

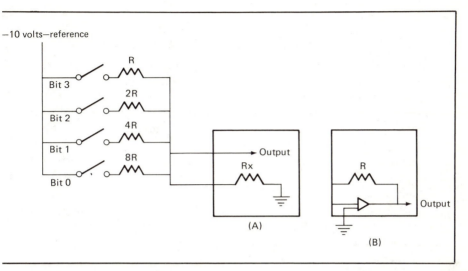

FIGURE 9.7. *Weighted ladder network of a 4-bit DAC: (A) with register and (B) with operational amplifier.*

second box. This uses an operational amplifier to create the high resistance needed.

Bit 0, when closed, will generate a voltage V, bit 1 a voltage $2V$, bit 2 a voltage $4V$ and the nth bit a voltage of $2^n \times V$. The overall voltage is obtained

TABLE 9.1. *Analog Voltage Generated by 4-Bit Ladder Network. c is closed, o is opened switch.*

Bit 0	Bit 1	Bit 2	Bit 3	Voltage
o	o	o	o	0.00
c	o	o	o	1.25
o	c	o	o	2.50
c	c	o	o	3.75
o	o	c	o	5.00
c	o	c	o	6.25
o	c	c	o	7.50
c	c	c	o	8.75
o	o	o	c	10.00
c	o	o	c	11.25
o	c	o	c	12.50
c	c	o	c	13.75
o	o	c	c	15.00
c	o	c	c	16.25
o	c	c	c	17.50
c	c	c	c	18.75

by summing all the voltages. In Figure 9.7 the values of the resistors are in the ratio 1, 2, 4, and 8, which results in gains of $-1/8$, $-1/4$, $-1/2$, and -1. With just bit 0 closed, the output through the operational amplifier is 1.25 volts due to the gain of $-1/8$ (-10 volts input). When bit 1 is closed 2.5 volts are added to the 1.25 volts. When bit 2 is closed 5.0 volts are added and when bit 3 is closed 10.0 volts are added, giving a total maximum output of 18.75 volts. This is summarized in Table 9.1. To evaluate a DAC, various parameters must be examined. The resolution is one of the most important parameters. It is determined by the number of bits in the DAC.

The resolution of a DAC is given by $1/2^n$ where n is the number of bits in the converter. Table 9.2 gives the resolution of DACs assuming a voltage range output of -10 to $+10$ volts.

TABLE 9.2. *Resolution of Various DACs.*

Bits	Resolution	Increment Value of Output
4	1/16	1.24 V
6	1/64	310 MV
8	1/256	78 MV
10	1/1024	19.5 MV
12	1/4096	4.8 MV
14	1/16384	1.2 MV
16	1/65536	0.31 MV

Another factor that should be considered is the output range. This is the voltage difference between the maximum voltage output and minimum voltage output of the DAC. The accuracy of a DAC is usually expressed as a percent of the full-scale output or of the least significant bit (usually $\pm 1/2$ LSB). This is the percentage error associated with a voltage output. The settling time, or conversion time, is the time it takes the DAC to generate an output from a digital input that meets the other specifications. Table 9.3 lists some commonly available DACs.

TABLE 9.3. *Some Commercial DACs.*

Manufacturer	No.	Resolution (no. of bits)	Speed
Motorola	MC1408	8	300 ns
Analog Device	AD7520	10	500 ms
Datel	DAC-4212D	12	1 μs

Analog-to-Digital Converters (ADC)

When the analog signal reaches the computer it must be converted into a digital signal. There are many different types of analog-to-digital (A/D) converters. Some are slow, some are fast, and there are numerous voltage levels available. Among the more common are the following.

Counter converters. The simplest type of ADC, these have a conversion time of 1 ms and thus can collect 1000 data points per second. They consist of a comparator, clock, counter, and a digital-to-analog converter (DAC). The analog signal is sent to the comparator. A start-of-conversion signal is generated, which sets the counter to 0, starts the counter, and presents a digital input to the DAC. The DAC sends an analog signal out in turn to the other input of the comparator. As the counter increases, the output of the DAC increases in corresponding steps. When the output of the DAC is equal to or greater than the analog signal from the external device, the comparator changes state. This turns off the clock and stops the counter. The digital output of the counter can then be read. Note that the time it takes to make a conversion depends upon the incoming analog voltage; the higher the voltage, the longer the time. This type of counter is also known as an up-counter. Other versions are available in which the counter starts at the highest value and counts down. These are known as down-counters. Up-counters and down-counters are the simplest and least expensive A/D converters available.

Continuous counters. A continuous counter can count either up or down. When the comparator realizes it has exceeded the voltage of the input analog signal, instead of turning the clock off it reverses the direction of the counter. This then proceeds to follow or track the analog signal. Digital outputs can be read at intervals from the counter. This counter is also known as an up-down counter. After the counter locks onto the signal, it is extremely fast in making conversions.

Successive approximation converters. This type of converter does not have a counter but uses a device known as a pattern generator. The pattern generator generates 1 bit at a time, and the voltage generated is compared with the input voltage. The bits are generated starting with the MSB. Since every bit must always be checked, this type of converter always takes the same amount of time, no matter what the analog input. Figure 9.8 shows how the bit pattern generated is compared with the analog input using a 4-bit ADC.

When the most significant bit is set in the bit generator, the voltage generated is less than the analog input. This bit remains set and the next bit is set. This time the voltage exceeds the analog input signal, so the bit is returned to 0 and the next bit is set. This continues until all bits are checked.

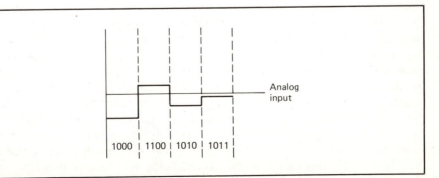

FIGURE 9.8. *Bit comparison of voltage to analog input signal.*

Analog integration. This type of converter is quite different from the others discussed above. In general, the time it takes to charge a capacitor by an unknown voltage is compared with the time it takes to discharge the capacitor under a known voltage. From the time ratios the voltage of the analog input is calculated.

Figure 9.9 shows the charging and discharging times of this dual-slope integrator, as it is called. Here a capacitor is charged by an unknown voltage for a fixed period of time. The capacitor is then discharged by a known voltage. The time it takes to discharge the capacitor will thus vary and be a function of the analog input voltage. These dual-slope conversion ADCs are slow compared with the successive approximation converters. They are usually found in pH meters.

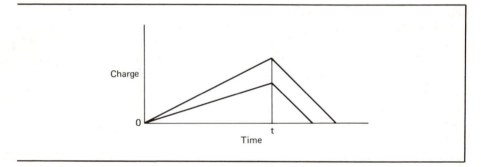

FIGURE 9.9. *Integration timing.*

In choosing an A/D, various parameters must also be evaluated. The range is the voltage difference between the maximum input voltage and minimum input voltage you can put on an ADC. In general, input voltages to ADCs fall between -10 and $+10$ volts. Some common examples are 0 to $+5$, -10 to $+10$, -5 to $+5$, 0 to $+1$, 0 to $+5$, and $-2\frac{1}{2}$ to $+2\frac{1}{2}$ volts. The resolution is also determined by the number of bits in the ADC as well as by the voltage range. It can be calculated by dividing the voltage range by 2^n, where n is the number of bits.

Sample and hold circuitry. Often the analog signal to be examined is changing with time. Since an ADC takes a short time to convert the analog signal to a digital signal, the analog signal must be stable during the conversion time. To handle this, a special circuit called a sample and hold circuit is built into an ADC. This circuit accepts the input voltage at a given time and stores its value until the next reading. It is the stored value that is converted by the ADC. Because of the conversion time, the reading of the ADC represents an analog signal in the past. It usually differs by microseconds or milliseconds from the present and for most applications the difference is meaningless. In some applications, though, this difference must be considered.

EXERCISE 9-3   D/A and A/D techniques

1. A 6-bit D/A converter has a resolution of:
    a. 1/16   b. 1/64   c. 1/256   d. 1/1024
2. An A/D converter that starts a count at 0 and counts up until the analog signal is matched is called:
    a. Successive approximation counter
    b. Analog integration converter
    c. Down-counter
    d. Up-counter
3. The A/D converter that always takes the same amount of time to make a conversion is known as
    a. Continuous counter
    b. Successive approximation converter
    c. Analog integration
    d. Up-down counter

SAMPLING

The rate at which data are sampled is very important in analog-to-digital conversions. Improper sampling can lead to numerous types of errors. Figure 9.10 illustrates one type of sampling error.

In Figure 9.10 the analog signal is a simple sine wave. Sampling is done at a constant rate corresponding to the (0). In this case the sampling rate is so slow it would appear as if no signal were being input.

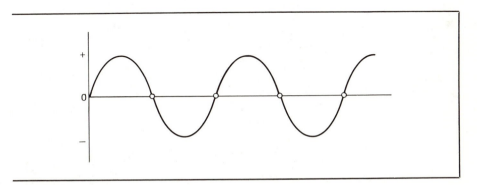

FIGURE 9.10.   *Infrequent sampling of an analog signal.*

The maximum frequency of a sine wave that can be sampled by a given converter is given by the "sampling theorem." This states that the sampling frequency must be at least twice the highest frequency of the analog signal under investigation. The frequency *above* which you can no longer sample successfully is called the "Nyquist" frequency. This relationship is given by:

$$\text{Nyquist frequency} = \text{Sampling rate}/2$$

If we double our sampling rate in Figure 9.10, our converted signal looks like that given in Figure 9.11. The dotted line corresponds to the digitized signal as compared with the analog signal. In general, it is better to sample at ten or more times the highest frequency to ensure successful conversions.

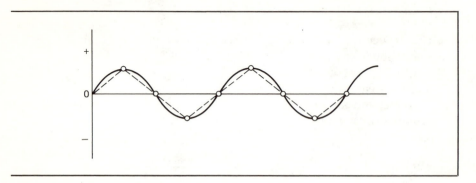

FIGURE 9.11. *Proper sampling of an analog signal.*

FILTERING TECHNIQUES

Often when a signal is received by the computer it is filled with "noise." Noise is a component of a signal that interferes with the observation, detection, or analysis of the signal. Noise can be categorized in two classes:

- Endogenous noise: This is noise inherent to the system. An example is thermal noise in detectors due to the movement of electrons or other carriers. Since this noise is random in origin, it can be averaged out over a period of time.
- Exogenous noise: This is noise created by external influences on the system. Radiofrequency and electromagnetic interference are examples. This noise is limited in its frequency range.

The reduction of noise can be treated in many different ways. Some common techniques are discussed in the following.

Analog Filtering

By using a resistor/capacitor combination along the path of transmission, high-frequency components can be removed, while low-frequency components are passed with little distortion. Figure 9.12 is a schematic of an analog filtering circuit.

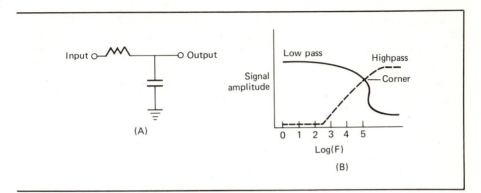

FIGURE 9.12. *Analog filter (A) and frequency transmitted curve (B).*

At a given frequency F the signal passed through the filter drops off. This is called a "corner" frequency and is given by the expression $F = 1/(2\pi RC)$. The resistor/capacitor combination should be chosen such that the corner frequency is ten times the highest frequency desired to be passed. Such a filtering system is known as a low-pass system since it allows low frequencies to pass and shuts off the higher frequencies.

By reversing the capacitor and resistor, a high-pass analog filter can be built. This allows high frequencies to pass and shuts off the low frequencies. Its characteristic curve is the dotted line in Figure 9.12. Various combinations of these two types of filters can be used to restrict the frequencies that can be passed into a circuit.

Digital Filtering

Additional filtering of a signal may be accomplished by using software filters based on numerical techniques.

Boxcar averaging. If the analog signal varies slowly compared with the rate of sampling of the ADC, then the signal can be sampled many times and averaged. The relationship between a single sample, signal-to-noise ratio, and multiple samples is as follows:

$$(S/N)_n = n^{1/2} \cdot (S/N)$$

where n is the number of times the signal has been measured. The signal-to-noise ratio is improved by the square root of the number of times the signal is sampled. Thus, to improve the signal-to-noise ratio by a factor of 2, four readings must be taken. To improve the ratio by a factor of 3, nine readings must be taken. In boxcar averaging the analog signal is broken into boxes. The width of each box depends upon how many times you wish to sample the signal and the rate at which the analog signal is changing. In general, a boxcar average can be done by averaging so many samples taken at 1-ms intervals. The time depends upon the speed of the ADC. In taking the sample, we have to consider the time it takes an ADC to make a measurement (20–25 μs) as well as the time it takes the computer to average and store the results (70–75 μs). An average time of 100 μs per sample is a reasonable assumption. Figure 9.13 shows what a boxcar analysis would look like.

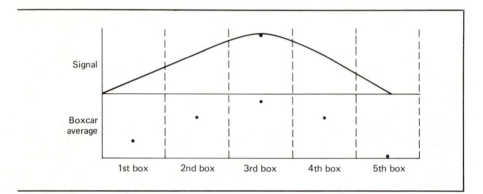

FIGURE 9.13. *A boxcar average of a signal.*

Ensemble averaging. This technique is used where the incoming signal is repetitive in nature. By sampling the same signal over and over again and averaging the results, the noise is reduced since it is random in nature. The improvement in the signal-to-noise ratio is given by the same relationship as in boxcar averaging. This is the basic technique used by a computer of average transients (CAT) in nuclear magnetic resonance (NMR) analysis.

EXERCISE 9-4 Sampling and Filtering Techniques

1. Define Nyquist frequency.
2. Which of the following types of noise is random and can be averaged out using filtering techniques?
   a. Endogenous   b. Exogenous
3. Which of the following techniques should be used to minimize exogenous noise?
   a. Analog filtering   b. Digital filtering
4. If a signal is sampled 16 times, the signal-to-noise ratio is improved _____ times.
   a. 4   b. 16   c. $\frac{1}{4}$ d. $\frac{1}{16}$
5. Which of the following digital filtering techniques can be used for a nonrepetitive analog signal?
   a. Boxcar averaging   b. Ensemble averaging

REVIEW QUESTIONS

1. Match column A with the correct answer in column B.

A	B
1. Transducer	a. Generates a clean signal from a noisy signal.
2. Schmitt trigger	
3. Monostable multivibrator	b. Used to store an analog signal for conversion.
4. Sample and hold circuit	
	c. Converts one physical form of energy into another.
	d. Stretches pulses.

2. The Nyquist frequency is
   a. The highest frequency you can detect in an ADC.
   b. The highest frequency you can detect in terms of your sampling rate.
   c. The corner frequency in an analog filter.
   d. The frequency at which sampling should be done to get the best results in an analysis.
3. Which of the following is not used as an ADC?
   a. Dual-slope converter   b. Analog-integration converter
   c. Successive approximation converter   d. Up-counter
4. The increase in signal-to-noise improvement in taking 25 samples of the same signal is
   a. 5X   b. 25X   c. 625X   d. 1/25X
5. Draw a diagram of a high-pass analog filter.
6. What is the resolution of an 8-bit DAC?
   a. 1/8   b. 1/64   c. 1/256   d. 1/512
7. What is the resolution of an 8-bit D/A converter with an output range of 0 to +5 volts? (Give the resolution in terms of the voltage change needed to cause a bit in the D/A to change.)
8. Suppose you have to measure a signal that varies from −5 to +5 volts with an accuracy to the nearest 0.01 volt. What size (how many bits) A/D should you use?
9. What is meant by the term "polling"?
10. Though a one-shot is normally an analog device, you can accomplish the same thing with a software program. Discuss in general how this might be done.
11. What is the difference between an input transducer and an output transducer.
12. Give some examples of ways interference signals can be generated in a computer.
13. In each of the following examples, tell whether you would use ensemble or boxcar averaging.
    a. Repetitive scans over a series of wavelengths.
    b. Setting up a calibration curve for a thermocouple.
    c. Following the change in conductivity of a solution as a function of time.

REFERENCES

1. Austin Lesea and Rodnay Saks, *Microprocessor Interfacing Techniques*, 2nd ed. Sybex, 1978.
2. Sam Perone and David Jones, *Digital Computers in Scientific Instrumentation*. McGraw-Hill Book Company, New York, 1973.
3. Raymound E. Dessy, *Microprocessors and Minicomputers, Interfacing and Applications Using the LSI-11*. American Chemical Society, Washington, D.C., 1977.
4. Bruce A. Artwick, *Microcomputer Interfacing*. Prentice-Hall, Englewood Cliffs, N.J., 1980, Chapter 5.
5. H. V. Malmstadt and C. G. Enke, *Digital Electronics for Scientists*. The Benjamin/Cummings Publishing Co., 1969, Chapter 7.
6. A. James Diefenderfer, *Principles of Electronic Instrumentation*. W. B. Saunders Company, Philadelphia, 1979, Chapters 11 and 14.

GLOSSARY

A/D converter	Analog-to-digital converter: generates a digital signal to represent an analog signal.
Boxcar averaging	Dividing a signal into equal widths in units of time, reading each "box" as many times as possible during this time, and averaging the readings.
D/A converter	Digital-to-analog converter; generates an analog signal to represent a digital signal.
Daisy chain	When an interrupt occurs, the computer sends an acknowledgement to the first peripheral in line; if this was not the peripheral requesting the interrupt, it passes the signal to the next peripheral, and so on down the line until the correct peripheral is found.
DMA	Direct memory access; direct deposit of data to and from memory and peripherals.
Endogenous noise	Random noise in a system.
Ensemble averaging	Used with repetitive signals. Signal is read over and over again and average determined.
Exogenous noise	Repetitive noise in a system caused by external influences.
Hysteresis	The difference in the upper and lower threshold voltages in a Schmitt trigger.
Interrupt service routine	A software routine that stores the contents of the PC, accumulators, and flags in a cascade stack.
Maskable interrupt	An interrupt that can be temporarily ignored by the computer.
Monostable multivibrator	Analog device used to stretch pulses; also called a one-shot.

Nonmaskable interrupt	An interrupt that must be executed immediately by the computer.
Nyquist frequency	Maximum frequency that can be sampled with an A/D converter.
One-shot	See Monostable multivibrator.
Polling	Use of a software to check for flags in a peripheral while searching for an interrupt.
Programmed I/O	Same as Polling.
Priority-encoder chip	Chip that assigns an order of priority to peripherals during an interrupt.
Resolution of a D/A	Given by $\frac{1}{2^n}$ where n is the number of bits in the converter.
Schmitt trigger	Device with an upper and lower threshold voltage used to clean up noisy signals.
Signal-to-noise ratio	Ratio of intensity of signal to intensity of noise.
Transducer	Device that takes an analog signal in one form of energy and converts it to another form of energy.
Vectored interrupt	Interrupt and address of peripheral supplied to the computer from the peripheral.
Vectoring the interrupt	To branch to the I/O address of the peripheral.

ANSWERS TO EXERCISE 9-1

1. a. Polling of all input/output devices under software control to transfer data.
    b. Slow; wasteful of CPU time.
2. Chip used to assign priorities to various peripheral devices; it controls order in which devices are polled.
3. Signal that allows an external device to request or demand service from the CPU.
4. Maskable interrupts can be delayed by the CPU until it is ready to service the interrupt; nonmaskable interrupts require immediate service by the CPU.
5. a. Software program that stores the values of the registers and program counter before servicing an interrupt.
    b. Term used that means servicing the interrupt.
    c. Device that enables peripherals to pass a signal down the bus to the next device on the bus during polling of the devices.
    d. An interrupt in which the external device supplies its address as well as the interrupt request.
    e. Ability to halt the CPU temporarily and use this time to send information on busses.

ANSWERS TO EXERCISE 9-2

1. To generate a time delay; or stretch pulses.
2. By varying the resistors and capacitors.
3. Two voltage levels that a signal must pass through before the signal can change value (from 1 to 0 or 0 to 1).
4. Difference in value of the upper and lower threshold value.
5. Device that converts energy in one form to another; speaker, barometer, thermometer.

ANSWERS TO EXERCISE 9-3

1. b
2. d
3. b

ANSWERS TO EXERCISE 9-4

1. Frequency above which you can no longer sample successfully.
2. a
3. a (though b can be used)
4. a
5. a

ANSWERS TO REVIEW QUESTIONS

1. 1—c
   2—a
   3—d
   4—b
2. b
3. d
4. a
5.

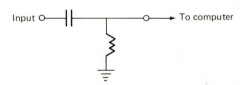

6. c
7. 0.0195 volt.
8. Ten-bit voltage change is 0.00976 volt.
9. Having the computer search along the bus to see the status of each peripheral attached to the bus.
10. By generating a high or a low on a line for more than two clock pulses.

11. Input transducer: converts an outside signal to an electrical signal.
    Output transducer: converts an electrical signal to some other physical form.
12. Capacitance in a circuit where wires come too close together or are not connected to a common ground; radiofrequency inductance in wires from overhead lights; thermal "noise" of electrons in tubes.
13. a. Ensemble
    b. Boxcar
    c. Boxcar

CHAPTER 10

A SURVEY OF THE FIELD

There are no specific learning objectives in this chapter. The information presented here is for reference purposes only.

INTRODUCTION

Throughout this text the emphasis has been placed on one particular microprocessor, the Motorola MC6800. This was used as a typical example of an 8-bit microprocessor. The number of different microprocessors available is quite large and cannot possibly be covered in one text. Table 10.1 lists some of the common general-purpose microprocessors. Microprocessor-based microcomputers are available in 2, 4, 8, or 16 bits, with 32 bits recently announced by Intel and Hewlett-Packard. The following discussion will cover some of the more common 8- and 16-bit micros.

8-BIT MICROS

Motorola 6800 Series

Since this has been discussed in detail only a few comments will be made here. Other versions of the 6800 are available with faster clocks: MC68A00 with a 1.5-MHz clock and MC68B00 with a 2-MHz clock. As most manufacturers do, Motorola makes a complete line of support devices for use with the 6800, that is, chips to handle parallel and serial transmission, memory units, and so on. Other useful devices include a MC6828/8507 priority interrupt controller (PIC), which allows eight levels of interrupts, and another version of the PIA called a MC6821. This latter is identical to the MC6820 in operating characteristics but not in physical layout.

The MC6802 is a MC6800 with a clock on the same chip, and 128 bytes of RAM, 32 bytes of which can be saved with a battery back-up during a power failure. The maximum clock rate is 4 MHz. The MC6808 is identical except that it does not have the RAM.

TABLE 10.1. Some Common Microprocessors.

Manufacturer	Processor	Technology	Word Size	No. of Instructions	Comments
Intel	4004	PMOS	4	46	The original micro.
Intel	4040	PMOS	4	60	Very popular 4-bit.
Texas Instrument	TMS100	PMOS	4	Depends upon series	Single-chip microcomputer. A series of six different micros.
Fairchild	3850 (F8)	NMOS	8	69	Very popular two-chip system.
Intel	8080A	NMOS	8	78	Most popular micro.
Intel	8085	NMOS	8	80	Enhanced version of 8080A.
Motorola	MC6800	NMOS	8	72	Many versions.
Motorola	MC6801	NMOS	8	72	Microcomputer on a chip.
Motorola	MC6809	NMOS	8	59	One of the better 8-bit micros available.
Zilog	Z80	NMOS	8	150+	Enhanced version of 8080A.
MOS Technology	6502	NMOS	8	56	Very popular. Used in many home micro sets.
RCA	1802	CMOS	8	91	Known as COSMAC.
Data General	mN601	NMOS	16	42	Uses Nova instructions.
Fairchild	9440	I²L	16	42	Uses Nova instructions.
General Instruments	CP1600	NMOS	16	87	Minicomputer-like system.
Intel	8086 (IAPX86/10)	NMOS	16	97	Will work with some 8080A programs.
Intel	8088 (IAX88/10)	NMOS	16	97	Version of 8086 with 8-bit bus.
Motorola	MC68000	NMOS	16	61	Uses many of the 6800 chips. Has 32-bit registers.
Zilog	Z8000	NMOS	16	110+	Two versions.
Texas Instruments	TMS9980	NMOS	16	69	Basis of home computers.
Western Digital	MCP1600	NMOS	16	116	Basis of PDP-11 other computers.

The MC6801 is a microcomputer on a chip. It contains 2048 bytes of mask-programmable ROM, 128 bytes of RAM, a 16-bit counter/timer, and a programmable UART. It uses all the instructions of the 6800 and an additional ten instructions. Any program written for a 6800 can be run on the 6801.

The 6803 is a ROM-less version of the 6801. The 6805 is an expanded version with an 8-bit counter/timer and additional address-checking modes. The 6805 is a microcomputer on a chip. Programs written on a 6800 will run on all the microprocessors except the 6805.

The newest entry is the MC6809. This comes in three versions with the same three clock rates as mentioned for the 6800. It has fewer instructions (59) than the 6800 but more addressing modes. Many of the instructions now handle 16-bit operations with a 16-bit address bus. This is almost a hybrid between an 8-bit and a 16-bit micro. Seven flags are used here compared with the five in the 6800.

In order to put everything on a single chip using NMOS technology, a new version of the technology has been developed. It is called high-density NMOS or HMOS technology. The 6809 is built using HMOS technology. The 6809 is the microprocessor in Radio Shack's new "color" computer as well as many other new computers.

Intel 8080 Series

This is one of the most popular micros made. The MCS-80 (8080A) contains two temporary registers called W and Z, six general-purpose 8-bit registers, an 8-bit accumulator, an 8-bit program status word used to control five flags, a 16-bit stack pointer, and a 16-bit program counter. This is summarized in Figure 10.1-A. There are 78 basic instructions. Software support is plentiful since this model is so commonly used. Many of its instructions though are separate I/O or one-of-a-kind instructions.

The 8080A uses four basic addressing modes: direct, indirect, register, and immediate. Register addressing allows transfers between the accumulator and the six basic registers. All direct addressing is 3 bytes long. Three levels of power supplies are needed, $+12$ volts, $+5$ volts, and -5 volts. This microprocessor is manufactured by many sources; make sure these are compatible with the Intel product. NEC microcomputers, Inc., for instance, makes an authorized version, which it calls an "upward enhanced" version, as well as an exact product. Programs written for an 8080A may not run on the "enhanced version." For more details, see reference 8.

There are many support chips made for this system. A priority interrupt controller (PIC) 8214 is very versatile, though it cannot be used with non-8080A systems. It can handle up to 64 levels of priority by having one PIC control eight others. Each controller has eight levels of interrupts. This can become quite complicated.

The 8251A is a USART (Universal Synchronous/Asynchronous Receiver/Transmitter). It handles serial transmission in either synchronous or asynchronous format.

This is a most difficult support device to use with an 8080A because of complicated timing requirements. There are also two general-purpose I/O devices. The 8255 or 8255A programmable peripheral interface (PPI) is a very useful device that can be used with many other micro systems. It functions like the PIA of the 6800. The A version will work with faster clocks than the other version. There is also an 8212 8-bit parallel port, which is nonprogrammable. It is essentially an 8-bit data latch, and is a less expensive and less complicated part to work with.

A minimum system would consist of a processor, clock, bus controller on three separate chips, some memory, and memory decoding. All but the clock are TTL compatible. The 8080A is the CPU used in some home computers such as the H-8 by Heath and the "Sol" series by Processor Tech (no longer made).

Because of problems associated with the three power levels, various enhanced versions have appeared. The MCS-85 (8085A, 8085A-2) offers two more instructions than the 8080A with four levels of interrupts, a serial I/O line, and a 3-MHz clock on the same chip. The –2 version is a 5-MHz clock version. Programs written for the 8080A normally run on the 8085. You have to watch timing loops because of the difference in speeds.

Zilog Z-80

The Z-80 is Zilog, Inc.,'s enhanced version of an 8080A. The instruction set includes all of the 8080A instructions as a subset plus an additional 80 instructions. Pin compatibility does not exist between the two micros. Many of the support devices made for the 8080A will also work with the Z-80. There are two operating versions; the Z-80 has a 2.8-MHz clock and the Z-80A has a 4.5-MHz clock.

Two major improvements over the 8080A are the fact that the CPU is a single-chip unit while in the 8080A it was three chips, and only a single +5-volt voltage supply is needed compared with the three voltage levels needed in the 8080A. Other advantages of the Z-80 are

1. The complex two-phase clock of the 8080A has been replaced by a single clock signal.
2. Automatic dynamic refresh is part of the CPU unit.

The Z-80 has more than twice as many registers as the 8080A. Figure 10.1 compares the two. Note that the processor status word register, accumulator, and six general-purpose registers have been duplicated in the Z-80. In addition, two 16-bit index registers (IX and IY), an 8-bit interrupt vector (IV), and an 8-bit memory refresh center (R) have been added.

In addition to the four addressing modes in the 8080A, two new address-

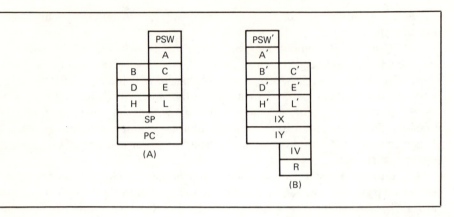

FIGURE 10.1. *Registers in an 8080A (A) and additional registers in the Z-80 (B).*

ing modes are found in the Z-80. It has a number of memory reference instructions using the IX or IY registers as indexes and it has 2-byte relative jump instructions. These last two items are similar to those used in the 6800.

The Z-80 is also available as a microcomputer on a chip called a Z-8. This has the Z-80 microprocessor, 2048 bytes of ROM, 124 bytes of RAM, 32 I/O lines, two counter/timers, and a programmable UART, all on a single chip.

The Z-80 has become an extremely popular 8-bit microcomputer because of its versatility and speed. It is the basic CPU used in Radio Shack "TRS-80" series, Bally's "Computer Series," and Exidy's "Sorcerer" computer.

MOS Technology—6500 Series

This series comes in two families—the 6502, which has an on-board one-phase clock, and the 6512, which works with an external two-phase clock. Both families have different versions that can address 4K, 8K, or 65K bytes of memory. The operating frequencies are 1 MHz, or 2 MHz for the A series (6502A or 6512A).

The 6500 series can be considered an enhancement of the MC6800 series. The philosophies behind the construction of the two series are similar, but the final results differ considerably. The instruction sets look alike but are significantly different. A single +5-volt power supply is used. All devices have TTL-compatible signals. The registers in any CPU in the 6500 series are given in Figure 10.2.

Note the differences from the 6800. The 6500 series has only one accumulator, the 16-bit index register of the 6800 has been broken into two 8-bit index registers (X and Y), and the stack pointer is also only an 8-bit register. The maximum width of the stack is thus only 256 bytes. The higher byte of the address is always fixed at 01_{16}; therefore, memory locations 0100_{16} to $01FF_{16}$ are reserved for the stack.

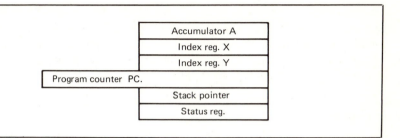

FIGURE 10.2.   *The registers in the 6500 series by MOSTech.*

There are essentially ten addressing modes available on the 6500 series:

1. Accumulator immediate
2. Absolute (direct)
3. Zero page
4. Indexed zero page
5. Indexed absolute
6. Implied
7. Relative
8. Indexed indirect
9. Indirect indexed
10. Absolute indirect

The direct addressing and page zero addressing are the same as for the 6800. Index addressing is also essentially the same. The second byte of the instruction is added to the contents of either the X or Y register (remember, though, these are 8-bit index registers). The indexed absolute addressing is done by adding a 16-bit address to the contents of either the X or Y register.

In indirect addressing each instruction is 3 bytes long, with the last 2 bytes an address of an address. With the indexed indirect and indirect indexed mode, all instructions are 2 bytes, with the second byte an 8-bit address. In the case of the indexed indirect instructions, this second byte is added to the contents of the X register to get a location in the first 256 bytes of memory where an address is to be found. With indirect indexed addressing, the second byte is an address in the first 256 bytes of memory. At this address is an indirect address that is added to the contents of the Y register to get the address the computer must go to. The other addressing modes are the same as the 6800.

The clock signals and cycles are identical to the 6800's. Because of its similarity to the 6800, many of the support devices of the 6800 can be used with the 6500 series. The PIAs are interchangeable to the extent that either can be used in either system. But one cannot simply be substituted for the other because pin configurations differ and the MCS 6522 PIA uses more hand-shaking logic than the MC6820.

Rockwell International produces an 8-bit microcomputer on a single chip using the 6502 as its CPU. This is the R6500/1. It contains the 6502 microprocessor, 2048 bytes of ROM, 64 bytes of RAM, 32 bidirectional I/O lines, four interrupts, and a 16-bit programmable counter/timer. The 6502 is used by many hobbyist computers. Better known ones are KIM, SYM, and PET by Commodore, and Apple II by Apple.

Fairchild F8

This microprocessor family is quite different from the others in the field. It was developed with the intention to make the system on as few chips as possible. Because of this the logic employed and the instruction set will seem strange to programmers used to other microprocessors or minicomputers. Because of the limited number of chips needed to use this as a controller, it is the most popular micro made. It is utilized in many consumer products where only two chips are needed, for example, toys and computer-based games. Any other microcomputer system would need seven or more chips to duplicate the ability of the F8 system. Because of the success of the F8 in the consumer field, it has influenced other single-chip products. Examples are the Intel 8048 and the MCS6530 from MOS Technology.

    The heart of the F8 family is the 3850 CPU. The CPU contains a 64-byte scratchpad RAM and 16 I/O lines. All devices require +5-volt and +12-volt power supplies. Clock frequencies of 0.1 MHz to 2 MHz are available. There is a single 8-bit accumulator, a 5-bit status register, and a 6-bit indirect scratchpad address register (ISAR). There are *no* program counter or data counters on the CPU. They are contained in other devices. The data counter is an implied address register. Since these are present on certain devices, they may be duplicated in a system.

    There are 76 basic instructions for the CPU. They can be placed in the following groups.

1. Accumulator
2. Memory reference
3. Branch and jump
4. Address modification
5. Scratchpad register
6. Control instructions

    Since there are no memory addressing registers on the 3850 CPU, there is no memory address logic. This is all handled by the support devices. Extended addressing is always done using implied addressing in an autoincrement mode. The 3850 is available as a single-chip microcomputer from MOS Technology Corporation as MK3870, MK3872, or MK3876. The 3870, which is available from various sources, is very popular as a controller because of its low cost and low power consumption. A single +5-volt power supply is used in the unit. It is the microcomputer in many of the microprocessor-based toys found in the home, such as the video games.

16-BIT MICROS

At present the major push in microprocessors is toward 16 bits. It may be a little surprising to learn that 16-bit micros have been available for some time, but have not been too popular.

The first 16-bit micro was produced by National Semiconductor Corporation in a single IC called "Pace." Its architecture was developed after Data General's Nova minicomputer. Pace did not catch on readily as it was built from slower PMOS technology. The NMOS 8-bit micros were almost as fast as the 16-bit. Later a NMOS version was introduced, but this is not popular either.

Other early 16-bit micros were General Instruments' CP1600, which also did not catch on, and Texas Instruments' Model 9900, a downward extension of its 990 minicomputer. The TI computer is well supported as it is compatible with the 990. Data General has come out with MicroNova, mN601, which is a downward extension of its Nova minicomputer. Neither has had any great success in the market.

The most popular of the 16-bit micros has been the Western Digital MCP-1600. This consists of four chips that are the basis of Digital Equipments' LSI-11 series. The MCP-1600 is microprogrammable; thus it can be set to implement the LSI-11 code or programmed differently to implement the code in the AM-100 computer of Alpha Microsystems. A new version of this same chip is used in the "Pascal" microengine. The newest 16-bit micros to become available are the 8086 of Intel, the Z-8000 of Zilog, and the MC68000 of Motorola. These are the basis of the more popular 16-bit microcomputers.

Intel 8086

The Intel 8086 is an upward enhancement of the 8080A. It contains a compatible subset of registers of the 8080A. It also contains four-segment address registers that enable it to address up to a mega-byte of storage. Individual instructions can address up to 64K bytes. The instruction set has 97 basic instructions with 24 different operand address modes.

The CPU contains two asynchronous processors, one to control the basic operations of the CPU and bus and the other to prepare and manipulate data. There are nine 16-bit registers accessible to the programmer. A unique feature is a 6-byte instruction queue maintained by the bus interface unit (BIU). The execution unit (EU) takes instructions from the queue and executes them. The BIU can add instructions to the queue while the EU is executing them. This increases the throughput of the processor. This microprocessor has been built to handle one program at a time.

Intel makes another version of the 8086 known as an 8088. The only difference between the two is that the 8088 connects to the outside world through an 8-bit bus even though it is capable of handling 16 bits internally. The 8088 is the microprocessor used in IBM's new microcomputer.

Zilog Z-8000

This 16-bit micro is available in two versions—a 48-pin chip that can address 8 Mbytes of storage, and a 40-pin chip that can address 64K bytes. It contains 16 general-purpose registers that can serve as accumulators and all but one can also serve as an index register. There are six other special-purpose registers. It would appear that this will compete against some minicomputers since it contains a resident operating system to control I/O flow and is capable of handling multiple programs.

Motorola MC68000

This product, which is more powerful than either the Z-8000 or 8086, has just started to hit the market. The MC68000 has sixteen, 32-bit registers that enable it to address up to 4 Mbytes of memory without having to use segmented addressing registers. It also contains a 24-bit program counter and a 16-bit status register. This micro has features useful for multiple program controls as well.

The instruction set contains only 61 basic commands, but combined with 14 different addressing modes, it becomes very versatile. A minor disadvantage is that it is on a 64-pin DIP. A big plus is that all the 6800 devices can be used with the 68000. This chip needs a single +5-volt power supply, as do the Z-8000 and 8086. All that is necessary for operation is an external clock (up to 8 MHz), memory, and I/O circuits.

More and more manufacturers have been announcing the production of microcomputers using one of these 16-bit microprocessors. IBM is the latest to enter the field with a 16-bit microcomputer. These 16-bit machines would seem to be most useful in the business area.

A 16-bit computer will handle calculations faster than a 8-bit computer and is capable of addressing a greater amount of main memory than most 8-bit computers.

The full capability of the 8-bit micros has not yet been fully exploited. In fact, a 16-bit may be overkill for many applications. Even though 16-bit machines are just beginning to make a dent in the market, 32-bit processors are being made. The technology in this field is moving ahead so fast, that the use of this technology has not been able to keep pace.

BIT-SLICE MICROPROCESSORS AND SINGLE-BOARD COMPUTERS

Two other products that are popular in the microprocessor field are the bit-slice microprocessor and the single-board computer (SBC).

Bit Slice

A bit-slice microprocessor has a somewhat different architecture than the microprocessors previously discussed. It is made from bipolar technology. This gives it greater speed in operation.

It can be pictured as a slice of n bits through a conventional microprocessor; n is normally 2 or 4 but some 8-bit slices are available. A larger microprocessor is made by concatenating these chip slices together. Thus four 4-bit slices can be put together to build a 16-bit micro.

The control signals for the fetch and execute states are contained in a separate ROM. Because of this bit slice micros are usually microprogrammable. Because the instructions used by the micro are controllable to some extent by the user, they are used to emulate other computers.

Single-Board Computers

Within the past year or so, the single-board computer has become quite popular. The SBC contains microprocessor, memory, and I/O support devices, all on a single board. Single-board computers are available built around either 8- or 16-bit microprocessors, although the 16-bit micros are beginning to dominate the field.

MICROCOMPUTERS

As the cost of the microprocessors decrease, more and more products are built using them. They are the basis of many toys and of the hobby microcomputers. For some time there were three major builders of home computers—the Apple II, Pet, and Sorcerer—but others did exist. With the development of the Radio Shack TRS-80, the sales of home computers have increased tremendously. Table 10.2 lists some of the more popular systems.

This table is in no way a complete listing. Other systems that are available are those from Tektronix (4051), Hewlett-Packard, Processor Tech (Sol I-A, etc.) based on the 8080A, Ohio Scientific, Challenger series based on the 6502, and Heath Corporation H-8 based on the 8080A and H-11, which is the PDP-11 series from Digital Equipment.

Those wishing to use the computer for home purposes would probably be satisfied with any of these systems. In buying a system, considerations should be given to service, to whether you want black and white or color, and whether you want to do your own programming. Disks are preferred since they normally are more reliable than cassettes. The four for home use are Apple II, PET (or CBM), TRS-80, and Atari—though Texas Instruments is pushing hard here.

If the system is to be used at a school, then its purpose would determine the type of system you would buy. For laboratory applications an expansion bus is necessary to add AD/DA convertors. The SWTPC, Altair, LSI-11 or its equivalent H-11, and the North Star are preferred. Disk systems would be best for program storage. If you wish to use the system for computer-assisted instruction (CAI), then a disk system is not always needed, but is very useful. Some manufacturers, such as Tektronix and Hewlett-Packard, have complete systems with cartridges that can be readily used, although most of these prepackaged programs are for scientific or business uses.

Someone who is interested in a limited home computer that is quite inex-

TABLE 10.2. *Some of the More Commonly Used Microcomputer Systems.*

System	Micro	Comments
TRS-80	Z-80	Model I no longer sold in the United States though other companies are making computers identical to it.
TRS-80 (Model III)	Z-80	Improved version of Model I costs about $1000.
TRS-80 (color)	MC6809E	Very inexpensive color computer ($400) can be used as a serious computer or with games.
Apple II	6502	Color, graphics capability, expansion bus, one of most popular systems ($1200). Needs video screen.
Apple III	6502	Enhanced version of Apple II for business uses. Can address more memory than Apple II.
PET (CBM)	6502	Complete system, black and white IEEE-488 bus. About $800.
VIC 20	6502	Commodores new color computer similar to Radio Shack's ($300).
ATARI 800	6502	Color, no expansion bus $1000; Model 400, available with color for about $500. Model 400 holds less memory than Model 800.
Texas Instruments TI 99/4	9900	Color, complete unit, no expansion bus, about $1150. No disk. Without monitor price is around $750. Excellent graphics and sound.
Sorcerer	Z80	B/W, S-100 expansion bus. About $1000.
Compucolor II	8080A	Complete system, color, no expansion bus, programs are almost compatible with Apple II. About $1700.
SWTPC	6800/6809	Not known as a home computer, has almost no dealer network, but excellent systems; used in many universities, in laboratories and for CAI with language Pilot. Many configurations available.
Altair 8800	8080A	S-100 expansion bus, has 8- or 12-bit DA/AD boards available. Not noted for home buyers. Excellent for colleges and universities.
North Star Horizon	Z-80	S-100 expansion bus, double-density disk.

pensive should consider Ohio Scientific Challenger—a black and white system available for around $350. However, it has very little expansion capability.

The most popular systems for CAI are the big three—TRS-80, Apple, II and PET. The PET is a complete integrated unit with nice graphic capabilities, while Apple II is noted for its color graphic capabilities. The Apple II has an outstanding amount of software that is easily obtainable. The TRS-80 and PET do have sufficient software available.

For teaching Basic, the Commodore Business Machines (PET's) and Radio Shack's TRS-80 Model III are hard to beat with the complete system (keyboard and video screen) in one unit. All of these systems have the ability to program in Basic, and most are able to use other languages as well. Commodore computers with a disk can use Fortran, and the Apple can use Fortran, Pascal, and Pilot. The SWTPC 6800/6809-based systems also can use Pilot. This is an interesting and easy language to learn for writing CAI programs.

Those systems with expansion busses can have printers or other peripheral devices added to them. For those interested in home computers, the following references provide reviews of the various computers. Readers who wish to keep up with the latest developments in the microprocessor field are referred to *Electronic Design* (references 9–11), which publishes annual reviews, usually in March on microcomputers and in November on microprocessors. Many of the trade journals (references 12–14) present surveys of the latest microcomputers and the hardware associated with them.

REFERENCES

1. John W. Moore et al., Computer-Aided Instruction with Microcomputers, Part I. *J. Chem. Education* 56 (12), p. 776, Dec. 1979. A review of TRS-80, Apple II, PET, SWTPC, North Star, Terak 8510, Altair.
2. John W. Moore et al., Computer-Aided Instruction with Microcomputers, Part II. *J. Chem. Education* 57 (2), p. 93, Feb. 1980. A review of TRS-80, Apple II, Compucolor II, Tektronix 4051, Altair, North Star, PET, SWTPC.
3. Carol Ogdin, Sixteen Bit Micros, *Mini-Micro Systems*, p. 64 Jan. 1979.
4. R. Shuford, A User Reviews the Radio Shack TRS-80, *On Computing*, 1 (1), p. 40, Summer 1979.
5. B. Liffick, A Review of the Commodore PET, *On Computing*, 1 (1), p. 32, Summer 1979.
6. R. G. A. Cote, The Apple II System, *On Computing*, 1 (1), p. 28, Summer 1979.
7. K. Barbier, The Sorcerer Computer, *On Computing*, 1 (1), p. 38, Summer 1979.
8. Adam Osborne, *An Introduction to Microcomputers, Volume II, Some Real Products*. Osborne & Associates, Berkeley, Calif., 1977.
9. *Electronic Design*, 28 (10), Special Computer Issue, May 10, 1980.

10. *Electronic Design*, 28 (24), Annual Microprocessor Special, Nov. 22, 1980.
11. *Electronic Design*, 29 (6), Annual Microcomputer Data Manual, Mar. 19, 1981.
12. Comparison Charts: A First-Buyer's Guide to Hardware, *Interface Age*, 5 (5), p. 94, May 1980.
13. Tom Fox, Comparison Charts Explained, *Interface Age*, 5 (6), p. 80, June 1980.
14. Tom Fox, Micro Systems, Survey, Let The Buyer Compare, *Interface Age*, 6 (1), p. 76, Jan. 1981.

APPENDIX A

THE 6800

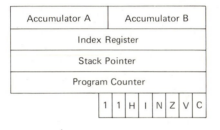

Accumulator A	Accumulator B
Index Register	
Stack Pointer	
Program Counter	

1	1	H	I	N	Z	V	C

The 6800 microprocessor contains two accumulators called accumulator A (ACCA) and accumulator B (ACCB). It has three 16-bit registers, an index register, a stack pointer, and a program counter. The index register stores 16 bits of a memory address. The stack pointer is a two-byte register that keeps track of a push-down/pop-up stack. The program counter contains the address of the next instruction in a program. There is an 8-bit condition code register in which only 6 bits are used. These bits indicate the result of an operation on an accumulator. Each symbol represents the following.

C = carry from bit 7
V = overflow from bit 6 to bit 7 (changing sign of number)
Z = accumulator has been set to zero
N = accumulator has become negative
 I = interrupt mask bit
H = half-carry from bit 3

Bits six and seven are set at 1 at all times and are not used.

Summary of Machine and Assembly Language Instructions Accumulator and Memory Instructions (Courtesy Motorola Semiconductor Products, Inc.)

OP CODE

Instruction	Mnemonic	Immediate	Direct	Index	Extended	Implied
Add	ADDA	8B	9B	AB	BB	
	ADDB	CB	DB	EB	FB	
Add accumulators	ABA					1B
Add with carry	ADCA	89	99	A9	B9	
	ADCB	C9	D9	E9	F9	
And	ANDA	84	94	A4	B4	
	ANDB	C4	D4	E4	F4	
Bit test	BITA	85	95	A5	B5	
	BITB	C5	D5	E5	F5	
Clear	CLR			6F	7F	
	CLRA					4F
	CLRB					5F
Compare	CMPA	81	91	A1	B1	
	CMPB	C1	D1	E1	F1	
Compare accumulators	CBA					11
One's complement	COM			63	73	
of accumulator A	COMA					43
of accumulator B	COMB					53
Two's complement	NEG			60	70	
or negate	NEGA					40
	NEGB					50
Decimal adjust A	DAA					19
Decrement	DEC			6A	7A	
	DECA					4A
	DECB					5A
Exclusive or	EORA	88	98	A8	B8	
	EORB	C8	D8	E8	F8	
Increment	INC			6C	7C	
	INCA					4C
	INCB					5C
Load accumulator	LDAA	86	96	A6	B6	
	LDAB	C6	D6	E6	F6	
Inclusive or	ORAA	8A	9A	AA	BA	
	ORAB	CA	DA	EA	FA	
Push data	PSHA					36
	PSHB					37
Pull data	PULA					32
	PULB					33
Rotate left	ROL			69	79	
	ROLA					49
	ROLB					59
Rotate right	ROR			66	76	
	RORA					46
	RORB					56
Arithmetic shift left	ASL			68	78	

Instruction	Mnemonic	Immediate	Direct	Index	Extended	Implied
	ASLA					48
	ASLB					58
Arithmetic shift right	ASR			67	77	
	ASRA					47
	ASRB					57
Shift right logic	LSR			64	74	
	LSRA					44
	LSRB					54
Store accumulator	STAA		97	A7	B7	
	STAB		D7	E7	F7	
Subtract	SUBA	80	90	AO	BO	
	SUBB	CO	DO	EO	FO	
Subtract accumulators	SBA					10
Subtract with	SBCA	82	92	A2	B2	
carry	SBCB	C2	D2	E2	F2	
Transfer accumulators						
	TAB					16
	TBA					17
Test, zero, or	TST			6D	7D	
minus	TSTA					4D
	TSTB					5D

Index Register and Stack Manipulation Instructions

Instruction	Mnemonic	Immediate	Direct	Index	Extended	Implied
Compare index register	CPX	8C	9C	AC	BC	
Decrement index register	DEX					09
Decrement stack register	DES					34
Increment index register	INX					08
Increment stack pointer	INS					31
Load index register	LDX	CE	DE	EE	FE	
Load stack pointer	LDS	8E	9E	AE	BE	
Store index register	STX		DF	EF	FF	
Store stack pointer	STS		9F	AF	BF	
Index regulator → stack pointer	TXS					35
Stack pointer → index register	TSX					30

Jump and Branch Instructions Addressing

Instructions	Mnemonic	Relative	Index	Extended	Implied
Branch always	BRA	20			
Branch if carry = 0	BCC	24			
Branch if carry = 1	BCS	25			
Branch if = zero	BEQ	27			
Branch if ≥ zero	BGE	2C			
Branch if > zero	BGT	2E			
Branch if higher	BHI	22			
Branch if ≤ zero	BLE	23			
Branch if < zero	BLT	2D			
Branch if minus	BMI	2B			
Branch ≠ zero	BNE	26			
Branch if overflow = 0	BVC	28			
Branch if overflow = 1	BVS	29			
Branch if plus	BPL	2A			
Branch to subroutine	BSR	8D			
Jump	JMP		6E	7E	
Jump to subroutine	JSR		AD	BD	
No operation	NOP				01
Return from interrupt	RTI				3B
Return from subroutine	RTS				39
Software interrupt	SWI				3F
Wait for interrupt (HALT)	WAI				3E

SUMMARY OF THE SIX ADDRESSING MODES

1. *Inherent*: 1-byte instruction; memory address and instruction are implied by the instruction.
2. *Immediate*: 2- or 3-byte instruction; operand is found in the next one or two memory locations.
3. *Direct*: 2-byte instruction; address is found in next memory location.
4. *Extended*: 3-byte instruction, first memory location following instruction contains the 8 bits of the higher byte of a 16-bit word, while the second memory location contains the lower byte.
5. *Indexed*: 2-byte instruction; the number found in the memory location following the instruction is added to the contents of the index register to form an address.
6. *Relative*: 2-byte instruction used to move 126 memory locations backward or 129 memory locations forward with branch instructions. Reference point for counting is present position + 2.

Assembler Symbols

Symbol	Meaning
No symbol preceding number	Decimal number follows.
#	Immediate addressing mode.
$	Hexadecimal number follows.
@	Octal number follows.
%	Binary number follows.
'	ASCII literal character follows (20–5F).

INSTRUCTIONS IN INCREASING OP CODE NUMBER*

Instruction	Mnemonic	OP Code	Cycle Time	Boolean/Arithmetic Operation or Branch Test
No operation	NOP	01	2	Advances PC + 1
Increment index regulator	INX	08	4	$X + 1 \rightarrow X$
Decrement index regulator	DEX	09	4	$X - 1 \rightarrow X$
Subtract accumulators	SBA	10	2	$A - B \cdot A$
Compare accumulators	CBA	11	2	A B
Trans accumulator $A \rightarrow B$	TAB	16	2	$A \cdot B$
Trans accumulator $B \rightarrow A$	TBA	17	2	$B \cdot A$
Decimal adjust A	DAA	19	2	Converts A to BCD
Add Accumulators	ABA	1B	2	$A + B \cdot A$
Branch always	BRA	20	4	None
Branch if higher	BHI	22	4	$C + Z = 0$
Branch if lower or same	BLS	23	4	$C + Z = 1$
Branch if carry clear	BCC	24	4	$C = 0$
Branch if carry set	BCS	25	4	$C = 1$
Branch if not equal to zero	BNE	26	4	$Z = 0$
Branch if = zero	BEQ	27	4	$Z = 1$
Branch if overflow clear	BVC	28	4	$V = 0$
Branch if overflow set	BVS	29	4	$V = 1$
Branch if plus	BPL	2A	4	$N = 0$
Branch if minus	BMI	2B	4	$N = 1$
Branch if greater = zero	BGE	2C	4	$N \oplus V = 0$
Branch < zero	BLT	2D	4	$N \oplus V = 1$
Branch > zero	BGT	2E	4	$Z + (N \oplus V) = 0$
Branch if ≤ zero	BLE	2F	4	$Z + (N \oplus V) = 1$

*(Courtesy Motorola Semiconductor Products, Inc.)

Instruction	Mnemonic	OP Code	Cycle Time	Boolean/Arithmetic Operation or Branch Test
Stack pointer → index register	TSX	30	4	$SP + 1 \rightarrow X$
Increment stack pointer	INS	31	4	$SP + 1 \rightarrow SP$
Pull data to A	PULA	32	4	$SP + 1 \rightarrow SP \ M_{sp} \cdot A$
Pull data to B	PULB	33	4	$SP + 1 \rightarrow SP \ M_{sp} \cdot B$
Decrement stack pointer	DES	34	4	$SP - 1 \rightarrow SP$
Index Register → stack pointer	TXS	35	4	$X - 1 \rightarrow SP$
Push data from A	PSHA	36	4	$A \cdot M_{sp} \ SP - 1 - SP$
Push data from B	PSHB	37	4	$B \cdot M_{sp} \ SP - 1 - SP$
Return from subroutine	RTS	39	5	
Return from interrupt	RTI	3B	10	
Wait for interrupt	WAI	3E	9	
Software interrupt	SWI	3F	12	
Two's complement A	NEGA	40	2	$00 - A \cdot A$
One's complement A	COMA	43	2	$\bar{A} \cdot A$
Logic shift right A	LSRA	44	2	
Rotate right A	RORA	46	2	
Arithmetic shift right A	ASRA	47	2	
Arithmetic shift left A	ASLA	48	2	
Rotate left A	ROLA	49	2	
Decrement A	DECA	4A	2	$A - 1 \cdot A$
Increment A	INCA	4C	2	$A + 1 \cdot A$
Test zero or minus A	TSTA	4D	2	$A \ 00$
Clear A	CLRA	4F	2	$00 \cdot A$
Two's complement B	NEGB	50	2	$00 - B \cdot B$
One's complement B	COMB	53	2	$\bar{B} \cdot B$
Logic shift right B	LSRB	54	2	
Rotate right B	RORB	56	2	
Arithmetic shift right B	ASRB	57	2	
Arithmetic shift left B	ASLB	58	2	
Rotate left B	ROLB	59	2	
Decrement B	DECB	5A	2	$B - 1 \cdot B$
Increment B	INCB	5C	2	$B + 1 \cdot B$
Test zero or minus B	TSTB	5D	2	$B - 00$
Clear B	CLRB	5F	2	$00 \cdot B$
				Addressing Mode
Two's complement	NEG	60	7	Index
One's complement	COM	63	7	Index
Logic shift right	LSR	64	7	Index
Rotate right	ROR	66	7	Index
Arithmetic shift right	ASR	67	7	Index
Arithmetic shift left	ASL	68	7	Index
Rotate left	ROL	69	7	Index
Decrement	DEC	6A	7	Index

Instruction	Mnemonic	OP Code	Cycle Time	Boolean/Arithmetic Operation or Branch Test
Increment	INC	6C	7	Index
Test zero or minus	TST	6D	7	Index
Jump	JMP	6E	4	Index
Clear	CLR	6F	7	Index
Two's complement	NEG	70	6	Extended
One's complement	COM	73	6	Extended
Logic shift right	LSR	74	6	Extended
Rotate right	ROR	76	6	Extended
Arithmetic shift right	ASR	77	6	Extended
Arithmetic shift left	ASL	78	6	Extended
Rotate left	ROL	79	6	Extended
Decrement	DEC	7A	6	Extended
Increment	INC	7C	6	Extended
Test	TST	7D	6	Extended
Jump	JMP	7E	3	Extended
Clear	CLR	7F	6	Extended
Subtract A	SUBA	80	2	Immediate
Compare A	CMPA	81	2	Immediate
Subtract with carry A	SBCA	82	2	Immediate
AND A	ANDA	84	2	Immediate
Bit test A	BITA	85	2	Immediate
Load accumulator A	LDAA	86	2	Immediate
Exclusive OR	EORA	88	2	Immediate
Add with carry	ADCA	89	2	Immediate
Inclusive OR	ORAA	8A	2	Immediate
ADD A	ADDA	8B	2	Immediate
Compare index register	CPX	8C	3	Immediate
Branch to subroutine	BSR	8D	8	Relative
Load Stack pointer	LDS	8E	3	Immediate
Subtract A	SUBA	90	3	Direct
Compare A	CMPA	91	3	Direct
Subtract with carry	SBCA	92	3	Direct
AND A	ANDA	94	3	Direct
Bit test A	BITA	95	3	Direct
Load accumulator A	LDAA	96	3	Direct
Store Accumulator A	STAA	97	4	Direct
Exclusive OR	EORA	98	3	Direct
Add with carry	ADCA	99	3	Direct
Inclusive OR	ORAA	9A	3	Direct
ADD A	ADDA	9B	3	Direct
Compare index register	CPX	9C	4	Direct
Load stack pointer	LDS	9E	4	Direct
Store stack pointer	STS	9F	5	Direct
Subtract A	SUBA	A0	5	Index
Compare A	CMPA	A1	5	Index

Instruction	Mnemonic	OP Code	Cycle Time	Boolean/Arithmetic Operation or Branch Test
Subtract with carry	SBCA	A2	5	Index
AND A	ANDA	A4	5	Index
Bit test A	BITA	A5	5	Index
Load accumulator A	LDAA	A6	5	Index
Store Accumulator A	STAA	A7	6	Index
Exclusive OR	EORA	A8	5	Index
Add with carry	ADCA	A9	5	Index
Inclusive OR	ORAA	AA	5	Index
ADD A	ADDA	AB	5	Index
Compare index register	CPX	AC	6	Index
Jump to subroutine	JSR	AD	8	Index
Load stack pointer	LDS	AE	6	Index
Store stack pointer	STS	AF	7	Index
Subtract A	SUBA	B0	4	Extended
Compare A	CMPA	B1	4	Extended
Subtract with carry	SBCA	B2	4	Extended
AND A	ANDA	B4	4	Extended
Bit test A	BITA	B5	4	Extended
Load accumulator A	LDAA	B6	4	Extended
Store accumulator A	STAA	B7	5	Extended
Exclusive OR	EORA	B8	4	Extended
ADD with carry	ADCA	B9	4	Extended
Inclusive OR	ORAA	BA	4	Extended
ADD A	ADDA	BB	4	Extended
Compare index register	CPX	BC	5	Extended
Jump to subroutine	JSR	BD	9	Extended
Load stack pointer	LDS	BE	5	Extended
Store stack pointer	STS	BF	6	Extended
Subtract B	SUBB	C0	2	Immediate
Compare B	CMPB	C1	2	Immediate
Subtract with carry B	SBCB	C2	2	Immediate
AND B	ANDB	C4	2	Immediate
Bit test B	BITB	C5	2	Immediate
Load accumulator B	LDAB	C6	2	Immediate
Exclusive OR	EORB	C8	2	Immediate
Add with carry	ADCB	C9	2	Immediate
Inclusive OR	ORAB	CA	2	Immediate
ADD B	ADDB	CB	2	Immediate
Load index register	LDX	CE	3	Immediate
Subtract B	SUBB	D0	3	Direct
Compare B	CMPB	D1	3	Direct
Subtract with carry	SBCB	D2	3	Direct
AND B	ANDB	D4	3	Direct
Bit test B	BITB	D5	3	Direct
Load Accumulator B	LDAB	D6	3	Direct

Instruction	Mnemonic	OP Code	Cycle Time	Boolean/Arithmetic Operation or Branch Test
Store accumulator B	STAB	D7	4	Direct
Exclusive OR	EORB	D8	3	Direct
Add with carry	ADCB	D9	3	Direct
Inclusive OR	ORAB	DA	3	Direct
ADD	ADDB	DB	3	Direct
Load index register	LDX	DE	4	Direct
Store index register	STX	DF	5	Direct
Subtract B	SUBB	E0	5	Index
Compare B	CMPB	E1	5	Index
Subtract with carry	SBCB	E2	5	Index
AND B	ANDB	E4	5	Index
Bit test B	BITB	E5	5	Index
Load accumulator B	LDAB	E6	5	Index
Store accumulator B	STAB	E7	6	Index
Exclusive OR	EORB	E8	5	Index
Add with carry	ADCB	E9	5	Index
Inclusive OR	ORAB	EA	5	Index
ADD B	ADDB	EB	5	Index
Load index register	LDX	EE	6	Index
Store index register	STX	EF	7	Index
Subtract B	SUBB	F0	4	Extended
Compare B	CMPB	F1	4	Extended
Subtract with carry	SBCB	F2	4	Extended
AND B	ANDB	F4	4	Extended
Bit test B	BITB	F5	4	Extended
Load accumulator B	LDAB	F6	4	Extended
Store accumulator B	STAB	F7	5	Extended
Exclusive OR	EORB	F8	4	Extended
Add with carry	ADCB	F9	4	Extended
Inclusive OR	ORAB	FA	4	Extended
ADD B	ADDB	FB	4	Extended
Load index register	LDX	FE	5	Extended
Store index register	STX	FF	6	Extended

For the 6800 with a 1-MHz clock, 1 cycle time is 1 μs.

$\quad$ Boolean AND or transfer into

$\oplus$ Boolean exclusive OR

$+$ Boolean inclusive OR

0 Bit zero

00 Byte zero

M_{sp} Memory location pointed to by stack pointer

$\rightarrow$ Transfer into

APPENDIX C

SUMMARY OF MACHINE AND ASSEMBLY LANGUAGE INSTRUCTIONS FOR MC 6809*

OP	Mnemonic	Mode	—	#
00	NEG	Direct	6	2
01	*			
02	*			
03	COM		6	2
04	LSR		6	2
05	*			
06	ROR		6	2
07	ASR		6	2
08	ASL,LSL		6	2
09	ROL		6	2
0A	DEC		6	2
0B	*			
0C	INC		6	2
0D	TST		6	2
0E	JMP		3	2
0F	CLR	Direct	6	2
10	Page2	—	—	—

*(Courtesy of Motorola Semiconductor Products, Inc.)

OP	Mnemonic	Mode	—	#
11	Page3	—	—	—
12	NOP	Inherent	2	1
13	SYNC	Inherent	2	1
14	*			
15	*			
16	LBRA	Relative	5	3
17	LBSR	Relative	9	3
18	*			
19	DAA	Inherent	2	1
1A	ORCC	Immediate	3	2
1B	*	—		
1C	ANDCC	Immediate	3	2
1D	SEX	Inherent	2	1
1E	EXG		8	2
1F	TFR	Inherent	6	2
20	BRA	Relative	3	2
21	BRN	↑	3	2
22	BHI		3	2
23	BLS		3	2
24	BHS,BCC	↓	3	2
25	BLO,BCS	Relative	3	2
26	BNE	Relative	3	2
27	BEQ	↑	3	2
28	BVC		3	2
29	BVS		3	2
2A	BPL		3	2
2B	BMI		3	2
2C	BGE		3	2
2D	BLT		3	2
2E	BGT	↓	3	2
2F	BLE	Relative	3	2
30	LEAX	Indexed	4+	2+
31	LEAY	↑	4+	2+
32	LEAS	↓	4+	2+
33	LEAU	Indexed	4+	2+
34	PSHS	Inherent	5+	2
35	PULS	↑	5+	2
36	PSHU		5+	2
37	PULU		5+	2
38	*			
39	RTS		5	1
3A	ABX		3	1
3B	RTI		6,15	1
3C	CWAI		20	2
3D	MUL		11	1

OP	Mnemonic	Mode	—	#
3E	*	↓		
3F	SWI	Inherent	19	1
40	NEGA	Inherent	2	1
41	*			
42	*			
43	COMA		2	1
44	LSRA		2	1
45	*			
46	RORA		2	1
47	ASRA		2	1
48	ASLA,LSLA		2	1
49	ROLA		2	1
4A	DECA		2	1
4B	*			
4C	INCA		2	1
4D	TSTA		2	1
4E	*			
4F	CLRA	Inherent	2	1
50	NEGB	Inherent	2	1
51	*			
52	*			
53	COMB		2	1
54	LSRB		2	1
55	*			
56	RORB		2	1
57	ASRA		2	1
58	ASLB,LSLB		2	1
59	ROLB	Inherent	2	1
5A	DECB	Inherent	2	1
5B	*			
5C	INCB		2	1
5D	TSTB		2	1
5E	*			
5F	CLRB	Inherent	2	1
60	NEG	Indexed	6+	2+
61	*			
62	*			
63	COM		6+	2+
64	LSR		6+	2+
65	*			
66	ROR		6+	2+
67	ASR		6+	2+
68	ASL, LSL		6+	2+
69	ROL		6+	2+
6A	DEC		6+	2+
6B	*			
6C	INC		6+	2+

OP	Mnemonic	Mode	—	#
6D	TST	↓	6+	2+
6E	JMP	Indexed	3+	2+
6F	CLR	Indexed	6+	2+
70	NEG	Extended	7	3
71	*			
72	*			
73	COM		7	3
74	LSR		7	3
75	*			
76	ROR		7	3
77	ASR		7	3
78	ASL, LSL		7	3
79	ROL		7	3
7A	DEC		7	3
7B	*			
7C	INC		7	3
7D	TST		7	3
7E	JMP	↓	4	3
7F	CLR	Extended	7	3
80	SUBA	Indexed	2	2
81	CMPA		2	2
82	SBCA		2	2
83	SUBD		4	3
84	ANDA		2	2
85	BITA		2	2
86	LDA		2	2
87	*			
88	EORA	Indexed	2	2
89	ADCA	Indexed	2	2
8A	ORA		2	2
8B	ADDA	↓	2	2
8C	CMPX	Immediate	4	3
8D	BSR	Relative	7	2
8E	LDX	Immediate	3	3
8F	*			
90	SUBA	Direct	4	2
91	CMPA		4	2
92	SCBA		4	2
93	SUBD		6	2
94	ANDA		4	2
95	BITA		4	2
96	LDA		4	2
97	STA		4	2

OP	Mnemonic	Mode	—	#
98	EORA		4	2
99	ADCA		4	2
9A	ORA		4	2
9B	ADDA		4	2
9C	CMPX		6	2
9D	JSR		7	2
9E	LDX		5	2
9F	STX	Direct	5	2
A0	SUBA	Indexed	4+	2+
A1	CMPA	Indexed	4+	2+
A2	SBCA		4+	2+
A3	SUBD		6+	2+
A4	ANDA		4+	2+
A5	BITA		4+	2+
A6	LDA		4+	2+
A7	STA		4+	2+
A8	EORA		4+	2+
A9	ADCA		4+	2+
AA	ORA		4+	2+
AB	ADDA		4+	2+
AC	CMPX		6+	2+
AD	JSR		7+	2+
AE	LDX		5+	2+
AF	STX	Indexed	5+	2+
B0	SUBA	Extended	5	3
B1	CMPA		5	3
B2	SBCA		5	3
B3	SUBD		7	3
B4	ANDA		5	3
B5	BITA		5	3
B6	LDA		5	3
B7	STA		5	3
B8	EORA	Extended	5	3
B9	ADCA	Extended	5	3
BA	ORA		5	3
BB	ADDA		5	3
BC	CMPX		7	3
BD	JSR		8	3
BE	LDX		6	3
BF	STX	Extended	6	3
C0	SUBB	Immediate	2	2
C1	CMPB		2	2
C2	SBCB		2	2

OP	Mnemonic	Mode	—	#
C3	ADDD		4	3
C4	ANDB		2	2
C5	BITB		2	2
C6	LDB		2	2
C7	*			
C8	EORB		2	2
C9	ADCB		2	2
CA	ORB		2	2
CB	ADDB		2	2
CC	LDD		3	3
CD	*			
CE	LDU	Immediate	3	3
CF	*			
D0	SUBB	Direct	4	2
D1	CMPB		4	2
D2	SBCB		4	2
D3	ADDD		6	2
D4	ANDB		4	2
D5	BITB		4	2
D6	LDB		4	2
D7	STB		4	2
D8	EORB		4	2
D9	ADCB		4	2
DA	ORB		4	2
DB	ADDB		4	2
DC	LDD		5	2
DD	STD		5	2
DE	LDU		5	2
DF	STU	Direct	5	2
E0	SUBB	Indexed	4+	2+
E1	CMPB		4+	2+
E2	SBCB		4+	2+
E3	ADDD		6+	2+
E4	ANDB		4+	2+
E5	BITB		4+	2+
E6	LDB		4+	2+
E7	STB		4+	2+
E8	EORB	Indexed	4+	2+
E9	ADCB	Indexed	4+	2+
EA	ORB		4+	2+
EB	ADDB		4+	2+
EC	LDD		5+	2+
ED	STD		5+	2+

OP	Mnemonic	Mode	—	#
EE	LDU	↓	5+	2+
EF	STU	Indexed	5+	2+
F0	SUBB	Extended	5	3
F1	CMPB	↑	5	3
F2	SBCB		5	3
F3	ADDD		7	3
F4	ANDB		5	3
F5	BITB		5	3
F6	LDB		5	3
F7	STB		5	3
F8	EORB		5	3
F9	ADCB		5	3
FA	ORB		5	3
FB	ADDB		5	3
FC	LDD		6	3
FD	STD		6	3
FE	LDU	↓	6	3
FF	STU	Extended	6	3
1021	LBRN	Relative	5	4
1022	LBHI	↑	5(6)	4
1023	LBLS		5(6)	4
1024	LBHS, LBCC		5(6)	4
1025	LBCS, LBLO		5(6)	4
1026	LBNE		5(6)	4
1027	LBEQ		5(6)	4
1028	LBVC		5(6)	4
1029	LBVS		5(6)	4
102A	LBPL		5(6)	4
102B	LBMI		5(6)	4
102C	LBGE		5(6)	4
102D	LBLT		5(6)	4
102E	LBGT		5(6)	4
102F	LBLE	Relative	5(6)	4
103F	SW12	Inherent	20	2
1083	CMPD	Immediate	5	4
108C	CMPY	↕	5	4
108E	LDY	Immediate	4	4
1093	CMPD	Direct	7	3
109C	CMPY	↑	7	3
109E	LDY	↓	6	3
109F	STY	Direct	6	3
10A3	CMPD	Indexed	7+	3+
10AC	CMPY	↑	7+	3+

OP	Mnemonic	Mode	—	#
10AE	LDY	↓	6+	3+
10AF	STY	Indexed	6+	3+
10B3	CMPD	Extended	8	4
10BC	CMPY	↑	8	4
10BE	LDY	↓	7	4
10BF	STY	Extended	7	4
10CE	LDS	Immediate	4	4
10DE	LDS	Direct	6	3
10DF	STS	Direct	6	3
10EE	LDS	Indexed	6+	3+
10EF	STS	Indexed	6+	3+
10FE	LDS	Extended	7	4
10FF	STS	Extended	7	4
113F	SW13	Inherent	20	2
1183	CMPU	Immediate	5	4
118C	CMPS	Immediate	5	4
1193	CMPU	Direct	7	3
119C	CMPS	Direct	7	3
11A3	CMPU	Indexed	7+	3+
11AC	CMPS	Indexed	7+	3+
11B3	CMPU	Extended	8	4
11BC	CMPS	Extended	8	4

Legend:
—Number of MPU cycles (less possible push-pull or indexed-mode cycles).
Number of program bytes.
* Denotes unused OP code.
Note: All unused OP codes are both undefined and illegal.

INDEX